Technical Yacht Design

Technical Yacht Design

Andrew G. Hammitt

VNR VAN NOSTRAND REINHOLD COMPANY
New York Cincinnati

Van Nostrand Reinhold Company Regional Offices:
New York Cincinnati Chicago Millbrae Dallas

First published in Great Britain by
Crosby Lockwood Staples

Printed in Great Britain

First published in the U.S.A. in 1975 by
Van Nostrand Reinhold Company
A Division of Litton Educational Publishing, Inc.
450 West 33rd Street, New York, N.Y. 10001

16   15   14   13   12   11   10   9   8   7   6   5   4   3   2   1

Library of Congress Cataloging in Publication Data

Hammitt, A G
  Technical yacht design.

  1. Yacht-building—Design and construction. I. Title.
VM331.H32   623.82′2   75–2324
ISBN 0–442–23096–6

Contents

Nomenclature

a	Width to length ratio of a panel.
a	Velocity change ratio through propeller
a_{cg}	Acceleration of center of gravity
A	Amplitude of wave motion; cross-sectional area of structural member
A_b	Underwater lateral hull area
A_c	Underwater cross-sectional area
A_f	Frontal area
A_k	Area of keel
A_p	Area of propeller disc
A_r	Area of rudder
A_s	Sail area
A_v	Area of air cushion vehicle
A_w	Wetted area
A_{wl}	Area of waterline plane
AR	Aspect ratio
b	Beam: panel width
C	Coefficient for cross-section in apparent mass formula; chord of hydrofoil; slope of lift angle attack curve; constant in mast design formula; circumference of ACV
C_{D_*}	Cross-flow resistance coefficient, drag coefficient
C_{DA}	Wave drag coefficient based on wetted area
C_{Di}	Induced resistance coefficient
C_f	Skin friction coefficient
C_F	Chord of flap
C_H	Lateral sail force coefficient; hinge moment coefficient
C_L	Lift coefficient

C_{Lb} Lift coefficient based on beam

C_M Moment coefficient

C_N Total sail force coefficient

C_p Propulsive sail force coefficient; pressure coefficient

C_p^* Net propulsive force coefficient

C_{pR} Rotating power coefficient

C_T Thrust coefficient

C_{TR} Rudder torque coefficient

C_{WR} Rudder work coefficient

d   Draft; propeller diameter; distance between rudder post and center of pressure; deflection; diameter

D   Displacement

E   Elastic modules

f   Acceleration in wave; freeboard

F   Fetch; propeller thrust; force of sails on hull; force on keel or rudder

F_1, F_2 Factor to specify hull loads on planing boats

Fr   Froude number

g   Acceleration due to gravity

G   Distance from chine to keel

h   Height of sail; height of air cushion

h_{cp} Height of center of effort of sails above center of lateral resistance of hull

h_m Metacentric height

H   Wave height; lateral sail force

HM   Heeling moment

I   Area moment of inertia

J   Polar moment of inertia

k   Apparent mass constant; roughness size; radius of gyration

K   Factor in column formula

l   Length of member

L   Boat length; waterline length; length; lift force

L_{cp} Distance to center of pressure from leading edge of hydrofoil or distance of center of pressure forward of transom

L_{KR} Distance between center of pressure of keel and rudder

LOA   Overall length

LWL   Waterline length

m   Cross-sectional mass

m_a Cross-sectional apparent mass

$\dot{m}_a$ Mass flux of air

M   Bending moment; stiffness parameter (Equation 6.38)

M_a Total apparent mass

MS   Midship section

N   Normal force

p   Pressure; propeller pitch; distributed load (total value)

p' Change in pressure through propeller

p_1 Pressure in front of propeller

p_o Pressure far ahead of or behind propeller; reference pressure on planing hull

P   Power; propulsive force

P_d Design pressure on planing hull

P_{sm} Pressure caused by slamming

P_R Rotating power

P_V	Pressure on hull (related to forward speed)
q	Dynamic pressure
Q	Resistance side force ratio of hull
r	Radius in wave; $(PR^2/V_{a_1}^5)^{\frac{1}{4}}$; cross-section dimension of mast
R	Radius of wave propagation circle; radius of curvature; force of water on hull; speed of rotation; turning radius, radius of gyration
R_f	Frictional resistance force
R_H	Resistance force caused by lateral forces
R_w	Wave resistance force
Re	Reynolds number
RM	Righting moment
S	Propeller slip; section modules $(2I/t)$; hydrofoil area, planing area
S_w	Water slip
t	Time; thickness
T	Duration; tension load, tangential force on propeller
T_R	Rudder stock torque
u	Water velocity on surface
U	Wave energy
$v = aV_b/V_w$	
V_1	Velocity ahead of propeller
V_a	Apparent wind velocity; relative water velocity
V_b	Boat velocity
V_R	Water velocity relative to propeller blade
V_r	Tangential component of velocity relative to the propeller
V_w	Wave velocity; wind velocity

V_2 Velocity behind propeller

w   Specific weight

w_a Specific weight of air

w_w Specific weight of water

W   Weight per unit length; load on column

x   Horizontal distance

z   Vertical distance

α Angle between wind direction or wave and boat direction

β Rudder deflection coefficient; coefficient related to apparent mass; angle between direction of apparent wind and boat; relative flow angle to propeller blade

β_e Deadrise angle

γ Leeway angle; angle of attack

Γ Wave-induced flow angle at rudder

δ Deflection angle of rudder; wind turning angle caused by sail or airfoil

ε_p Lift/drag ratio for propeller blade

ε Lift/drag ratio for sails

η Overall efficiency of propeller

η_p Pumping efficiency of propeller

η_w Water efficiency of propeller

θ Angular position of wave-generating circle; pitch or roll angle; angle of discharge of jet

λ Wave length

ν Kinematic viscosity

σ Prismatic coefficient; stress

σ_{max} Maximum stress

τ Wave or boat period; boat turning time; shear stress

ϕ Slope of wave surface

ω Rate of rotation

Chapter One
Design of the Hull

The hull is the basic boat: it must be designed to accomplish the uses to which the boat is to be put. It is required to have both static and dynamic characteristics. The static characteristics can be listed as follows:

1. It must contain and support the cargo and accommodation as required.
2. It must be stable in the desired position under all circumstances to which it may be subjected.

In addition to the static requirements, there are dynamic requirements concerned with the water flow about the hull. The nature of this flow depends very much upon the speed with which the boat moves through the water. This dynamic behavior is very important in determining the hull shape and will be considered in detail later. For present purposes, the dynamic requirements can be listed as follows:

1. The hull shape must be such that it can reach the desired speed with acceptable propulsive thrust.
2. The hull's reaction to waves must be acceptable for the service required.

The general restrictions imposed by requirements of this type are well known. The hull should be relatively long and narrow. It should have smooth lines, and it should have easy sections that allow it to negotiate waves without excessive shock. It also should control spray so that reasonably dry decks are maintained whenever possible.

With these general requirements in mind, let us consider how to go about putting them into practice and then determining whether the product lives up to the desired requirements.

1.1   Hull specifications

The hull is a rather complicated three-dimensional shape. The lines of the hull are specified by means of a series of planes. These planes are taken parallel to the waterline, and called waterlines; perpendicular to the waterline and parallel to the centerline, called buttocks; and perpendicular to the waterline and the centerline, called stations. The intersections of these planes with the hull surfaces are then used to describe the hull contours. This system is illustrated in Figure 1.1. The table of offsets is used to describe these lines by giving the coordinates, at the various stations, of the intersections of the waterline and buttock planes with the hull. The number of stations which should be used is at the discretion of the designer, but it is often convenient to divide the waterline length into ten equal spaces. The table of offsets typically contains of the order of two hundred entries to describe a hull. These two hundred entries represent a considerable mass of data which must be assimilated in some way if intelligent engineering judgements are to be made of the performance and behavior of the boat. It is therefore useful to sum up this information in a few parameters which represent the most useful combinations of these individual numbers.

It is useful to specify both dimensional and non-dimensional parameters to describe the boat. Since the non-dimensional parameters could be the same for any boat of similar shape regardless of the size, these parameters provide a useful means of comparison. A set of parameters for describing a hull are shown in Table 1.1. The dimensional form is shown first and then a useful non-dimensional form.

Table 1.1　Hull parameters

Quantity	Ab	Dimension	Non-dimensional
Length overall	LOA	ft	$\dfrac{\text{LOA}}{\text{LWL}}$
Length waterline	LWL	ft	
Beam waterline	b	ft	$\dfrac{b}{\text{LWL}}$
Draft	d	ft	$\dfrac{d}{b}$
Freeboard	f	ft	$\dfrac{f}{b}$
Displacement	D	tons	$\dfrac{D}{w_w(\text{LWL})^3}$
Area midship section	MS	ft^2	$\dfrac{\text{MS}}{bd}$
Block coefficient			$\dfrac{D}{w_w(\text{LWL})bd}$
Prismatic coefficient	σ		$\dfrac{D}{w_w(\text{MS})(\text{LWL})}$
Metacentric height	h_m	ft	$\dfrac{h_w D}{w_w(\text{LWL})b^3}$

The dimensionless displacement, the displacement/length ratio, is usually written in a semi non-dimensional form $D/(\text{LWL}/100)^3$ with units of tons per 100 feet cubed. The density of water w_w is left out since it is a constant

$$\left(65\ \frac{\text{lb}}{\text{cu ft}} \text{ or } \frac{1}{35}\ \frac{\text{ton}}{\text{cu ft}} \text{ for seawater} \right)$$

In later sections the relations between these various quantities and the boat's performance will be considered. Initially, however, it seems worthwhile to examine present day practice to determine typical values for the various parameters.[4]

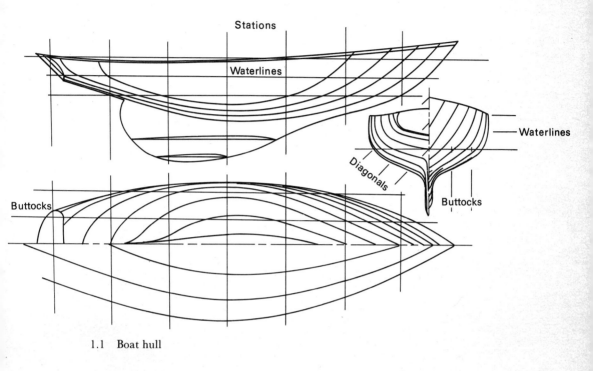

1.1   Boat hull

1.2   Typical range of hull parameters

1.2.1   LENGTH

The length overall/length waterline ratio has a variety of values depending upon the type of boat being considered. For most powerboats this value is close to 1. For sailboats, it varies depending upon the type of boat and the measurement rule to which it is designed. Typical values for sailboats are as follows:

	Avg.	*Max.*	*Min.*
Cruising boats	1·32	1·43	1·17
International Rule boats	1·55	1·65	1·4
Centerboard day sailers	1·15	1·28	1·02
Fin-keel day sailers	1·47	1·65	1·15

1.2.2   BEAM

The beam/length overall ratio is shown for typical motorboat designs in Figure 1.2. Planing and displacement types do not differ noticeably in this characteristic.

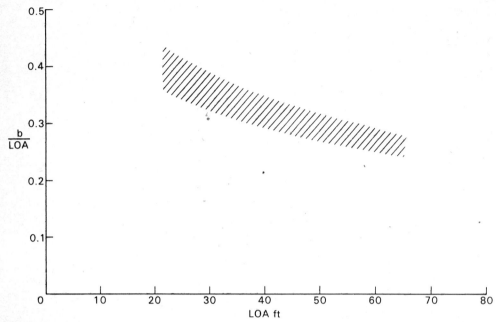

1.2   Typical beam/length ratios for motorboats

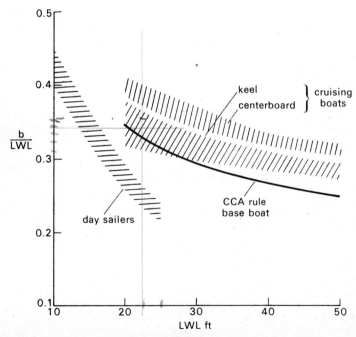

1.3   Typical beam/length ratios for sailboats

Typical values of the beam/waterline length ratio for sailboats are shown in Figure 1.3.

1.2.3   DRAFT

The draft/length ratio is shown in Figure 1.4 for typical motorboats. The Figure shows that the drift of planing type motorboats is less than for displacement boats. The draft/beam ratio for sailboats is shown in Figure 1.5.

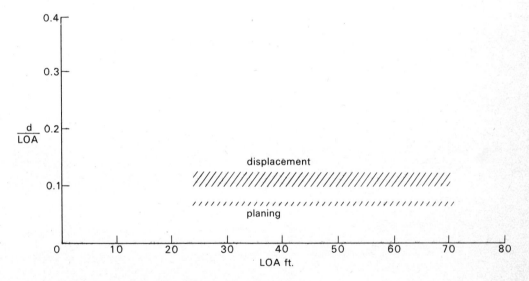

1.4   Typical draft/length ratios for motorboats

1.2.4   FREEBOARD

Typical freeboard ratios are presented in Figure 1.6 for cruisers and day sailers. The ratio of the freeboard at the forward end of the load waterline is compared to that at the after end and also to the waterline length. The values for motorboats vary considerably according to the purpose of the boat and cabin arrangement.

1.2.5   DISPLACEMENT/LENGTH RATIO

The displacement/length ratio of a boat is usually expressed in the units of tons per 100 feet cubed instead of the more fundamental non-dimensional form. It can be considered a measure of the average cross-sectional area of the boat. For boats of different size, the displacement increases rapidly with length if the displacement/

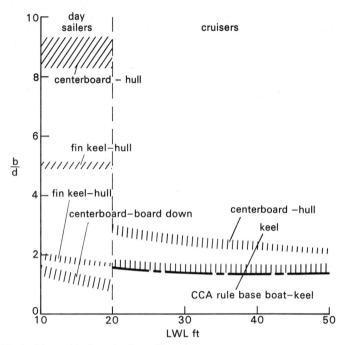

1.5   Typical beam/draft ratios for sailboats

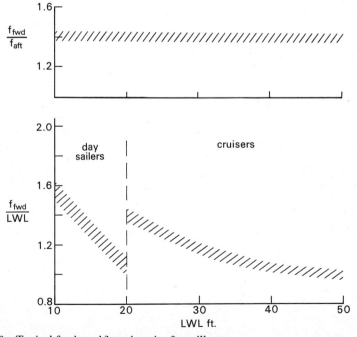

1.6   Typical freeboard/length ratios for sailboats

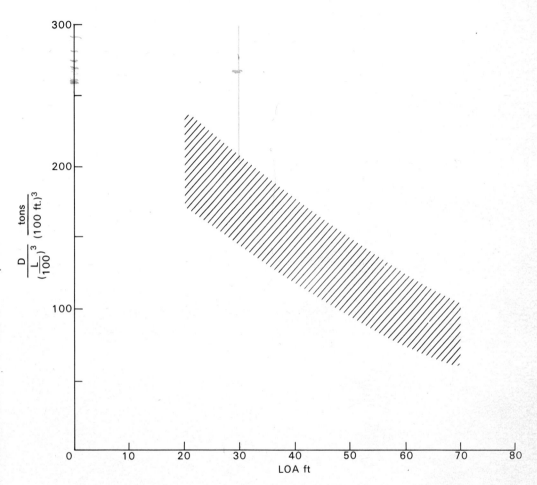

1.7   Typical displacement/length ratios for planing and light displacement
motorboats

length ratio is to remain constant (a factor of 8 if the length is doubled). Typical
values of this parameter are shown for motorboats in Figure 1.7 and for sailboats in
Figure 1.8. Figure 1.7 shows a rather rapid decrease of the displacement/length
ratio with size. Typical ship values are:

	LWL	D	$\dfrac{D}{(LWL/100)^3}$
Cargo ship	271 ft	3000 T	$150T/(100\ ft)^3$
Destroyer	374	3000	57

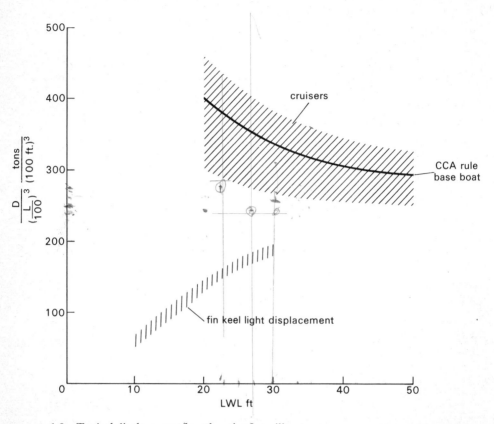

1.8   Typical displacement/length ratios for sailboats

The motorboat trend appears to extrapolate fairly smoothly to the destroyer value. Heavy duty motorboats (not shown) would be more consistent with the cargo ship displacement/length ratio. Sailboats vary over a wide range from light to heavy displacement types; there is a general decrease in displacement ratio with size similar to the motorboat trend.

1.2.6   STABILITY COEFFICIENT

The metacentric height coefficient is a measure of the actual stability of a boat non-dimensionalized by a quantity based on the length and beam. For a normal shape of the waterline plane with the center of gravity occurring at the center of buoyancy, this coefficient would be about 0·03. For a rectangular centerline plane, such as a barge, it would be 0·083. A smaller value would be obtained if the center of gravity were appreciably above the center of buoyancy and a larger value if the reverse were true.

1.2.7   CURVE OF AREAS

Another useful guide to the naval architect is the curve of transverse areas of the hull below the load waterline. This curve represents the distribution of displacement of the hull in the longitudinal direction. In 1897 Colin Archer proposed the wave-form distributions which required that the area curve of the forebody be a versed sines for 60% of the waterline length and a trochoid for the remaining 40%. Pre-viously accepted practice had been to locate the section of maximum cross-section further forward. At present there seems to be a trend to move the maximum cross-section somewhat forward of the 60% point, nearer to the 50% point.

This description of the curve of areas is limited to displacement boats operating below 'hull speed'. Boats trimmed for operation at high speed must have a curve of areas with the maximum cross-section further aft. As a first approximation, the curve of areas for the high speed boat in the trimmed condition should be that of a longer boat which would be operating at hull speed cut off at the length of the desired boat. This will leave an appreciable area at the stern. A boat designed to travel at $\sqrt{2}$ times its hull speed should have a curve of areas in the trimmed condition with the maximum area at the stern. It may also be desirable to have the curve of areas go smoothly to zero at the stern when at the trim angle for low speed operation. This requirement leads to the broad flat stern typical of many motorboats.

A prismatic coefficient is a measure of the fullness of the hull. A hull with a constant transverse section for the full length of the hull would have a prismatic coefficient of 1. Smaller values indicate that the sections fore and aft of the midship sections are reduced. For boats designed to operate below hull speed a prismatic coefficient of 0·5 to 0·55 appears to give the lowest resistance. For higher speeds, near hull speed, values of 0·55 to 0·60 give lower resistance.

1.3   Stability

The conditions under which a boat is stable are not immediately obvious. If the center of gravity of a boat is below the center of buoyancy (the center of gravity of the displaced water) it seems obvious that the boat is stable. This is a sufficient but not necessary condition for stability, and one which is seldom fulfilled. For any floating object of uniform density, the center of gravity is always above the center of buoyancy and the object is stable in at least one position.

To carry this reasoning a step further, consider the cylindrical floating object of uniform density shown in Figure 1.9a. The center of gravity is at the center of the cylinder while the center of buoyancy is at the center of the submerged segment. Symmetry or experience tells us that this cylinder is neutrally stable in any position; that is, it will stay in any position in which it is put but will not return to that position if disturbed from it. Define a point called the metacenter, which is a point so selected that if the boat were suspended from this point, the righting moment at a small

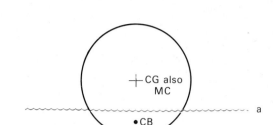

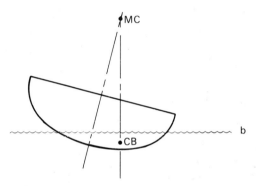

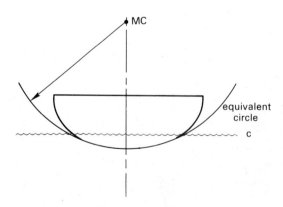

1.9 a, b, c   Concept of a metacenter

angle of heel would be the same as for the actual boat. For the case of the cylinder, the metacenter is clearly the center of the cylinder.

Two effects are involved with determining the position of the metacenter. As the boat is heeled, a wedge-like area of the cross-section is submerged on one side, and a corresponding area is raised on the other side. This increase in displacement on one side and decrease on the other clearly shifts the center of buoyancy towards the submerged side of the body. A vertical line drawn through the shifted center of buoyancy intersects the centerline of the cross-section of the boat at some point. For all small angles of heel about the neutral position, this intersection occurs at approximately the same location, which is called the metacenter (Figure 1.9b). Since the vertical supporting buoyancy force passes through the metacenter, the boat can be considered to be suspended from this point. The righting moment depends on the distance from the metacenter to the center of gravity; the location of the metacenter depends upon the dimensions of the waterline plane, which determines the volume of the immersed wedges, and the displaced volume and center of buoyancy in the neutral position. It follows that the metacenter will be the same for all shapes that have the same waterline, displacement, and center of buoyancy. A crude method for estimating the location of the metacenter for a given cross-sectional shape is to determine the circle with the same waterline and the same immersed volume (Figure 1.9c). The distance from the center of this circle to the center of buoyancy of the immersed segment of the circle will be the same as the distance from the metacenter of the given shape to its center of buoyancy.

The actual determination of the metacenter can be carried out as shown in Figure 1.10. Consider dA, a small element of the horizontal projected area of the bottom. The pressure on dA is the depth of submergence which consists of the static depth d plus that due to heel angle θ. Therefore the pressure on dA is:

$$(d + x \sin \theta) w_w$$

where x is the horizontal distance from the centerline and w_w is the specific weight of water. The vertical force on area dA is:

$$(d + x \sin \theta) w_w \, dA$$

The moment about the centerline caused by the force on dA is:

$$(d + x \sin \theta) x w_w \, dA$$

The total moment is found by adding the contributions of all the small elements dA. Since the boat floats in the $\theta = 0°$ position without any moment, all the contributions involving d must add up to zero, so the resulting moment is:

$$w_w \sin \theta \int x^2 \, dA$$

The integral expresses the summation over the whole waterline plane. Because this integral is of importance in many engineering applications, it is called the moment of inertia (I) and may be found for different common shapes in handbooks. Therefore,

$$\text{Moment} = w_w \sin \theta \int x^2 \, dA = w_w I \sin \theta$$

This moment is caused by the horizontal motion of the center of buoyancy as the boat is heeled, and can be expressed in terms of the distance from the metacenter to the center of buoyancy MB.

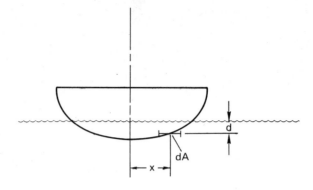

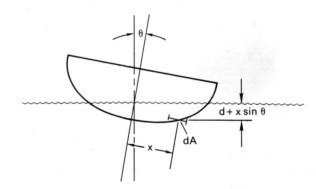

1.10　Terminology for development of metacenter relation

Moment $= (MB)D \sin \theta = w_w I \sin \theta$ where D is the displacement.

Therefore,

$$MB = \frac{w_w I}{D}$$

The actual righting moment depends upon the distance of the metacenter from the center of gravity or h_m.

Righting moment $= h_m D \sin \theta$

The concept of the metacenter just described is only applicable at small angles of heel. The point at which the vertical through the center of buoyancy intersects the cross-sectional centerline does not remain at the same point as the angle of heel becomes large. The simple calculation just described is not adequate to describe the righting moment of the boat at large angles of heel. The method used to calculate the righting moment at large angles is as follows. The boat is placed at the desired angle of heel and the waterline upon which it would float determined. The center of buoyancy of all the submerged cross-sections is then determined and, by a weighted average, the center of buoyancy for the entire hull. The horizontal displacement of the center of buoyancy in the inclined position from its location in the level position is the righting arm and determines the metacenter. In carrying out this calculation it is commonly assumed that the trim of the boat does not change as this makes the process of determining the inclined waterline much easier and does not cause an important error. If a boat is to be stable in the level position, the boat will usually rise out of the water in this inclined position so that the center of gravity of the boat is actually raised. The actual requirement is that the center of gravity must rise with respect to the center of buoyancy if the boat is stable. If the mean beam is greater than the mean draft, this condition will result in the inclined waterline being below the design waterline. A useful means of carrying out the righting moment calculations is to assume two inclined waterlines, one passing through the intersection of the design waterline and the centerline, and one below this waterline. If the displacement and righting moments are calculated for both of these waterlines, then an interpolation or extrapolation can be made to determine the actual righting moment on the desired waterline. The steps are as follows:

1. Find the displacement for the two assumed waterlines.
2. Determine the center of buoyancy for the various cross-sectional areas. (This can be done by making cut-outs of the sections and balancing them to find the centers of gravity.)
3. Determine the mean center of buoyancy by calculating the average horizontal distance from the centerline to the center of buoyancy, by multiplying the value for each section by the cross-sectional area, and then dividing by the sum of the cross-sectional areas. Determine the horizontal distance from center of buoyancy to center of gravity: this is the desired righting arm. The righting moment is the displacement times the length of the righting arm.

A typical righting moment curve for a sailboat is shown in Figure 1.11 by curve 1. A keel sailboat should be self-righting from the 90° heel angle so the crossing of the curve with the horizontal axis should be beyond the 90° point. Actually it is possible to have only one crossing of the axis, in addition to the 0° crossing, which occurs at the 180° position, curve 2. The crossings with positive slope such as occur at 0° and 180° for curve 1 and only at 0° for curve 2, are stable crossings and a boat would tend to float stably at these positions. The crossings with negative slope, at 120° and 240° for curve 1 and 180° for curve 2, are unstable and a boat would roll from this unstable point to the nearest stable one. The boat with a stability curve similar to 1 would be stable in the inverted position while one similar to 2 would not. A cylinder with an offset center of gravity would have a stability curve such as curve 2. Stability curves with more crossings of the axis than those shown are possible but unlikely for a usual boat design. The slope of the righting moment curve at the point of zero heel is the distance from the metacenter to the center of gravity times the displacement.

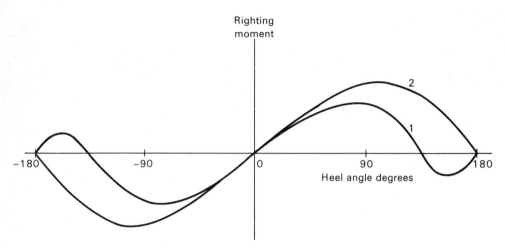

1.11   Typical righting moment curves

The righting moment curve for several simple shapes is of interest. Consider the flat-bottomed boat and catamaran configurations shown in Figure 1.12.

$$\text{Flat bottom} \qquad MB = \frac{b^3}{12V}$$

$$\text{Catamaran} \qquad MB = \frac{b^3 - (b-a)^3}{12V}$$

For equal beams and equal displaced volumes, it is clear that the flat bottom has the higher metacenter. However, when the catamaran has heeled sufficiently far that one hull has lifted clear of the water, then its righting moment is:

$$RM = \frac{D}{2}\left(b - \frac{a}{2}\right)$$

For the same angle, the center of buoyancy for the flat bottomed boat will not be a distance $(b - a/2)$ from the centerline since it will displace a wedge of water giving a lower righting moment. Beyond this angle, the righting moment for the catamaran begins to fall off.

The location of the metacenter and the center of buoyancy at angles of heel can be determined fairly accurately from the lines of the boat. To locate the center of gravity accurately is more difficult because of the numerous parts which must be considered in determining a weight balance. It is therefore useful to measure the moment required to obtain a given angle of heel. This measurement can be made on a boat fairly easily. A known weight is suspended from a pole guyed out perpendicular to the centerline; a fairly small weight will produce a measurable angle of heel. The angle can most easily be measured by suspending a plumb bob from overhead into a bucket of water placed on the cabin sole. A measurement of the sideward motion of the plumb bob and the distance from the point of suspension to the point of measurement gives the sine of the angle of heel, and the righting moment at this angle of heel is then known.

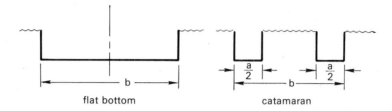

flat bottom   catamaran

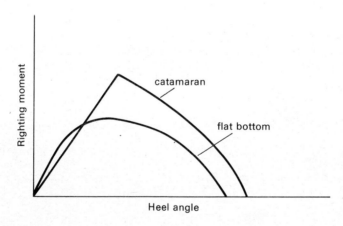

1.12   Righting moment curves for simple shapes

Chapter Two
Ocean Waves

Since a boat floats on the surface of the water the characteristics of this surface are of great importance. It is only the deeply submerged submarine which is effectively free of the surface behavior. Water is much heavier than air, about 800 times as heavy. It might be expected that the water would lie in a uniform surface below the air, and this condition does exist if there are no disturbing forces. Under some conditions this smooth surface can be considerably disturbed causing important consequences. Disturbances of most interest to the yacht designer are those caused by the passage of vessels and by the wind. In the first instance, the formation of waves causes a major increase in the resistance to forward motion of the boat, and in the second instance the waves caused by the wind have a large effect on its behavior.

The waves that occur on the water's surface impart to the water an oscillatory motion while the wave itself travels across the water surface with a continuous motion. The speed of travel of the wave front can be quite large, while the motion of the water is considerably slower. The water particles essentially oscillate about the same location as the wave front passes by them.

The forces that are involved in the propagation of surface waves are the inertial and the gravitational or weight forces and in some cases surface tension. If dimensional analysis is applied to a physical problem involving inertial and gravitational effects it is found that a suitable dimensionless parameter is $V_w/\sqrt{gL}$ which is called the Froude number and is the important parameter in wave theory.

2.1 Trochoidal wave theory

One of the simplest and oldest theories for describing waves is called trochoidal wave theory. The name stems from the fact that in this theory the surface of the water is assumed to follow the shape of a trochoidal curve. While this theory is not an entirely satisfactory description of all wave characteristics, it does present a reasonable description of many of them and provides a model upon which an initial understanding of wave motion is easily obtained.

In trochoidal wave theory we prescribe a reasonable behavior for the water particles and water surface. We then determine the velocity of the wave front from the equilibrium of the particles of water on the surface with the gravitational and inertial forces which act upon them. This condition requires that the sum of these gravitational and inertial forces be perpendicular to the water surface.

In trochoidal wave theory, we assume that the motion of the water is described by the particles moving in circular orbits while the wave front progresses at a uniform speed. This assumption agrees quite well with the observed facts. Referring to Figure 2.1, the motion of a surface particle of water is described by a circle whose center is at the mid-height of the wave and with a radius equal to the half height. This water particle rotates with uniform velocity ω and radius r. The wave front propagates with uniform velocity, equal to the tip speed of a wheel turning at velocity ω with a radius R, greater than r. We can look at this wave from two different frames of reference: the one which was used above is a stationary frame of reference in which the little wheel with radius r revolved describing the water particle motion and the larger wheel, radius R, rolled the wave forward (in this frame of reference the center of the large wheel is stationary). We may also consider a frame of reference which rides with the wave front and in which the center of the wheel rolls away at a velocity ωR, the tip speed of the large wheel. If we take this latter point of view (Figure 2.1) the motion of point P at the end of radius r describes

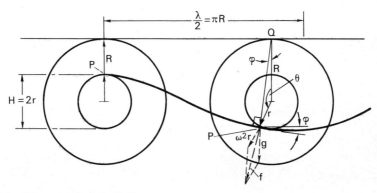

2.1   Diagram of trochoidal wave

the motion of the surface, and a curve of this shape is called trochoidal. In this frame of reference, the point at the top of the wheel of radius R which is in contact with the imaginary line at point Q is stationary with respect to the wave front, and at that instant, point P acts as if it were rolling about point Q with a radius of PQ. Therefore, since point P is sweeping out the surface of the wave, this surface must be perpendicular to the line PQ. If point P is to satisfy the conditions on the surface, the sum of the inertial and gravitational forces must be perpendicular to the surface. If the force is perpendicular to the surface, then

$$\frac{\omega^2 r}{g} = \frac{r}{R} \tag{2.1}$$

since the force triangle is similar to the triangle whose sides are r and R; therefore

$$\omega^2 = \frac{g}{R} \tag{2.2}$$

The wave front is propagating with a speed

$$V_w = \omega R \tag{2.3}$$

Therefore:

$$\omega^2 = \frac{V_w^2}{R^2} = \frac{g}{R} \tag{2.4}$$

The wave length L is the distance over which the wheel of radius R would roll in one revolution, so: $\lambda = 2\pi R$

Therefore

$$\frac{V_w^2}{g\lambda} = \frac{1}{2\pi} \tag{2.5}$$

By assuming the motion of the wave surface to be given by the trochoidal shape and the resultant of the inertial and gravitational forces to be perpendicular to the surface, we find that the Froude number is the proper non-dimensional wave speed parameter and that its value is $\sqrt{1/2\pi}$.

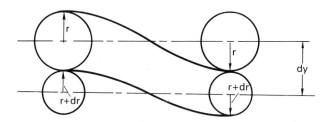

2.2   Diagram of trochoidal wave at different depths

It is also of interest to examine the magnitude of the force perpendicular to the surface. This force is caused by the weight of the water and its acceleration resulting in an effective modified acceleration due to gravity in the water. The surface water particles are at a constant pressure equal to one atmosphere during the wave; and similarly the water particles below the surface should remain at constant pressure during the wave cycle. The two accelerations, centrifugal and gravitational, are shown in Figure 2.1. The resulting acceleration f can be determined by employing the law of cosines: $f^2 = g^2 + (\omega^2 r)^2 - 2g\omega^2 r \cos \theta$

$$\frac{f}{g} = \sqrt{1 + \left(\frac{\omega^2 r}{g}\right)^2 - 2\frac{\omega^2 r}{g} \cos \theta} \tag{2.6}$$

but since:

$$\frac{\omega^2 r}{g} = \frac{r}{R}, \frac{f}{g} = \sqrt{1 + \left(\frac{r}{R}\right)^2 - 2\frac{r}{R} \cos \theta} \tag{2.7}$$

This relation can be simplified at the crest and trough of each wave where $\theta = 0°$ and $180°$.

$$\frac{f}{g} = 1 - \frac{r}{R} \text{ at the crest}$$

and

$$\frac{f}{g} = 1 + \frac{r}{R} \text{ at the trough} \tag{2.8}$$

If the pressure on each underwater particle is to remain the same through the waves, the actual depth of submergence must be greater at the crest than at the trough because of the difference in effective acceleration. If the pressure is constant, a relation for the way the wave motion decreases with depth can be found. The motion of particles below the surface is given by the rule which described the surface particles, except that the center of the circle must be lowered by the depth of submergence. The value of r need not be the same.

Referring to Figure 2.2, it can be seen that the distance between two particles a distance dy apart in still water is:

$$dy - \cos \theta dr$$

where dr is the change in r between the two depths. If pressure is to be constant for each of the particles, then:

$$f(dy - \cos \theta dr)$$

should be equal at the crest and the trough where the acceleration f lies along the direction y. Therefore

$$g\left(1 - \frac{r}{R}\right)(dy - dr) = g\left(1 + \frac{r}{R}\right)(dy + dr)$$

or

$$\frac{dr}{r} = -\frac{dy}{R}$$

Integrating gives

$$\log_e \frac{r}{r_0} = \frac{-y}{R} \quad \text{or} \quad \frac{r}{r_0} = e^{-\frac{y}{R}} \tag{2.9}$$

where r_0 is the value of r at $y = 0$.

The value of r/R can easily be related to the height/length ratio,

$$\frac{H}{\lambda} = \frac{r}{\pi R} \tag{2.10}$$

For small H/λ, the shape is very close to a sine wave but for larger values of H/λ the crests become relatively sharp and the troughs broad. For $r/R = 1$ and $H/\lambda = 1/\pi$, the crests become points. This is also the condition of the effective gravity equal to zero at the crests. Waves of different values of H/L are shown in Figure 2.3. $H/\lambda = 1/\pi$ is the largest value of H/L for which this theory has any physical meaning and considerably beyond the value at which white caps would have formed. An examination of Figure 2.1 will show that the slope of the wave surface ϕ is given by the relation

$$\tan \phi = \frac{r \sin \theta}{R - r \cos \theta} \tag{2.11}$$

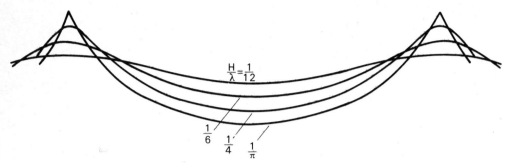

$$\frac{H}{\lambda} = \frac{1}{12}$$

2.3   Trochoidal wave shapes

for the maximum value of ϕ:

$$\sin \phi_{max} = \frac{r}{R} = \frac{\pi H}{\lambda} \tag{2.12}$$

Another interesting relation is the ratio of the velocity of water particles to wave speed. This ratio is easily seen to be:

$$\frac{u}{V_w} = \frac{r}{R} = \frac{\pi H}{\lambda} \tag{2.13}$$

At the crest or trough the water particle velocity is horizontal and parallel to the local water surface. Typical values of these parameters are given in the following table:

H/λ	f/g crest	ϕ_{max}	u/V_w
$1/\pi = 0.3$	0	90°	1·0
0·1	0·686	18°	0·314
0·05	0·844	9°	0·156

Another interesting relation is the total energy involved with the wave motion:

$$U = \tfrac{1}{8} w \lambda H^2 \left(1 - \frac{r^2}{2R^2}\right) \tag{2.14}$$

per unit length of crest. For waves of small r/R:

$$U \approx \tfrac{1}{8} w \lambda H^2 \tag{2.15}$$

If L = 100 ft and H/λ = 0·05

$$U = 2 \times 10^4 \ \frac{\text{ft lb}}{\text{ft of crest}}$$

or the power associated with the waves passing a given point is:

$$P = \frac{UV_w}{\lambda} \approx \tfrac{1}{8}wV_wH^2 = \tfrac{1}{8}w\lambda^2 \sqrt{g\lambda} \left(\frac{H}{\lambda}\right)^2 \tag{2.16}$$

which for the same conditions give $8\cdot25 \dfrac{HP}{\text{feet of crest}}$.

This figure is an interesting one to keep in mind when considering the possibility of surfing on a wave.

The trochoidal wave theory gives relations between velocity, period, and wave length which can be summarized in the following table:

$$V_w^2 = \frac{g}{2\pi}\lambda \quad = \left(\frac{g}{2\pi}\right)^2 \tau^2$$

$$\tau^2 = \frac{2\pi\lambda}{g} \quad = \left(\frac{2\pi}{g}\right)^2 V_w^2 \tag{2.17}$$

$$\lambda = \frac{2\pi}{g}V_w^2 = \frac{g}{2\pi}\tau^2$$

It is useful also to express these relations in units of feet seconds and knots.

$$V_w = 1\cdot34\sqrt{\lambda} = 3\cdot03\tau$$
$$\tau = 0\cdot442\sqrt{\lambda} = 0\cdot33V_w \tag{2.18}$$
$$\lambda = 0\cdot557V_w^2 = 5\cdot12\tau^2$$

It is interesting to observe actual waves to see how they correspond with these relations. In order to make worthwhile observations the period should be timed with respect to a stationary object, such as a patch of foam. The wave length can be estimated relative to some object of known length such as a boat and is done most easily if the boat is lined up with the wave direction. The wave height does not depend on the length and is difficult to measure accurately. A reasonable estimate can be made if the eye can be located so that when the boat is in the trough the crest of the waves just intercept the horizon. The height of the eye above the water is then the wave height. Even if the eye cannot be located in this position, to try to determine where this position would be is a useful way to estimate the height. This method of determination reduces the tendency to underestimate small waves and overestimate large ones.

2.1.1   PHASE AND GROUP VELOCITY

There are two velocities of interest to the propagation of water waves and for that matter waves of any type. These velocities are the phase and group velocities. The phase velocity is the speed with which an individual wave front moves and is the velocity which has been discussed for trochoidal waves. The group velocity is the velocity with which a group of waves moves. It might be expected that these two velocities would be the same, and indeed this is the case when the phase velocity is the same for waves of all lengths. For the case of water waves, the phase velocity varies as the square root of the wave length. The group velocity of a packet of waves of a given wave length is one-half of the phase velocity.

Each wave in a packet of waves is moving with the phase velocity V_w, but the group of waves is moving at $\frac{1}{2}V_w$. A wave which is near the rear of the packet will propagate more rapidly than the packet and approach the front where its amplitude diminishes and it disappears. New waves continually appear at the rear of the packet of waves and disappear at the front.

The most easily observed example of this type of behavior occurs in the bow wave of a boat. While this case is not exactly the one which has been described, it is a commonly observed one. The group of waves propagates outward from the boat at an angle of 19·5° while the individual waves lie at about 35° (Figure 2.4). The individual waves start behind the group, pass through the group, and then disappear in front of the group.

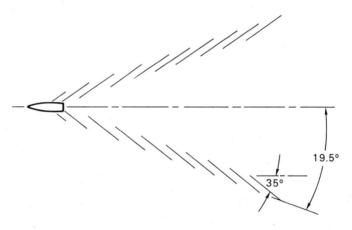

2.4   Ship's bow wave

2.1.2   CAPILLARY WAVES

Short waves are dominated by surface tension forces and not gravity forces and are therefore called capillary instead of gravity waves. The results presented for gravity wave theory are not applicable to capillary waves. For capillary waves the velocity of propagation increases as the wave length decreases, in contrast with gravity waves which have the opposite behavior. Figure 2.5 shows the wave propagation speeds as a function of wave length over a range which encompasses both gravity and capillary waves. The surface tension forces used are those for a clean surface. A minimum propagation velocity is reached at a wave length of about 0·7 in. This is often taken as distinguishing capillary from gravity waves, although capillary and gravity effects are both important for waves close to this length. Short capillary waves and long gravity waves both propagate at the same velocity, a fact thought by some to be significant in the coupling of wind energy into the generating of waves. Capillary waves are of significance to the yachtsman in only two ways. In model testing, the tests must be carried out on a large enough scale so that the wave field created is in the range of gravity waves. On a calm day capillary waves are also an indication of wind since they are the first waves generated on the surface by a wind passing over it. The little waves that cause the surface to sparkle in a wind rift are capillary waves. It is also thought that the small capillary waves moving along with the larger gravity waves are important in the energy transfer mechanism that extracts energy from the wind and uses it to build up and maintain large gravity waves.

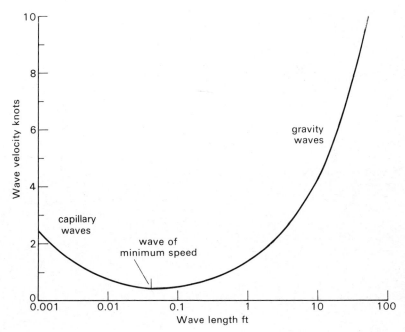

2.5   Wave propagation velocity as a function of wave length for capillary and gravity waves

2.1.3   INTERNAL WAVES

Internal waves are another interesting form of wave motion unknown to most yachtsmen and of only limited interest to him. Surface waves occur at the interface of the air and water at which there is a major change in density from that of water to air. The water in the ocean, however, is not of uniform density. These density differences are caused by differences in temperature and salinity. The denser water lies below the lighter water just as the water lies below the air. If the horizontal water layers are disturbed, then gravity causes them to return to their original position and a wave motion is set up as on the surface. The difference in density between the water on top and that underneath is often very slight so that orbital motions in the waves are very slow and the wave propagation speed is low.

Internal waves have two consequences that are of limited practical interest to yachtsmen. They do cause movement within the entire body of water and result in slow sloshing motions on the surface. These sloshing motions can be important in compacting and spreading out surface contamination which may exist on the surface of the water, and can result in the presence of surface slicks and clean areas. If a light wind is blowing, capillary waves will form in the clean areas and not in the slick areas, giving the appearance of wind rifts. Gifford Ewing of the Scripps Oceanographic Institute in La Jolla, California performed a very interesting series of experiments in which he was able to show a very strong relation between the apppearance and motion of wind rifts and the action of internal waves.[32] This condition may account for the disappointment that most sailors have experienced when they have sailed their boat from a slick area into an area of capillary waves and noticed no improvement in wind conditions.

Another effect of internal waves that is important in a few selected parts of the world is the presence of so-called dead water areas. In these areas the speed of a low-powered boat is greatly reduced. To sailors many years ago this was a frightening experience that led to a wide variety of supernatural explanations. It was the Swedish oceanographer V. W. Ekman who first described the true cause of this phenomenon and related it to internal waves. In some areas of the world where heavy rainfall or large runoffs from melting snow fields occur with suitable geographical features, a layer of relatively pure fresh water can form over the salt water resulting in a large density gradient. These conditions are found in the Norwegian fjords and those in British Columbia and in areas of the Bay of Bengal. A ship moving through such an area at a speed slow enough so that it is generating only minor surface waves may generate large internal waves and experience a large wave drag. For a faster ship, operating at a speed that is already causing considerable surface wave drag, the proportional change in drag is not as pronounced and the change in speed may be small.

2.2   Sea conditions

While numerous attempts have been made to describe sea heights in terms of the wind conditions, it has become obvious that an accurate description of the sea could only really be given in statistical terms. It is not possible to specify one size for the waves, but a spectrum of sizes is required giving the probability that waves of any one size will appear. To understand the nature of waves on the surface of the ocean, two different conditions must be considered. One type, called seas, is caused by the wind and exists in the region in which the wind is blowing. These seas grow with time or distance as the duration (the length of time the wind has been blowing) or the fetch (ths distance over which the wind has blown over the water) increases. After long duration or fetch, the seas will reach a fully risen state when the energy supplied to the waves by the wind, the energy dissipated by the waves in breaking, and other mechanisms are equal. When the wind stops blowing, or the wave trains move out of the area in which the wind is blowing, the waves decrease in size and become much more regular. These waves are called swells. This distinction between seas and swells can be made in two ways. First, they can be differentiated by the location in which they are found: seas in the area in which the wind which generates them is blowing, and swells in the area in which the wind that generates them is not blowing. Second, their appearance is quite different: seas provide an irregular appearance consisting of waves of different sizes and directions, while swells are regular and uniform.

2.2.1   SEAS

Seas may be thought of as the sum of many small waves of different wave lengths moving in different directions. At some points these various small waves interfere constructively to form large seas and at others destructively. The crests are not regular and the surface consists of many peaks and hollows. The crest of a sea can be followed for a short interval but not for long because that particular sea no longer continues to exist. Since the small waves which formed it are of different lengths and moving at different velocities, their phases shift with respect to each other so that, while they interfere constructively at one time, a short time thereafter the interference is destructive and the sea simply disappears. Similarly a new sea will rise up where one had not existed before. Since these waves which form the seas are all moving in different directions, peaks and hollows are formed as the waves interfere with each other in different ways.

One of the better ways of describing and predicting the behavior of waves is given by the US Navy Hydrographic Office's publication HO 603. This approach describes seas by the energy contained within the wave motion which at any given location depends on the strength and duration of the wind and the fetch. The value of this energy determines the properties of the seas, the height and the period.

The relation between the wave heights and the value of the wave energy U is shown in Figure 2.6. The wave size varies from 0 to ∞ times $\sqrt{U}$. There is no cut-off of the spectrum that prohibits the presence of a very small wave or a very large wave; however, it is very unlikely that one of these extreme waves will occur. To specify the height of waves by one number is not a reasonable thing to do; however, different types of averages can be made which help to characterize them.

The most frequent wave has a height of $1 \cdot 41 \sqrt{U}$ which is that which would

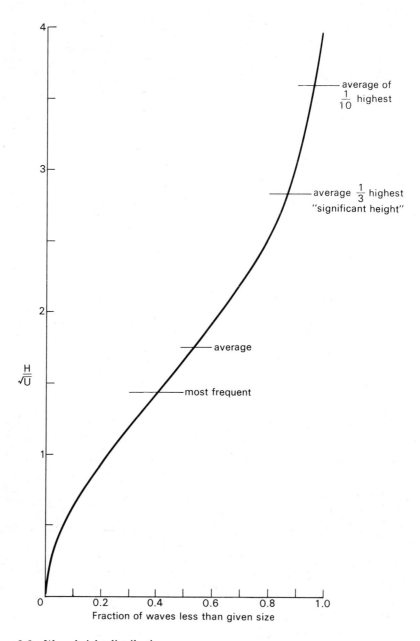

2.6   Wave height distribution

appear most frequently in a series of measurements. The average wave height is equal to $1.77\sqrt{U}$. This number represents an average of the heights of all the waves weighted by the probability of their occurrence. The significant wave height is taken as the weighted average of the highest third of the waves. This height is probably the one most representative of the sea state and is equal to $2.83\sqrt{U}$.

The average of the highest tenth of the waves represents the expected size of the large waves and is equal to $3.60\sqrt{U}$. A wave of this size should appear about every tenth wave but does not represent a really large wave which may occur occasionally.

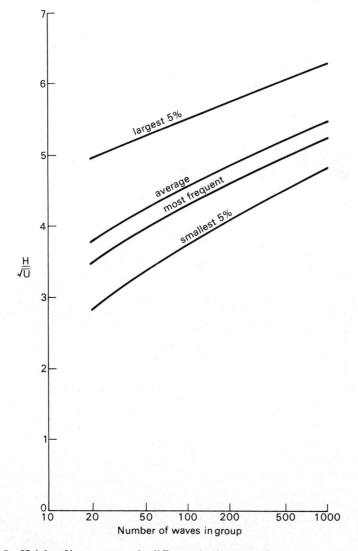

2.7   Height of largest waves in different sized groups of waves

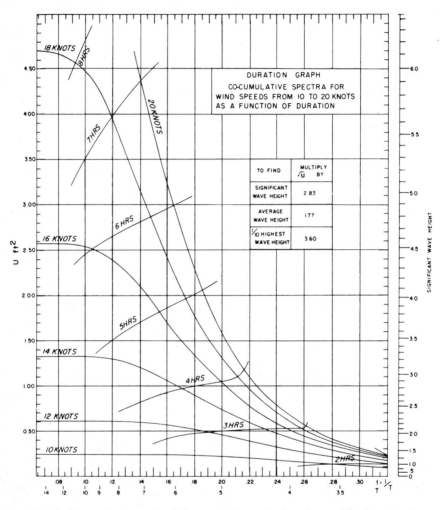

2.8 a-f   Energy in waves for different wind speeds, duration and fetch

A useful way to describe the frequency of occurrence of really large waves is to consider different sized groups of waves and select the largest waves in these groups (Figure 2.7). The larger waves shown here are really very infrequent. For instance a wave in the top 5% of the largest waves in groups of 1000 would only be expected to occur once in 20 000 waves. If the period of the waves is 5 seconds, then 28 hours are required for 20 000 waves to pass a given location.

The value of U, the energy in the wave system, depends on the strength of the wind, and its duration and fetch. The value of U for various values of these quantities is given in Figure 2.8, which shows that for a given wind strength the waves grow with duration or fetch depending upon which is the limiting factor. For moderate

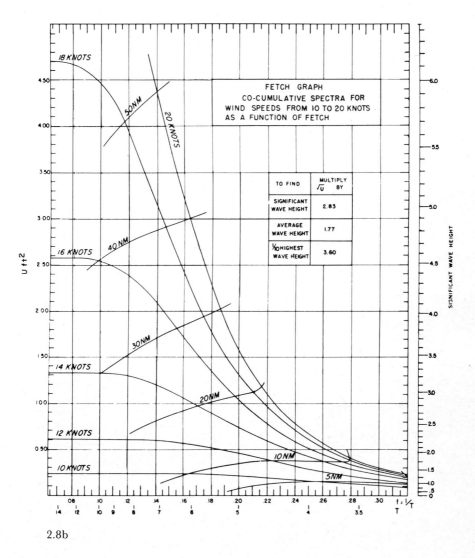

2.8b

winds, the sea can achieve close to its fully developed conditions in moderate values of duration or fetch. For a 20-knot wind, 8 hours of duration or 75 miles of fetch give seas which approach their fully developed height but are still considerably short of their fully developed period. For longer durations or fetch, the height does not increase greatly at this wind strength but the period and wave length do increase. Since initially the height increases more rapidly than the period, the waves become steeper; then as the period becomes longer, the steepness decreases.

The occurrence of a fully developed sea for winds of 45 knots or more is unlikely over most areas of the ocean. To produce fully developed seas the wind would have to blow for more than 50 hours over a distance greater than 1000 miles. For these

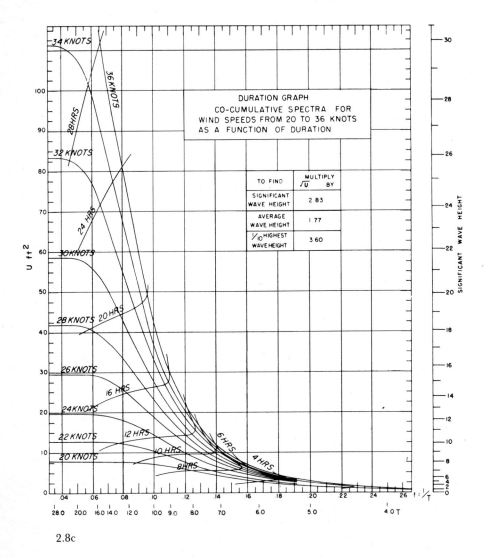

2.8c

reasons, sea states characterized by the larger values of U will seldom be obtained even in the strongest winds. It is only in the high latitudes of the Southern Ocean where winds blow for long durations uninterrupted by land that the really large waves are to be expected.

A few simple relations, which approximate the curves in Figure 2.8, exist between the wind velocities and the wave parameters. The value of U is given by the relation:

$$U(\text{ft}^2) = 0\cdot242\left(\frac{V(\text{kt})}{10}\right)^5$$

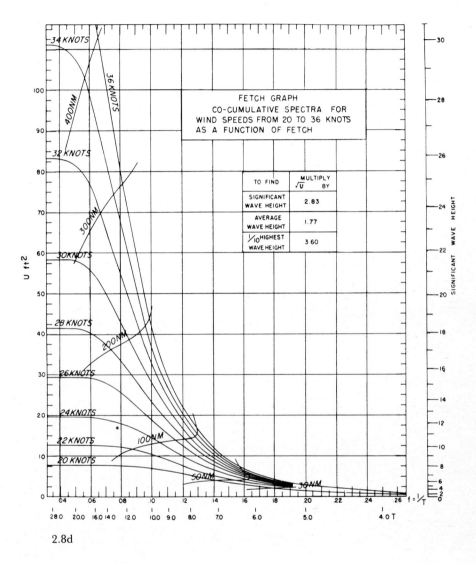

2.8d

The significant height H is:

$$H(ft) = 1 \cdot 4\left(\frac{V(kt)}{10}\right)^{2 \cdot 5}$$

The relation for the minimum duration and fetch to establish fully developed waves is:

$$F_{min} \text{ (miles)} = 0 \cdot 01(V(kt))^3$$
$$T_{min} \text{ (hrs)} = 0 \cdot 025(V(kt))^2$$
$$F_{min} \text{ (miles)} = 0 \cdot 4 T_{min} \text{ (hrs)} V(kt)$$

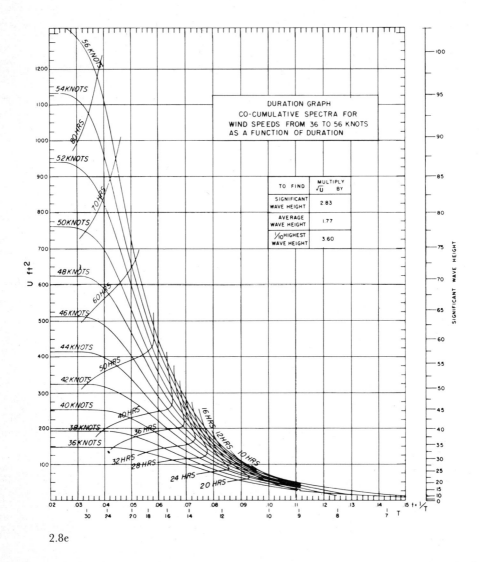

2.8e

This last relation is reasonably consistent with the concept that the group velocity of waves, with a phase velocity equal to the speed of the wind, times the minimum period, should equal the minimum fetch.

The waves of a fully risen sea are not all traveling in the same direction. The difference in the direction of travel is why the seas are short-crested. The angular distribution is given in Figure 2.9.

Many attempts have been made to correlate the observations of maximum wave sizes. These observations are usually presented as a function of wind velocity only. Two of the better accepted correlations have been accomplished by Niederman and Zimmerman. These correlations are reasonably consistent with each other and

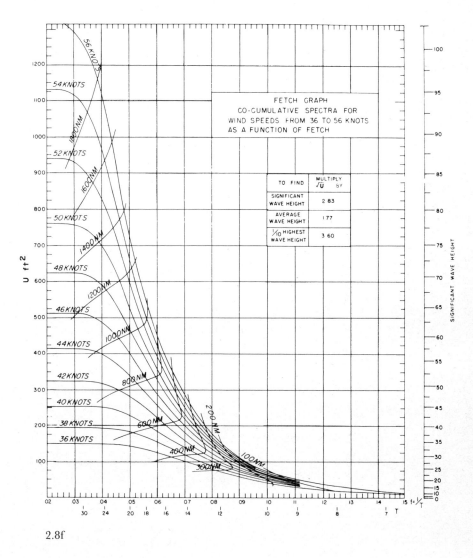

2.8f

correspond closely to the relation

$$H(ft) = 0.8V(kt)$$

This relation and the significant height previously considered are shown in Figure 2.10. The significant height curve is considerably different than the other two. Niederman's correlation is only applicable above about 20 knots but Zimmerman shows the results down to zero wind speed. The wave heights given by this correlation seem very large for low wind velocities. It is hard to believe that they are not simply an extrapolation of wave heights at higher velocities. At the higher wind velocities, these observations fall considerably below the predictions for the fully risen sea.

If, however, they are compared with the predicted wave heights for limited fetch or duration then the agreement is quite good. Figure 2.10 shows curves for 300 to 600 miles of fetch which approximately correspond to 20 to 36 hour durations. It seems reasonable that these observed waves were for conditions of wind durations limited to 20 to 36 hours.

Fetch and duration both limit the energy of the sea in approximately the same way. Figure 2.8. shows that when the wind first starts to blow the energy of the waves is at first found in the waves of the shorter periods. In a relatively short time these short-period waves build up to contain the amount of energy that they would contain in a fully risen sea. As the wind continues to blow, energy is fed into the waves of longer length while that in the shorter waves remains approximately the same.

Another interesting piece of information on wave growth comes from the work of Sverdrup and Munk.[32] They were able to show that the wave steepness is related to the ratio of wave speed to wind speed. This quantity is referred to as the age of the wave since the wave length and speed increase as the duration of fetch increases (Figure 2.11). Note that a maximum wave height/length ratio appears when the wave speed to wind speed ratio is of the order of about 0·4 and that this maximum is at about a height to length ratio of 0·1. Waves moving both faster and slower than this speed are less steep. At slower speeds, the actual height of the wave falls off rapidly since the wave length is also decreasing, and at higher speeds the

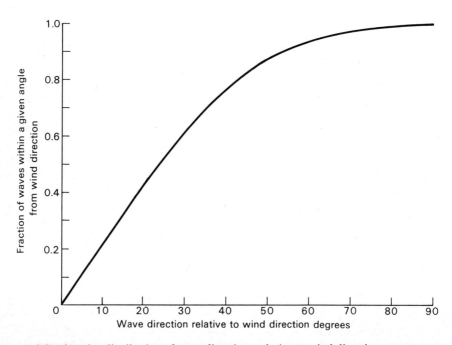

2.9   Angular distribution of wave directions relative to wind direction

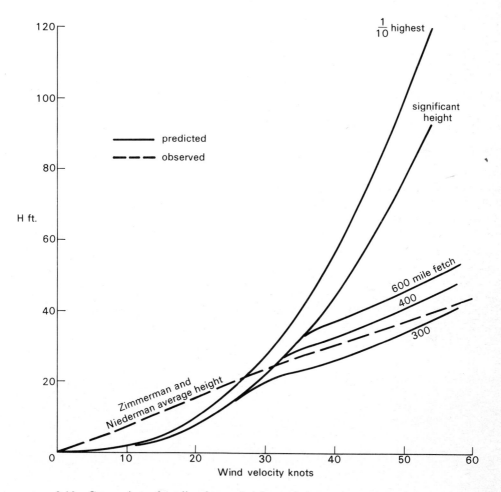

2.10   Comparison of predicted wave heights and observations

height falls off but not as rapidly since the wave length is increasing. When a wind initially starts to blow, the initial waves generated are of short length and travel at low velocities. As the wind's duration increases, the length and speed of the waves increase and they rapidly increase in height and steepness. Relatively quickly they reach a speed equal to half the velocity of the wind and achieve their maximum steepness. As the wind continues to blow, the length and speed of the waves increase but the steepness decreases.

It is these short steep waves that are often of the greatest concern to the yachtsman. Waves with lengths of a few boat's lengths are more important to the performance of a yacht than those that are much longer than it: long waves cause less of a problem because their period is longer and the boat has more time to respond to their motion.

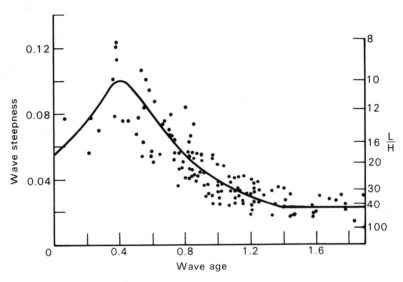

2.11   Relation between wave steepness and wave speed to wind speed ratio

Frequency	Period	Distance traveled in nautical miles	Length of disturbance in nautical miles
.050	20	1960	300
.067	15	1470	225
.083	12	1180	180
.100	10	980	150
.167	6	590	90

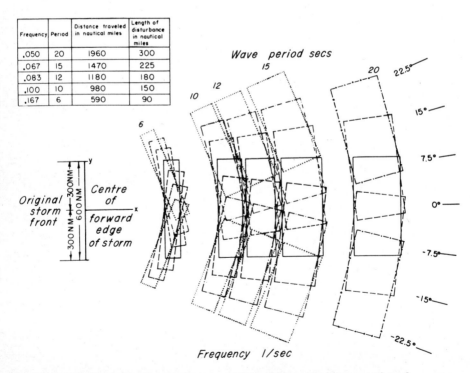

2.12   Propagation of waves from area of generation showing separation of waves of different period and direction after 64·6 hours

2.2.2 SWELLS

Swells are quite distinct from seas. They exist in areas removed from the wind which generated them and they are much more regular. As previously stated, seas can be thought of as combinations of waves of all frequencies and directions, while swells are made up of waves of a narrow frequency band and fairly uniform direction resulting in long-crested regular waves. Swells are the result of the natural dispersion process as waves travel over long distances (Figure 2.12). The storm area is filled with fully developed seas and the wind is blowing only in this area. When the waves in this area reach the limits of that area, they will continue to propagate with their group velocity. After a given period of time, the shorter waves which propagate slowly will only have gone a short distance and the longer waves with their higher velocity will have gone considerably farther. Actually only the waves of a limited band of wave length and direction will be found in any given area, while other waves of different lengths or directions will be found in different areas. The character of the waves in these different areas will be different. The total energy of the wave system in any one area will be considerable and persists after the storm. The frequency and direction distribution of the waves appearing in any one area will be small, but the energy in any frequency and direction that does appear will be about the same as in the storm area. The energy in the wave system is lost very slowly, but the spreading of this energy over large areas of the ocean causes a rapid decrease in energy density. The propagation characteristics of the waves provide a filtering action which decreases the variation in frequency and direction of the waves. As the total energy is reduced the size of the waves becomes smaller. The long waves travel fastest and are felt first at long distances from the source of the disturbance. The shorter waves which follow later may be lost or confused by the presence of waves of similar lengths caused by mild local winds.

Chapter Three
Seakeeping

3.1   Response to wave motion

Waves will cause several types of motion in boats. The most important are roll, the angular motion about the fore-and-aft axis; pitch, or angular motion about the athwartship axis; and heave, the vertical rise and fall. If the motion of the water is sufficiently slow, the boat has no trouble following the motion of the water and the actual waterline does not change appreciably. In this respect, the average waterline must be considered if the waves are not long compared with boat length. However, if the period of the waves is too rapid, the boat cannot respond and its motion may be considerably less than the waves. In between these two extremes is the case where the natural response frequency of the boat and the exciting frequency of the waves are about the same: a resonant condition is established in which the boat's motion may exceed the wave's motion.

In order to determine the response of a boat to the waves the magnitude of the exciting force and of the inertia effect must be determined. The period for heave of small amplitude about the design waterline will be considered first. The pitch and roll period are more complicated because the moments of inertia of a boat are difficult to calculate and general design results are not readily available.

The differential equation for the heave motion is written:

$$\frac{k_h D}{g} \, z'' + z A_{wl} w_w = 0 \tag{3.1}$$

where z = the change from normal draft
A_{wl} = the area of waterline plane
D = displacement
k_h = the factor to account for virtual mass of water
z'' = the second derivative of z with respect to time

In this equation the first term represents the inertial and the second term the gravitational force. Since when the boat heaves an adjacent mass of water also is moved, the actual inertia of all the moving mass is somewhat larger than that of the boat alone. The factor k_h is used to take into account the additional effect and will be discussed in greater detail later.

A solution to this equation is of the form:

$$z = A \sin \omega t \tag{3.2}$$

Then, by differentiation

$$z'' = -\omega^2 A \sin \omega t \tag{3.3}$$

If these relations are substituted into the original equation:

$$\frac{k_h D}{g} \, \omega^2 A \sin \omega t = A_{wl} w_w A \sin \omega t \tag{3.4}$$

38

therefore:

$$\omega^2 = \frac{A_{wl}W_wg}{k_hD} \qquad (3.5)$$

the period:

$$\tau = \frac{2\pi}{\omega} = 2\pi\sqrt{\frac{k_hD}{A_{wl}W_wg}} = 2\pi\sqrt{\frac{k_hd}{g}} \qquad (3.6)$$

where $d = D/A_{wl}w_w$ is the mean draft.

Similarly, the periods in pitch and roll can be determined. In these cases the basic differential equations are:

$$k_pJ_p\theta_p'' + D(h_m)_p\theta_p = 0 \qquad (3.7)$$

the period is:

$$\tau_p = 2\pi\sqrt{\frac{k_pJ_p}{D(h_m)_p}} = 2\pi\sqrt{\frac{k_pR_p^2}{g(h_m)_p}} \qquad (3.8)$$

and:

$$\tau_r = 2\pi\sqrt{\frac{k_rJ_r}{D(h_m)_r}} = 2\pi\sqrt{\frac{k_rR_r^2}{g(h_m)_r}} \qquad (3.9)$$

where the subscripts p and r indicate pitch and roll:

k = the factor that accounts for the mass of associated water
$R = \sqrt{Jg/D}$ = the radius of gyration
J = the mass moment of inertia
h_m = the metacentric height
D = the displacement

It is probably worth noting that while the righting moment of the boat can be described as if the boat behaved as a pendulum suspended at the metacenter, the period of pitch or roll cannot be considered in this way. This is because the boat in pitching does not swing about the metacenter as the pendulum analogy would suggest, but rather rotates about the center of gravity.[*] The metacenter concept is useful in calculating the force term but not the inertia term.

When a body moves within a fluid, the fluid must also move. If the body is accelerated, the fluid must also be accelerated, so the total mass being accelerated is larger than that of the actual body. The apparent mass of the fluid is that amount

[*] Actually, in pitching the center of gravity does not remain motionless. The correct way to handle the problem is to consider all rotations about the center of gravity and all motions as motions of the center of gravity. Coupling terms between the different forms of motion must then be considered. The approach presented here assumes that these coupling terms are zero.

of mass which must be added to the mass of the body to account for this effect. For typical boat hull shapes relations have been developed to predict this apparent mass. While these relations are based on solutions to the fluid flow equations, they are not applied in a rigorous way and they must be considered semi-empirical. For a relatively long narrow body such as a boat, the apparent mass for a section cut perpendicular to the centerline is given by the relation

$$m_a = \frac{\pi}{8} \frac{Cw_w b^2}{g}$$ (3.10)

where C is a coefficient which depends upon the shape of the cross-section. Define the block coefficient β so that

$$\beta = \frac{A_c}{bd}$$ (3.11)

where A_c is the cross-section of the underwater area.

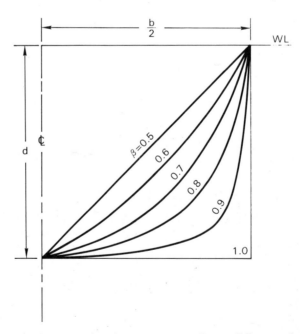

3.1   Typical hull cross-section shapes, corresponding to different values of β

Figure 3.1 shows typical shapes and the related values of β. For shapes typical of keel sailboats it is better to use the draft and cross-section without considering the keel in calculating β. Once β is determined, Figure 3.2 can then be used to find C. The range of d/b values of greatest interest to yacht designers is less than $\frac{1}{2}$ so the value of C is never much different than 1.

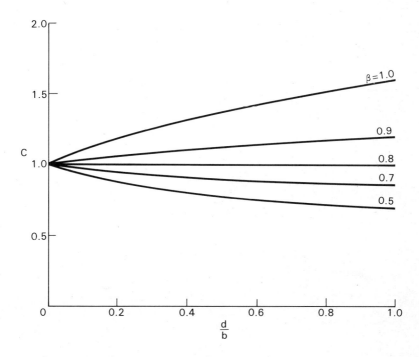

3.2   Values of C as a function of d/b and β

To judge the importance of the apparent mass it is interesting to compare its value with the mass of the cross-section as given by the displacement:

$$\frac{m_a}{m} = \frac{\dfrac{\pi}{8}\dfrac{Cw_w b^2}{g}}{\beta \dfrac{w_w}{g} bd} = \frac{\pi}{8}\frac{C}{\beta}\frac{b}{d} \tag{3.12}$$

Since b/d is usually considerably greater than 1, m_a/m can easily be 1 or higher. The value of k previously introduced can be related to m_a by

$$k = \frac{m_a}{m} + 1 \tag{3.13}$$

The apparent mass and its effect on the pitch moment of inertia can be determined for the entire boat by integrating along the length of the boat. The expression for the total apparent mass is simply

and

$$\begin{aligned} M_a &= \int m_a dx \\ J_a &= \int x^2 m_a dx \end{aligned} \tag{3.14}$$

where x is integrated from the forward to after end of the load waterline and must be measured from the center of gravity for the moment of inertia calculation. In one case the value of the apparent mass for a typical yacht was calculated to be 185% of the mass of the actual boat and the increase in the moment of inertia was 69% of the moment of inertia of the hull itself.[29]

To obtain a better understanding of the important physical effects that influence the periods in pitch and roll it is useful to consider a simple example. A shallow low-freeboard boat with a flat bottom and the mass distributed uniformly, proportional to the local displacement, is a particularly simple example.

First, consider the case for pitch. For this restricted case the radius of gyration of the waterline area about the pitch axis and of the mass of the boat about the pitch axis are the same. The metacentric height is:

$$(h_m)_p = \frac{w_w I_p}{D} = \frac{w_w A_{wl} R_p^2}{D} \tag{3.15}$$

therefore

$$\tau_p = 2\pi \sqrt{\frac{k_p D}{g A_{wl} w_w}} = 2\pi \sqrt{\frac{k_p d}{g}} \tag{3.16}$$

where d is the draft. Similarly, the period in roll is:

$$\tau_r = 2\pi \sqrt{k_r d/g} \tag{3.17}$$

The relations for the periods in pitch and roll are very similar to each other and also to the period in heave, and depend on the mean draft. A convenient non-dimensional representation for these periods is $\tau \sqrt{g/L}$ where L is the length of the boat.

For this particular case:

$$\tau \sqrt{g/L} = 2\pi \sqrt{kd/L} \tag{3.18}$$

with appropriate subscripts on τ and k. For all similar boats of different sizes the non-dimensional period will stay the same.

There is very little data on the natural periods and moment of inertia of boats. The calculation of the moment of inertia of a boat is a rather tedious procedure similar to a weight calculation in which every part has to be considered and then added to the others. Two types of experiments can be performed. For a boat in the water the natural period in pitch or roll can be excited simply by pushing up and down on one end or the side of the boat; the pushing must be synchronized with the natural period but this is not difficult to do. The period is thus obtained directly, which is probably the quantity really desired. If the metacentric height is determined, the moment of inertia can be calculated, and will be the moment of inertia including the apparent mass of the water. There is no way from this experiment to determine the moment of inertia of the hull itself and that of the apparent mass of water that moves with the hull. Once the moment of inertia of the hull plus apparent water mass is determined, then the change in period caused by shifting mass can be determined. One of the difficulties with this experiment is that the relatively high damping of the oscillatory motion requires a fairly large exciting force, and it is more difficult to synchronize a large exciting force exactly with the natural period so that the boat moves with its true natural period.

For a small boat which is kept on a two-wheeled trailer the exercise can be run on land by suspending the tongue of the trailer with a spring. This arrangement has much less damping so it might be expected to give a more accurate result, but it is considerably more trouble to set up. This experiment gives the moment of inertia of the boat itself with no apparent mass of water included. This result is probably less useful than the result including the effect of the water and it is somewhat difficult to convert from one to the other. Experiments carried out in both ways for the same boat would give a direct measure of the apparent mass effect.

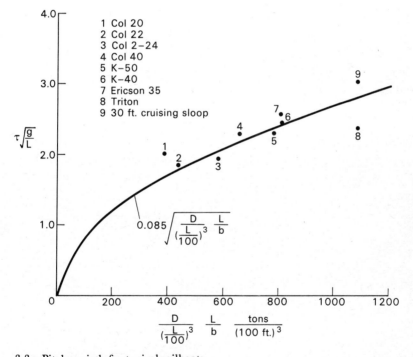

3.3   Pitch periods for typical sailboats

The available data on this subject is rather limited. A general result is that the radius of gyration is about 25% of the length overall.[29] Some results are shown (Figure 3.3) which were made on a variety of stock boats. The abscissa is:

$$\frac{D}{(L/100)^3}\frac{L}{b}$$

which is proportional to d/L for similar shaped boats. A line drawn for

$$\tau\sqrt{\frac{g}{L}} = 0{\cdot}085\sqrt{\frac{D}{(L/100)^3}\frac{L}{b}}$$

for the units of tons and feet roughly correlates much of this data.

It is also of interest to estimate the effect of weight changes within the boat upon the natural period. An example has been reported for a 12 Meter type boat.[7] In this example weights equal to about 5% of the displacement were moved from the center to a distance 55% of the waterline length forward and aft of the center. The result was about a 10% change in the natural period. Another example is obtained from a test of a Lightning, a one-design day sailer. Here the change of frequency with a crew of three (580 lb out of 1300 lb) shifting between a bunched up and spread out distribution is about a 5% change in period. This result is higher than would be expected in the water because of the increase in moment of inertia caused by the effect of the apparent mass of the water. These results seem to indicate that changes in natural period brought about by reasonable redistributions of weight are limited to a few per cent.

3.2. Relation of natural period to wave period

The effective period of the waves as seen by a boat is determined by the speed and course of the boat and the period of the waves. In general we are interested in how the period with which a boat meets the waves compares with its natural period. Also, the waves must be of a certain size and length before they can have much effect on the boat's motion. Waves which have a length of only one-tenth of the boat's length do not cause pitching or heaving. Therefore we would like to know the period of waves of various wave lengths related to the natural period of the boat.

The apparent period of the waves passing the boat is:

$$\tau = \frac{\lambda}{V_w + V_b \cos\theta} \tag{3.19}$$

which can be written in non-dimensional form:

$$\tau\sqrt{\frac{g}{L}} = \frac{1}{\dfrac{V_w}{\sqrt{g\lambda}}\sqrt{\dfrac{L}{\lambda}} + \dfrac{V_b\cos\theta}{\sqrt{gL}}\dfrac{L}{\lambda}} \tag{3.20}$$

If classical trochoidal wave theory is used to describe the relation between velocity and wave lengths then this relation becomes:

$$\tau\sqrt{\frac{g}{L}} = \frac{1}{0{\cdot}4\sqrt{\dfrac{L}{\lambda}} + \dfrac{V_b\cos\theta}{\sqrt{gL}}\dfrac{L}{\lambda}} \tag{3.21}$$

This relation has been plotted for the case of a boat going directly to windward ($\theta = 0$). Lines for various values of λ/L are shown (Figure 3.4). The motions in which we are primarily interested here are pitch and heave since roll can be controlled by various means such as sails or stabilizing devices. For illustration, take a boat with a natural period of $\tau\sqrt{g/L} = 1\cdot25$. Then Figure 3.4 shows that if the boat is not

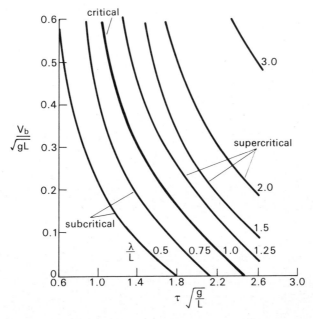

3.4   Boat's response to waves

moving through the water only waves of less than half the boat's length will have the frequency equal to the natural frequency of the boat and all longer waves will have a longer period. We would therefore expect the boat to be unaffected by short waves and to follow the longer waves since it can easily respond to the motion of these longer waves in the time available. If the boat proceeds at reasonable speed to windward, for instance $V_b/\sqrt{gL} = 0\cdot4$, then the boat meets waves of its own length at its natural frequency of $\tau\sqrt{g/L} = 1\cdot25$. Under this condition the boat can be expected to react rather violently to the waves. It will be resonant with the waves and the motion can become very large. At a higher speed the boat will meet longer waves with a period equal to its natural period and the performance will continue to be poor. If the boat's speed is high enough to meet almost all of the waves that exist with a period shorter than the natural period, it reacts hardly at all and tends to go through the waves: actually the boat's motion and the waves will become 180° out of phase. These three modes of operation are called subcritical, critical, and supercritical.

The natural period for a boat with zero forward motion which is the same as the wave period for waves equal to the length of the boat is $\tau = \sqrt{g/L} = 2 \cdot 5$. This value is not much above those measured for many boats. For a displacement hull limited to a hull speed of $V/\sqrt{g/L} = 0 \cdot 4$ a natural period of $\tau\sqrt{g/L} \langle 1 \cdot 25$ is desirable for good windward performance. If the boat does not head directly into the waves the frequency with which it meets waves of a given length will be reduced. However, the frequency with which it encounters waves of length equal to its own length projected in the direction of waves is increased. For instance, if $\theta = 45°$ and $\lambda/L = \cos 45°$ then $\tau\sqrt{g/L} = 1 \cdot 035$ instead of $1 \cdot 25$. It probably is pointless to carry this line of reasoning beyond $\theta = 45°$ since for greater angles the beam, instead of the length, becomes the important dimension. Figure 3.3 shows that for common design practice $\tau\sqrt{g/L}$ is considerably above these desired limits.

Chapter Four
Hydrodynamic Resistance

When a boat moves through the water, a force is created which opposes this motion; this force can be called resistance or drag. In contrast to a solid object sliding on a solid surface, no force is developed when there is no relative motion, but the force increases as the relative velocity increases. This fact means that a very small force can cause a very heavy object to move slowly and makes it possible for very small forces to move large boats. However, since the resistance force increases rapidly with increasing velocity, a large force is required to move a boat at a large velocity. The result is that a ship is the most efficient way of moving objects slowly but one of the least efficient ways of moving them fast.

For a boat floating on the surface, the resistance to motion can be divided into two principal categories: frictional resistance and wave-making resistance. Frictional resistance is caused by the water sliding over the surface of the hull, and the amount of wetted surface is important in determining the frictional drag. The viscosity of the water provides the resistance to the shear caused by water passing over the wetted surface. Closely allied with frictional resistance is form resistance caused by separation behind various underwater parts of the hull. The boat's contours must be kept sufficiently slim so that large areas of separated flow cannot develop. For a well designed boat, this form drag correction should be small. When a boat passes through the water, surface waves are created by energy put into the water by the passage of the boat. These waves cause an additional resistance which the boat must overcome. This force is actually applied to the boat in the form of greater pressures on the forward part of the boat than on the after part and causes a distortion of the surface of the water about the boat.

Air resistance is another force that a boat must overcome. Since water is so much more dense than air, the air resistance is usually negligible with respect to the water resistance. Even at high speeds, when the air resistance becomes a force of some magnitude, it is often a smaller part of the total than at low speed because the water resistance increases so much more rapidly. However, in going to windward against a strong wind, where the relative air speed is much greater than the water speed, the air resistance can become important.

4.1 Frictional resistance

The frictional resistance of water moving over the surface of a boat depends upon the amount of surface, the smoothness of that surface, and the local velocity. Since the water is dragged forward by the hull surface, the sections of the hull further aft will be operating in water which has been affected by the forward portions of the hull and the relative velocities will not seem as high. A proper measure of the effective length of the hull with respect to this effect is the Reynolds number. Because of the displacement of the hull the local water velocities about the hull are different than they would be for a thin object. This effect is usually fairly small and is often neglected in calculations of the skin friction.

The skin friction can be expressed by the following relation:

$$R_f = \frac{w_w}{2g} V_b^2 C_f S \tag{4.1}$$

where V_b = boat velocity
  A_w = surface area
  C_f = skin friction coefficient

The skin friction coefficient is dimensionless and any consistent set of units can be used. If w_w is given in lb/ft^3, V_b in ft/sec and A_w in sq. ft, then R_f is in lb.

  C_f depends upon Reynolds number and surface roughness. The Reynolds number is

$$Re = \frac{V_b L}{v} \tag{4.2}$$

where L is the length for which the water has been flowing along the hull and v is the kinematic viscosity of the water. v has a value of about $1 \cdot 3(10^{-5})$ ft^2/sec. The skin friction depends upon Reynolds number because of the effect of the surface area ahead of a given station changing the velocity at that station. As the friction slows down the water passing down the side of the ship a friction layer or boundary layer of reduced velocity is built up along the hull. The flow in this layer may be either laminar or turbulent. As the friction layer builds up from the bow, the layer is initially laminar and then when it has reached a Reynolds number of about 10^5 to 10^6 it becomes turbulent. Since Reynolds numbers of interest in yacht design are usually higher than this value, the turbulent layer is of greater practical interest.

  The surface roughness is also important in determining the skin friction. When the Reynolds number based on roughness size exceeds a given value, then the friction coefficient is greater than on a smooth surface. This critical Reynolds number is about 100:

$$Re_{crit} = \frac{V_b k}{v} = 100 \tag{4.3}$$

where k is the size of the roughness. Typical surface roughnesses for common ship construction materials are as follows:

Type of surface	k (mil)
Polished	0
Fiberglass gel coat (new)	0·01
Fiberglass gel coat (fine sanded)	0·02
Smooth marine paint	2
Bare steel plating	2
Galvanized plate	6
Ordinary wood	20
Average barnacle growth	200

The Reynolds number for a boat moving through the water is:

$$Re = 1·5(10^5)V_bL \qquad \text{for } V_b \text{ in knots and L in feet} \qquad (4.4)$$

If the relation for critical roughness Reynolds number is considered, then the roughness size to give $Re = 100$ is:

$$k_{crit} = \frac{8}{V(knots)} \qquad \text{for k in mils} \qquad (4.5)$$

Therefore, the roughness values of typical surfaces will exceed this critical value for reasonable boat speeds and all but very smooth surfaces. Figure 4.1 shows the relations between skin friction, Reynolds number and roughness size.

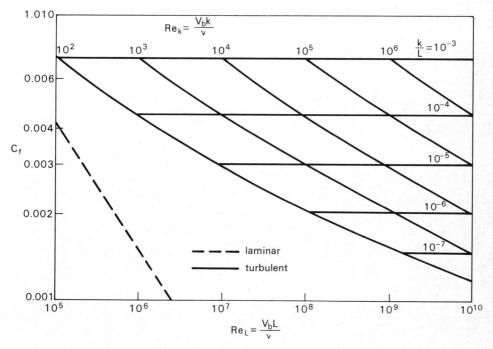

4.1   Friction coefficient as function of Reynolds number and surface roughness

In Figure 4.1 a laminar skin friction line is shown as well as turbulent skin friction curves. For Reynolds numbers greater than 10^5 to 10^6 it is very unlikely that the laminar flow condition will exist and the turbulent results are appropriate. For smooth surfaces the skin friction is given by the lower curve marked $Re_k < 10^2$. For this condition the skin friction coefficient decreases as the Reynolds number increases. For two different sized boats moving at the same speed with equally smooth hulls the larger boat would have the lower skin friction coefficient since it would have a larger Reynolds number. For the same boat moving at different speeds the Reynolds number will be larger when the boat is moving faster. The k/L will be the same for both conditions, so the roughness Reynolds number will also be larger when the boat is moving faster. If the k/L is greater than the critical value for the slow speed case, then the skin friction coefficient will not decrease as the boat speed increases. However, if the roughness is below the critical size at the slower boat speed, the skin friction will decrease until the roughness Reynolds number reaches its critical value.

While a typical value for barnacle size is given in the table, obviously the state of fouling depends upon the time the boat has been in the water. Tests seem to indicate that the bottom starts to foul as soon as the boat is put in the water no matter what kind of bottom paint is used. A good bottom paint greatly decreases the rate of fouling but frequent bottom cleaning is still worthwhile. Figure 4.2 shows some results of measurements made under different operating conditions. The location and the season are both important. The skin friction is shown to double in a few months because of fouling and the rate of increase seems fairly constant.

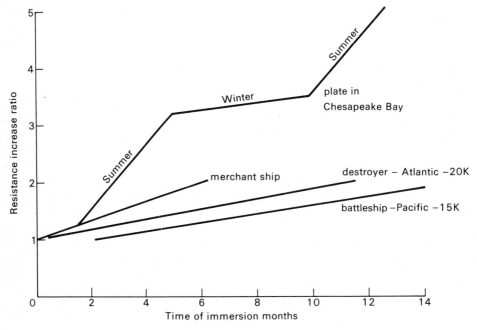

4.2   Rate of fouling under different sea conditions

4.1.1   SPECIAL DRAG REDUCTION COATINGS

The smoothness of the surface is very important in reducing the skin friction, as discussed. In addition to a smooth surface, are there any other changes to the surface that would be effective in further reducing friction? There have been various claims made for different surfacing materials but few of these have been substantiated. The various possibilities that have been suggested are, in order of demonstrated or probable usefulness:

1. Polymer added to the friction boundary layer to reduce turbulence.
2. A flexible skin to reduce turbulence.
3. Change in the wetting properties of the surface or change in surface tension.
4. Producing a slippery surface along which the water flows more easily.

The use of polymer additives has been shown to reduce skin friction when the boundary layer is turbulent, and has been the subject of a rather extensive investigation sponsored by the United States government. Figure 4.3 shows a typical result for the amount of additive that must be used to obtain a given reduction in skin friction.[16] Unfortunately, a fairly large amount of additive is needed to reduce the skin friction. The general conclusion is that for a powerboat the additive required is more than the amount of fuel saved. This quantity should be compared with the specific fuel consumption for an engine of about 0·5 lb fuel/hp hour (see Chapter 10). For a sailboat, the trade-off is more difficult to make, but it seems clear that the speed of a sailboat could be increased. The amount of polymer needed, however, would be too large to be useful on a cruising boat and racing rules rightly prohibit its use.

A satisfactory polymer coating material has not yet been developed that would dissolve from the surface of a hull. If it acted with the same efficiency as the liquid polymer then it would have to dissolve at the rates shown in Figure 4.3 (assuming a specific weight of 100 lb/ft^3). It is readily seen that thick coatings are required and the rate of dissolving must be drastically reduced when the boat is at anchor. On the basis of these numbers the idea does not appear to be very attractive. However, there does appear to be some reason to hope that a dissolving coating might be much more effective than the liquid injection of the polymer since it would put the material into the boundary layer along the hull with greater efficiency. However, this has not yet been demonstrated.

The action of the polymer in reducing the skin friction is at least qualitatively understood. The polymer's molecules are in the form of long strings of atoms which are long enough to substantially increase the damping of the small-scale turbulent motions in the boundary layer and decrease the turbulence. Decreased turbulence reduces the skin friction.

The use of a flexible skin to reduce turbulence has also been the subject of some research. The idea was originated by studying porpoises and other fish who were thought to be able to swim faster than would be possible if subject to the usual amount of skin friction. It was conjectured that a flexible or compliant skin could absorb energy from the turbulent fluctuations in the boundary layer and thereby reduce turbulence and skin friction. Claims for the success of this technique seem to vary; there does not yet seem to be sufficient data available so that demonstrated results can be presented. If a suitable material of this type could be developed, it would be of direct interest for yachting applications. It would not require expendibles and there would appear to be no reason to outlaw its use in sailboat racing. However, the surface constructions which have been considered so far are rather complicated and appear to be too expensive and fragile for practical use in addition to not yet being of proven effectiveness.

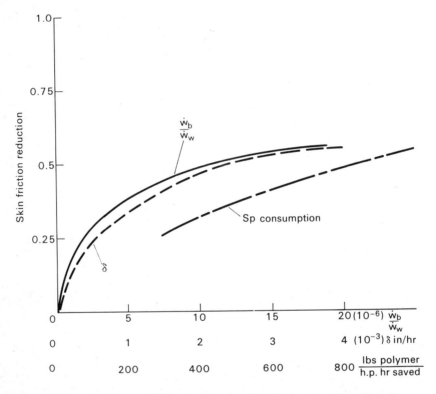

4.3   Effect of polymer additives in reducing skin friction, showing effect of polymer to water weight ratio in the boundary layer, rate of surface dissolving for solid polymer coating of a density of 100 lb/ft^3 at 10 ft/sec boat speed, and specific polymer consumption for power saving at the same boat speed

The properties of the hull surface with respect to wetting has been thought by some to affect the frictional resistance of a boat. However, there does seem to be some variation in opinion on whether better or poorer wetting is desirable. However, tests have never demonstrated any measurable effect of surface wetting on skin friction. Teflon at one time was promoted for such applications but tests showed no measurable effects. However, it does seem possible that surface wetting may influence the action of the water breaking free from the hull at the stern of the boat. On sailboats with long low overhangs the amount that the water clings to and follows up along the hull surface above the waterline may be influenced by the surface wetting properties. Any tendency for the water to cling to the surface above the waterline will cause a reduced pressure on this surface and will contribute to the drag if on an aft facing surface as well as increasing the wetted area. This effect is one of both pressure resistance and friction resistance. To minimize this adverse effect a non-wetting surface material would appear advantageous.

The fourth possibility, that of a slippery surface, may be very closely related to the wetting condition. When a liquid flows over a surface, hydrodynamic theory and experimentation have shown that a very thin layer of fluid directly on the surface is stationary with respect to the surface. If a surface material could be found over which the fluid molecules could slip freely then the friction would be reduced. However, up to the present time there is no reliable indication that such a material does exist and most hydrodynamicists do not expect it to be found.

To summarize this situation, the only practical technique of skin friction reduction is a smooth surface. The polymer additives have been proven to reduce skin friction but do not appear practical for yachting applications. The other techniques have not yet been demonstrated to be effective.

4.2   Wave resistance

Wave resistance is different from frictional resistance in that it does not depend upon the viscous property of the water. The motion of a boat along the surface of the water causes gravity waves on the surface of the water. These gravity waves cannot occur unless the moving body is near the interface of fluids of different density, e.g. the air/water interface. There is no wave resistance for a deeply submerged submarine or for an airplane. In order to create waves on the surface the boat must do work on the water which requires that a force must resist the motion of the boat. In the absence of viscosity, there would be no force resisting the motion of the deeply submerged submarine. If the surface of the water is undisturbed, then the pressure force is balanced by the gravity force. The pressure is hydrostatic and water displaced from a particular position has no tendency to return to that position. If the surface is disturbed, then the pressure at a given depth below the mean surface varies and the gravity force acts to restore the surface to its original position. This gravity force is the additional force which acts on the surface and causes a change in pressure about the boat resulting in resistance to motion and surface waves.

The wave pattern set up around a boat in motion contains two families of waves, the bow waves which spread at an angle to the direction of the boat's motion, and another set of waves which appear at right angles to the direction of the boat's motion. It is this latter set of waves which most influences the boat itself.

The time for the boat to push the water aside in its passage through the water is proportional to L/V_b and the velocity which the water must reach is proportional to V_b. So the acceleration of the water is $V_b/(L/V_b)$ or V_b^2/L. The Froude number is the square root of the ratio of this acceleration to the acceleration of gravity

$V_b/\sqrt{gL}$. In pushing this water aside, the hull must exert forces on the water which will result in higher pressures about the bow sections tending to resist the forward motion of the boat. To cause the water to return and fill in behind the boat the local pressures on the hull must be reduced from their normal static condition. These reduced pressures will also act to resist the forward motion of the boat.

These increased pressures about the forward part of the boat and reduced pressure on the after part would tend to move the center of the upward components of pressure further forward on the boat. Since the center of gravity is fixed, the trim of the boat must change. The boat will squat, the stern will sink, and the bow will rise until the center of pressure of the upward forces again falls under the center of gravity.

The distance it takes the water to return to its undisturbed position under the influence of gravity forces is the natural wave length of a wave moving at the speed of the boat. If the boat is moving at a speed of less than that corresponding to the natural speed of a wave of length equal to the boat's length, the water can easily fill in behind the boat as it passes through the water and the boat's cross-sectional area distribution should taper smoothly to zero at the stern. If the boat is going faster than the speed of a wave of length equal to the boat's length, then the water will not be able to follow the boat's hull if the section tapers smoothly to zero cross-sectional area at the stern, so the stern section should have a cross-section greater than zero. The area curve may be thought of as a wave-shaped area curve of a length equal to the full length of a wave travelling with the boat's speed, and then cut off at the actual boat length.

A good high-speed displacement hull design must be able to accommodate to the changing requirements to be effective at both high and low speed. A relatively wide-sterned boat, so designed that the draft of the hull proper is very small at the stern when stationary, can have the correct low-speed area distribution. A small change in trim will cause the displaced cross-section at the stern to increase rapidly so that a proper high speed area curve can be obtained.

The waves caused by a boat are a good way to judge her speed when the water is calm enough to distinguish the position of the stern wave. If the stern wave appears directly under the transom, then the boat is traveling at about wave speed or a Froude number of 0·4. At double this speed (Froude number 0·8) the stern wave should appear at about three boat lengths astern. The long closing distance behind a high-speed boat with the stern wave appearing many boat lengths behind is a familiar characteristic.

Two types of hulls are often considered, displacement and planing hulls. Displacement hulls are designed to operate at low Froude number (Fr < 0·4); such speeds are too low to give much dynamic lift and the boat displaces a weight of water equal to its own weight. For a displacement hull the curve of areas should approach zero at the stern. A planing hull is designed to operate at high Froude number (Fr > 0·6), to be lifted by dynamic pressure and skim along the surface of the water. At planing trim, the area curve should have reached a maximum at the stern and the buttock lines should be straight towards the stern, slanting downwards. Both hulls cause waves and their motion is resisted by the pressure forces which cause these waves. For the displacement hull, it is easier to think of the energy needed to cause these waves as the source of resistance and not to consider the pressure forces on the hull in detail. For the planing hull the opposite is true. It is easiest to consider the pressure forces which only act on the forward facing portions of the hull. The water breaks clean from the rearward facing portions and no pressure force is exerted on them.

There are several accepted ways for expressing the wave resistance of a boat. All of these forms have some advantages and disadvantages.

R_w/D Resistance/displacement ratio, often expressed in lb per ton.

$$C_{DD} = \frac{R_w}{\frac{w_w}{2g} V_b^2 \left(\frac{D}{w_w}\right)^{\frac{2}{3}}} \tag{4.6}$$

$$C_{DA} = \frac{R_w}{\frac{w_w}{2g} V_b^2 A_w}$$

where A_w is wetted area.

Since wave resistance is not a function of the velocity but the Froude number, dividing by the velocity squared is not particularly useful. Wave resistance depends on the displacement and not the wetted area so there is some logic in dividing by displacement. The coefficient involving wetted area is useful in that this number can then be directly compared with the skin friction to see which is predominant. These three forms can be related as follows:

$$\frac{R_w}{D} = \tfrac{1}{2} C_{DD} \left(\frac{V_b^2}{gL}\right) \left(\frac{w_w L^3}{D}\right)^{\frac{1}{3}} = \tfrac{1}{2} C_{DA} \left(\frac{V_b^2}{gL}\right) \frac{w_w A_w L}{D} \tag{4.7}$$

All of the wave resistance parameters depend upon Froude number.

The Froude number $\sqrt{V_b^2/gL}$ is a dimensionless number. Any consistent set of units can be used for V_b, g and L, for instance V_b in ft/sec, g in ft/sec^2 and L in ft. A less common but consistent set would be V_b in knots, g in nautical miles/hr^2 or knots/hr, and L in miles. Actually the naval architect often uses the specific speed $V_b/\sqrt{L}$ where V_b is in knots and L in feet. The use of the specific speed in place of Froude number is perfectly satisfactory since g is a constant. It should be remembered that a gravity wave moves with a speed given by $Fr = 0\cdot4$ or $V_b/\sqrt{L} = 1\cdot34$ knots/$\sqrt{ft}$.

The wave resistance is related to the Froude number and increases as the Froude number increases. Whenever the boat's length is some even multiple of the natural length of a wave moving at the boat's speed, a bump may appear in the wave drag curve. The size of these bumps depends on the hull shape parameters such as prismatic coefficient, but they are usually quite small, except for that occurring when the wave length equals the boat length. The drag coefficient rises rapidly near a Froude number of $0\cdot4$ causing the phenomenon referred to as hull speed. It is

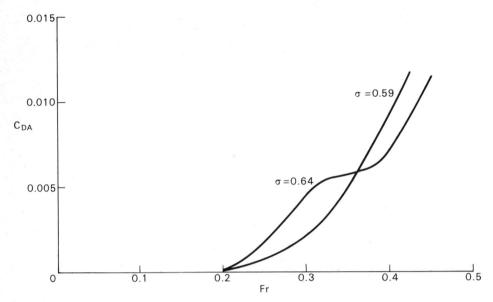

4.4   Wave resistance of typical hulls. Displaced volume to length cubed ratio
$= 0.011$

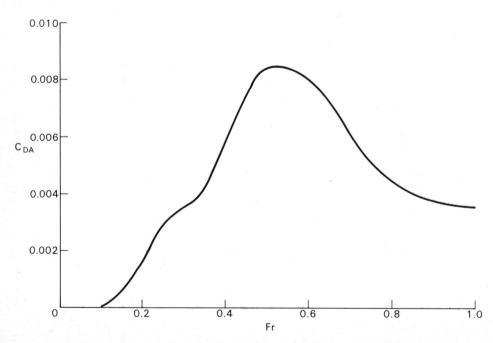

4.5   Wave resistance of high speed hull. $D/w_w L^3 = 0.043$, $\sigma = 0.65$, $L/b = 5.2$,
$b/d = 3.6$, $A/L^2 = 0.18$

possible for a boat to exceed Froude numbers of the order of 0·4 and, for a properly designed hull, the wave drag need not be too large at higher speeds.

Figure 4.4 shows a typical wave drag curve for boats of different prismatic coefficients. The bumps in the curves tend to appear at slightly higher values of Froude number than the integral wave length values of 0·4 and 0·284. They are closer to 0·45 and 0·3. Only the higher prismatic coefficient curve shows the bump at Fr=0·3, but it also gives a lower drag near Fr=0·4. The best prismatic coefficient as a function of Froude number is shown in Figure 4.6.

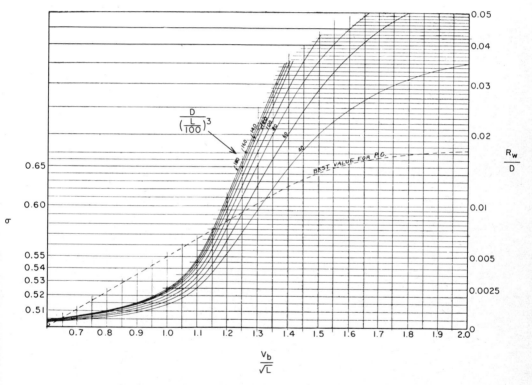

4.6   Wave resistance for displacement hulls for various length/displacement ratios and best prismatic coefficient

Figure 4.5 shows a resistance curve for a high speed boat. Notice the decrease in wave drag coefficient at Fr>0·45. The value of drag coefficient at Fr=1 is down to about 0·0035, and since this is the coefficient based on wetted area, can be compared with a skin friction coefficient of about the same order.

Ignoring the small local bumps, the wave drag can be expressed as a function of Fr approximately as $R_w/D \approx (Fr)^4$ for Fr between 0 and 0·45. R_w/D is relatively constant for different beam/draft ratios with a tendency to be somewhat higher for wide shallow boats than deep narrow ones. This ratio is also fairly independent of length/displacement ratio at values greater than 200 but decreases somewhat at lower values.

A useful set of curves for wave drag as a function of Fr and length/displacement ratio is shown in Figure 4.6. These curves are for the best prismatic coefficient at each Fr. The value of the best prismatic coefficient is also shown.

4.3   Air resistance

The resistance to motions caused by the air is usually quite small. Because boats are usually not designed to have particularly low-resistance shapes above the waterline they can in general be treated as blunt bodies with a drag coefficient of the order of 1·0 to 1·5 based on frontal area. Therefore:

$$R_A = \frac{w_a}{g} V_b^2 C_D A_f \tag{4.8}$$

The value of w_a is about 0·07 lb/ft^3.

4.4   Resistance calculations

To demonstrate how the resistance to motion of a typical auxiliary sailboat hull can be calculated, consider a boat of the following dimensions:

$$L = 25 \text{ ft}$$
$$D = 13{,}450 \text{ lb} \qquad \frac{D}{(L/100)^3} = 360$$
$$A_w = 275 \text{ ft}^2$$

For the hull above the waterline, the frontal area of the hull is 40 ft^2 and the mast 20 ft^2 giving a total of 60 ft^2. The wave resistance, frictional resistance and air resistance have been calculated and are as follows.

$V_b/\sqrt{L}$	R_w/D	R_w	V_b	R_f	R_a	R_{Total}	Power
knots	lb	lb	knots	lb	lb	lb	hp
$\overline{\sqrt{ft}}$	ton						
0·6	0·9	5·3	3·0	22·0	2·2	29·5	0·274
0·8	2·0	11·8	4·0	36·8	3·9	52·5	0·656
1·0	5·0	29·5	5·0	55·9	6·1	91·5	1·42
1·2	22·0	130·0	6·0	77·8	8·8	217·0	4·05
1·4	74·0	436·0	7·0	105·0	12·0	553	12·0

It is interesting to consider the part of the total resistance caused by each type.

$V_b/\sqrt{L}$	R_w/R_T	R_f/R_T	R_a/R_T
0·6	0·18	0·75	0·07
0·8	0·23	0·70	0·07
1·0	0·33	0·61	0·06
1·2	0·60	0·36	0·04
1·4	0·79	0·19	0·02

Notice that the wave resistance starts to predominate between $V_b/\sqrt{L}$ of 1·0 and 1·2 and that the air resistance becomes less important at higher speeds.

The air resistance would be more important under head wind conditions. The values of wind resistance for different head wind velocities relative to the boat speed are shown in the following table. For strong head winds the air resistance can be very important.

V_a knots	R_a lb
10	25·8
20	102
30	233
40	413

Consider what would happen if the dimensions of our basic boat were changed. Keep the displacement constant but increase the length; also keep the same relative cross-sections. Then:

$$d \sim b \sim 1/\sqrt{L} \qquad \text{Wetted surface} \sim (b+d)L \sim \sqrt{L}$$

If L is increased by 50% then the following results are obtained:

$$A_w = 335 \text{ ft}^2 \qquad D/(L/100)^3 = 107$$

V_b knots	$V_b/\sqrt{L}$ $\dfrac{knots}{\sqrt{ft}}$	Rw/D $\dfrac{lb}{ton}$	R_w lb	R_f lb	R_a lb	R_T lb	R_T/D $\dfrac{lb}{lb}$
3	0·49	0·8	4·4	27	2·2	33·6	2·5 $(10)^{-3}$
4	0·65	1·0	5·5	45	3·9	54·4	4·0 $(10)^{-3}$
5	0·85	2·0	11·0	68·5	6·1	85·6	6·4 $(10)^{-3}$
6	0·98	4·0	22·0	95·5	8·8	126·3	9·4 $(10)^{-3}$
7	1·14	12·0	66·0	129	12·0	207	1·54$(10)^{-2}$
8	1·30	36·0	198	161	15·7	375	2·8 $(10)^{-2}$
9	1·47	76·0	420	198	20·0	638	4·8 $(10)^{-2}$
10	1·63	106·0	585	238	24·5	848	6·3 $(10)^{-2}$

This slimmer boat can reach considerably higher speeds than the original boat and requires less power at high speeds but more power at low speed.

The last column shows the ratio of resistance to displacement. This varies from numbers of the order of 1 to 1000 to numbers of the order of 1 to 10, showing the great efficiency of a boat at low speeds and the rapid decrease as it is driven to higher speeds.

4.5   Wave effects

The effect of waves on the resistance and speed of a boat is a rather complex subject which is just beginning to be understood. For simplicity the effects can be divided into three separate categories which can be considered independently. These are:

1. The effect of the surface currents generated by the waves.
2. The effect of the slope of the water surface causing an additional thrust on the boat.
3. The change in resistance of the boat caused by the motion of the boat relative to the surface of the water.

If the surface motion caused by the waves is simply an orbital motion, then there is no net drift and an object stationary with respect to the water will not progress in any direction. However, if a boat is moving with respect to the water at a constant relative velocity the orbital motions can cause a change of speed and the average speed may be different from the speed with respect to the water at any instant. The fact that this can occur can easily be understood if the case of a boat moving with the waves at such a speed that the sum of the boat's velocity with respect to the water and the orbital velocity at the crest of the wave is equal to the wave velocity. Under this condition the boat will stay with the wave crest and move at wave velocity even though its relative velocity with respect to the water is less. If the boat is moving at a slower velocity it will not stay with the wave crest and the effect will not be as dramatic. However, it will spend a greater time on the wave crest where the orbital motion of the water increases its speed than in the trough where the orbital motion decreases its speed and the wave profile moves past more rapidly. In going against the waves the effect will be opposite: the boat will be slowed down by the orbital motion on the crest and speeded up by the motion in the trough. However, since the wave velocity and boat velocity are now in opposite directions, the boat will be in the region of the crest for a longer period of time than in the trough, resulting in reduction in average speed. The change in average speed depends upon the change in the relative velocity between the boat and wave in the crest and in the trough. In going against the waves the relative velocity is high and the fractional change is small, but in going with the waves the relative velocity is low and the fractional change is larger. Therefore the contribution of this effect to the change of average boat speed will be larger when going with the waves than against the waves.

In addition to the orbital motion of the water particles, the slope of the water surface has an effect on the average boat speed. In Section 2.1 it was shown that the resultant of the gravity and the orbital acceleration on a particle of water was that the resultant of the gravity and acceleration vector was always perpendicular to the water surface. In other words, the orbital accelerations of the water particles is just that caused by the fact that the gravity vector is not perpendicular to the water's surface. This balance holds for any object floating stationary on the surface of the water. However, if an object is moving with respect to the water, it will spend a different amount of time on the forward and after slopes of the wave with the result that it will be accelerated more or less than the water particle. If the boat is moving in the same direction as the waves, it will spend a longer time and be accelerated more, and if moving against the waves it will spend a shorter time and be accelerated less than the water particles. It is the increase or decrease in the wave's period with respect to the boat that is important, so the effect is largest when the boat is going with the waves and at a speed near the wave speed. In many ways this effect is similar to that of the effect of the orbital water particle motions; the orbital particle motions are the result of the accelerations caused in a particle stationary with respect to the water and the effect now being discussed is the effect due to the additional accelerations experienced by an object moving with respect to the water. Both of these effects cause an increase in boat speed when moving with the waves and a decrease when moving against the waves. However, the effect when moving against the waves is considerably less than when moving with the waves because the fractional change in period is smaller when moving against the waves.

The change in the speed of a boat when moving with a set of waves can be calculated based upon a few reasonable assumptions. The equation of motion is:

$$\frac{D}{g} \frac{d^2x}{dt^2} = D(P - R) - D \frac{dz}{dx} \tag{4.9}$$

The term on the left hand side is the inertia of the boat, the first term on the right hand side the difference between the driving force and resisting force, and the second term the forward force due to the boat's position on the wave. Assume the resistance depends on some power of the velocity

$$R = K \left(\frac{dx}{dt} - u\right)^n \tag{4.10}$$

where u is the local water velocity caused by the wave motion. Assume the wave shape can be represented as a sinusoid

$$\frac{z}{H} = \tfrac{1}{2}\cos \frac{2\pi}{\lambda} (x - V_w t) \tag{4.11}$$

then

$$\frac{dz}{dx} = \frac{\pi H}{\lambda} \sin \frac{2\pi}{\lambda} (x - V_w t) \tag{4.12}$$

and

$$\frac{u}{V_w} = \frac{\pi H}{\lambda} \cos \frac{2\pi}{\lambda} (x - V_w t) \qquad (4.13)$$

Assume that if the boat were in smooth water it would be traveling at some speed $(dx/dt)_0$ such that $P = K(dx/dt)_0^n$.
Then

$$\frac{1}{g} \frac{d^2x}{dt^2} = K\left(\frac{dx}{dt}\right)_0^n - K\left(\frac{dx}{dt} - \frac{\pi V_w H}{\lambda} \cos \frac{2\pi}{\lambda} (x - V_w t)\right)^n - \frac{\pi H}{\lambda} \sin \frac{2\pi}{\lambda} (x - V_w t) \quad (4.14)$$

This equation can be solved and typical solutions are shown in Figure 4.7. For this calculation, the smooth water boat speed was taken as 0·6 of the wave speed. The boat does not surf for $H/\lambda = 0·025$ and $0·05$. The curves for these cases are for one cycle of motion as a wave passes under the boat. For $H/\lambda = 0·075$ and $0·10$ the boat surfs at wave speed. These last two calculations are performed by having the boat moving at the smooth water speed on the crest of a wave and then following the motion as the wave passes under the boat. For these wave sizes, the boat reaches wave velocity on the forward face of the next wave. The speed shown is the absolute speed and not relative to the water. The negative velocity in the trough is caused by the negative water velocity at that point.

Figure 4.8 shows average boat speeds for different smooth water speeds and wave heights. The average boat speed increases because of the wave action. When the boat surfs at wave speed, then the average speed is the wave velocity and this is

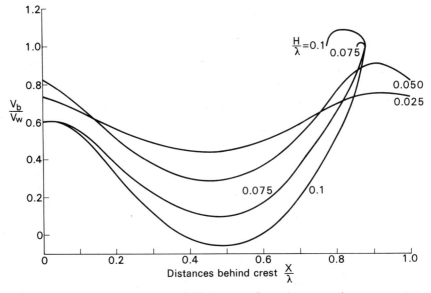

4.7 Surging motion caused by following seas. Smooth water resistance to weight ratio = 0·05, n = 4

the maximum speed obtainable. This calculation is based on waves of a single wave length. Actually, in a wind-driven sea there will be waves of many lengths. Even if the boat obtains wave speed surfing on one wave it cannot continue to do so (as this calculation shows) since the wave itself will not be continuous. The confused nature of the wind-driven sea was discussed in Chapter 2.

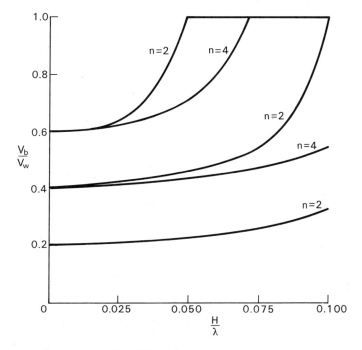

4.8   Average speed before following seas. Smooth water resistance to weight ratio = 0·05

The third effect, the change in the boat's resistance to motion is by far more complicated than the two effects just discussed. This problem has been studied for many years by hydrodynamicists but it is only recently that a reasonable understanding of the effect has been obtained. When a boat pitches a certain amount of energy is dissipated causing the pitching motion to decrease in magnitude if it is not fed by energy from some other source. This energy comes from the propulsion force of the boat and analysis based on this assumption predicts the additional drag caused by the waves. In the previous cases considered, the boat was assumed to be moving through waves with a length long compared with the boat, so the boat could pitch and heave so that it followed the surface of the water and continued to ride on its normal waterline. We are now interested in the case in which the boat is both pitching and heaving so as *not* to follow the surface of the water. The magnitude of this pitching and heaving will depend on the relation between the natural period of the boat in these two forms of motion and the period with which it is encountering waves. These effects have been discussed in Section 3.2 where it was shown that near the resonant conditions the motions could become large. In addition to the importance of the wave period, the theory also shows that the added resistance should be proportional to the square of the wave heights.

Several measurements have been made on this effect. One such experiment has been carried out on a model of a 12 Meter yacht hull towed through waves at an angle of 40° from the wave direction.[7] Figure 4.9 shows the added resistance over that in a smooth sea caused by the waves. This added resistance has been plotted against the period of wave encounter divided by the boat's natural period in pitch. The model was tested for two different weight distributions resulting in two different periods of pitch. The maximum increase in resistance equal to about 0·8 times the smooth water resistance occurs when the period of wave encounter is

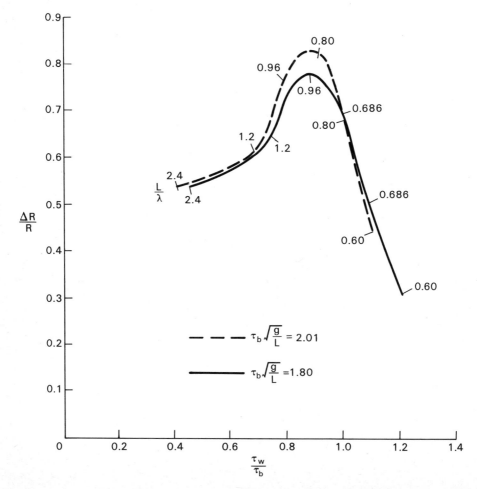

4.9   Increase in resistance of 12 Meter hull in head seas. Fr=0·323

about 0·9 of the boat's natural period in pitch and is the same for both pitching periods. This result is not surprising since the increase in wave resistance would be expected to depend only on τ_w/τ_b and λ/L. The pitching motion reaches a maximum at about $\tau_w/\tau_b = 1$ but the resistance maximum is at a somewhat reduced value. The added resistance peak is higher for the higher inertia model but the maximum pitching amplitude is about the same. Another interesting conclusion from this experiment is that the added resistance caused by the wave does not go to zero as the wave period and length become short compared with the boat pitching period and length, although the pitching motion does go to zero. Even though the boat is not pitching in this condition, the waves along the hull are causing a vertical water velocity and loss of energy.

An interesting combined analysis and experiment has been carried out on a model of a fast cargo ship.[28] In this case the theoretical calculations and experimental measurements have been compared and show that rather good agreement was obtained (Figure 4.10), except when the length of the waves was short compared with the length of the hull. The effect of different wave sizes was also investigated in these experiments, and the results confirmed that the added resistance was proportional to the square of the wave height as was also indicated by the experiments on the 12 Meter hull.

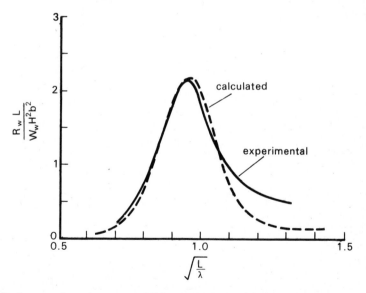

4.10   Increase in resistance caused by waves for cargo ship. $\mathrm{Fr} = 0·25$

The obvious conclusion from these results is that the boat should be designed so that its natural period will not correspond to the period with which it may be expected to meet waves. Figure 3.4 shows the relation between the boat's period, the wave length, and the boat's speed required to create these conditions. Figure 3.3

also shows the pitching period of typical yachts and shows that resonant conditions are likely to occur when sailing to windward at near hull speed. At first it might appear that either increasing or decreasing the boat's period would avoid these problems, but a more careful consideration will show that a decrease in the period is the only reliable solution. Unfortunately, a substantial decrease in the period is difficult to achieve. This is because typical waves in which the boat will be expected to operate will have their energy spread out over a rather wide range of frequencies and a substantial part of their energy concentrated at the lower frequencies. The result is that it is not practical to have the boat's natural period long compared with the period of encounter of all of the waves, and the best results can be obtained by making the period as short as possible in order to remain subcritical to all waves with a wave length equal to the length of the boat, and longer.

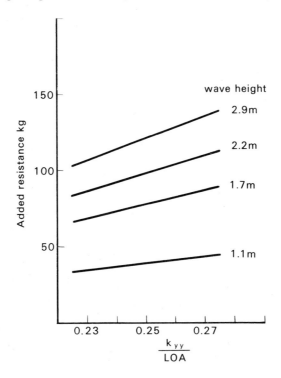

4.11   Increase in resistance caused by waves of a sailboat hull as a function of change in moment of inertia. Still ratio resistance = 154 kg, $V_b = 6.74$ k

An analysis of the performance of a boat sailing in waves with different values of the fore-and-aft radius of gyration which corresponds to different pitch periods has been performed.[29] A sea spectrum similar to those discussed in Section 2.2 was adopted. The added resistance was then calculated for waves of different heights. A result of this type of prediction is shown in Figure 4.11 and shows that a reduction in the pitching radius of gyration or moment of inertia can cause a substantial reduction in the added resistance caused by the waves, and that for the larger waves this added resistance is an important addition to the smooth water resistance of the boat.

4.6   Model testing

There is no exact system for scaling so that the important non-dimensional parameters are the same for both full-sized and model boats. The important scaling parameters are:

1. geometry
2. $Fr = V/\sqrt{gL}$
3. $Re = Vl/\nu$

There is no difficulty in scaling the geometry and making a model similar to the full-scale boat. Fr can be kept constant only by making $V \sim \sqrt{L}$ since g cannot be varied. However, if $V \sim \sqrt{L}$ then $\nu \sim L^{3/2}$ is required in order to make Re constant. No satisfactory fluid to accomplish this scaling has been found.

Luckily the effects that depend upon Fr (wave effects) are fairly independent of Re and the effect that depends upon Re (skin friction) is fairly independent of Fr and geometry. Therefore, the system is to measure skin friction on flat plates or any suitable surface to obtain the skin friction data of the type presented previously. The total drag of a model towed at the correct Fr can be measured and the skin friction drag subtracted to obtain the wave drag. The wave drag is the correct scaled value for the full-sized ship, and the skin friction for the full-sized ship can then be added.

To demonstrate this process, consider a test of the auxilary sailboat previously considered tested to $\frac{1}{16}$ scale. The test conditions and model dimensions are as follows:

	Yacht	Model
$V/\sqrt{L}$	1	1
L ft	25	$1\frac{9}{16}$
V knots	5	1·25
D lb	13 450	3·29
A_w ft^2	275	1·075

Assume that the measured model drag is 0·035 lb. The model skin friction drag is calculated as follows:

$$Re = \frac{VL}{\nu} = \frac{(1 \cdot 25)(6080)(1 \cdot 563)}{3600\,(1 \cdot 3)(10^{-5})} = 2 \cdot 54(10^5)$$

$$C_f = 0{\cdot}006 \text{ assuming the boundary layer is turbulent}$$

$$R_{FM} = \tfrac{1}{2}\frac{w}{g}V^2 C_f Aw = \frac{(1{\cdot}25)^2 (6080)^2 (0{\cdot}006)(1{\cdot}075)}{(3600)^2} = 0{\cdot}028$$

since
$$\frac{w_w}{2g} = 1 \text{ slug/ft}^3 \text{ for water}$$

$$R_{w_m} = R_T - R_F = 0{\cdot}035 - 0{\cdot}028 = 0{\cdot}007 \text{ lb}$$

$$\frac{R_{w_m}}{D_m} = \frac{0{\cdot}007}{3{\cdot}29} = 0{\cdot}00213$$

The full-sized yacht will have this same wave drag to displacement ratio. For the yacht

$$R_w = (13{,}450)(0{\cdot}00213) = 28{\cdot}6 \text{ lb}$$
$$Re = 1{\cdot}63(10^7) \qquad C_f = 0{\cdot}003$$
$$R_F = 58{\cdot}6 \text{ lbs}$$
$$R_T = 87{\cdot}2 \text{ lbs}$$

The ratio of wave and friction drag to the total drag for both the yacht and model are:

	Yacht	Model
R_w/R_T	33%	20%
R_F/R_T	67%	80%

The boundary layer on the model is often made turbulent by the use of a boundary layer trip. The friction drag is a fairly large part of the total model drag, so that the total and friction drag must be known with fair accuracy to obtain an accurate wave drag. Errors in wave drag will be relatively more important in the large boat.

The less the scaling the more accurate the process. For very small models surface tension forces become important and the results are not reliable. While this general method seems to be agreed upon, there is some difference of opinion about some of of the details so that accuracy is probably not better than a few per cent.

4.7   Planing hulls

A certain amount of force is needed to push the water out of the way of a boat's hull. This force results in higher pressure on the forward sections of the boat. As the boat moves faster through the water these inertia forces of the water can become quite large compared with the gravity or buoyancy forces and it becomes desirable to use these inertia forces to raise the boat out of the water both to decrease wetted friction area and to decrease the amount of water which must be pushed out of the way. When a large share of the weight of the boat is supported by these inertia forces the boat is said to be planing.

Similarity laws can be written for a planing boat. The pressure is proportional to the oncoming momentum of the water.

$$p \sim \frac{w_w}{g} V^2$$

The upward lift on the boat is the pressure times an area.

$$\text{Lift} \sim \frac{w_w}{g} V^2 L^2$$

The weight of the boat is the displacement:

$$D \sim w_w L^3$$

Since the total lift must be proportional to the displacement:

$$w_w L^3 \sim \frac{w_w}{g} L^2 V^2 \quad \text{or} \quad V \sim \sqrt{gL}$$

Similar boats of different sizes will have the same part of the total weight supported by the inertia forces if $V/\sqrt{gL}$ is the same. The quantity is the familiar Fr. Similar boats of different sizes start to plane at the same Fr and not at the same velocity.

The meaning of planing, or the speed at which a boat starts to plane, is not completely clear. Some parts of the boat are always under the mean water surface and there is always some buoyancy effect. In the same respect, there is always some inertia lift on any planing type hull at any reasonable speed. Planing effectively means that an appreciable part of the weight is supported by inertia forces or that the boat has risen out of the water an appreciable amount.

Planing cannot be related to any specific $V/\sqrt{gL}$. A very light boat could plane at $V/\sqrt{gL} < 0.4$ and a very heavy one could reach very high $V/\sqrt{gL}$ without planing. In practice there is an effective range where planing starts. This is because for similar boats of different sizes both displacement wave drag and planing lift are functions of $V/\sqrt{gL}$. Since wave drag on hulls with normal length/displacement ratios goes up very rapidly with increased speed in the regions of $V/\sqrt{gL} = 0.4$, and effective planing forces also are increasing, the result is that most planing boats start to plane by about $V/\sqrt{gL} = 0.6$.

The lift on a planing surface can be written:

$$\text{Lift} = \frac{w_w}{2g} V^2 SC_L \tag{4.15}$$

If the lift is equal to the displacement and S_w is taken as Lb (length $\times$ average beam) then the above relation can be written in terms of the length/displacement ratio.

$$\frac{D}{(L/100)^3}\frac{2280}{10^6} = \frac{w_w}{2g}V^2 Lb\, C_L$$

therefore

$$\frac{V^2}{gL} = \frac{4\cdot56(10^{-3})}{C_L}\frac{1}{w_w}\frac{D}{(L/100)^3}\frac{L}{b} \qquad (4.16)$$

or

$$\frac{V^2}{gL} = \frac{4\cdot56(10^{-3})}{C_L}\frac{1}{w_w}\frac{D}{(L/100)^3}$$

For an example take:

$$\frac{L}{b} = 4, \quad \frac{D}{(L/100)^3} = 250\,\frac{Ton}{100\,ft^3} \quad \text{and} \quad C_L = 0\cdot2$$

Thus:

$$\frac{V}{\sqrt{gL}} = 0\cdot6$$

The value of $C_L = 0\cdot2$ is a reasonable value for a high trim angle and this example shows that $Fr = 0\cdot6$ is a reasonable speed to start planing.

4.7.1   PLANING

If water is depressed by an object, and then that object is removed, it can only return at a given rate; in fact it will always take about the same time to come back regardless of the depth of the depression if the length is the same. This is because wave speeds and periods are independent of amplitude but depend on the length. When water passes behind the maximum area section of a boat, it must start returning, but it can only do this at a certain rate. If the boat is moving faster than $V/\sqrt{gL} = 0\cdot4$, the water cannot return as fast as the hull is receding. A high-speed boat will trim to assume a position so that water leaves it at points of maximum cross-sections and the water returns to the normal position in the wake. If the boat is moving at $V/\sqrt{gL} = 0\cdot56$ then it takes about another boat length for the water to return. Either a planing or displacement boat will behave in this way at high speed, and a boat should be able to maintain a proper trim with a large cross-section aft.

The total displacement of the hull and the depression behind the boat is equal to the weight of the boat. As soon as a depressed water area is left behind the boat, the hull proper must start to raise out of the water so that the total displacement of hull and depressed area astern of the boat is constant. When the hull rises appreciably it is said to be planing.

Water tends to flow reasonably straight down the buttock on a planing hull since the effective draft is usually small compared with the beam. If some buttocks are at different angles than others, the ones which are more horizontal or rising will have lower pressure and even negative pressure. A hull shape with all buttocks more or less parallel tends to give a more uniform lifting load and gets most benefit out of the wetted area exposed. This type of hull is called a monohedron and seems to be a very good shape.

If a boat is at one angle of trim and the lift is greater than the weight, it rises out of water. This rising moves the wetted surface aft which moves the center of pressure aft creating a moment to decrease the trim angle. The result is a decrease in wetted area and a decrease in trim angle. The boat will plane successfully over a rather wide range of center of gravity locations. If the center of gravity is moved aft the center of pressure must move aft also. This means the leading edge of wetted surface moves aft and the trim angle increases to allow the smaller surface to support the load.

This natural stability both with respect to speed and center of gravity location makes it easy to design a planing hull. The design of a hydrofoil boat is much more involved because it lacks this natural stability.

4.7.2   RESISTANCE AND LIFT OF A PLANING HULL

The resistance and lift of a planing hull will be considered both from a theoretical and empirical point of view. While planing is not subject to a rigorous theoretical solution some interesting analytic results are available. The lift coefficient of a rectangular planing surface may be written:

$$C_L = \frac{0.5 \, AR}{1+AR} \, \theta_p \cos^2 \theta_p \, (1 - \sin \beta) + (C_{Dc})_{\beta_e = 0} \cos^3 \theta_p \sin^2 \theta_p \cos \beta_e \qquad (4.17)$$

where C_{Dc} = cross-flow drag coefficient: equals 1·35 for flat and constant angle V surfaces
   AR = aspect ratio
   θ_p = trim angle measured between the planing surface and the horizontal
   β_e = deadrise angle

This expression for C_L consists of two terms. The first term depends on the aspect ratio and is predominant for short wide surfaces. It depends on θ_p to the first power. The second term is the force on a narrow object caused by the component of the velocity normal to the surface, the cross-flow. It is the term which is important for ski-like surfaces. The contribution of this term to the lift is proportional to θ_p^2 so it is more important at high trim angles.

The line of action of the force described by the first term is about $\frac{1}{4}$ of the wetted length behind the leading edge. The line of action of the force described by the second term is at the mid-point of the wetted length. The resulting center of pressure for any surface should be expected to be between $\frac{1}{4}$ and $\frac{1}{2}$ of the wetted length behind the forward edge of the wetted surface.

Because there is no leading edge suction effect, the force on a planing surface is perpendicular to the surface. Therefore the induced or pressure resistance depends on the angle of trim and is given by the relation:

$$C_{D_i} = C_L \tan \theta_p \qquad (4.18)$$

The induced or pressure resistance is the same as wave resistance. It is easier to think about the pressure forces on the planing hull and waves caused by the displacement hull, but they are the same thing. In addition to the pressure resistance there is also a skin friction resistance. A small trim angle is advantageous for obtaining a small pressure resistance, but a small angle will result in a small lift coefficient requiring a large wetted surface and large friction resistance. If the lift coefficient were proportional only to θ_p and the θ_p^2 term were missing, it can be demonstrated that the minimum resistance occurs when $C_{D_f} = C_{D_i}$ and this result will hold approximately for most practical planing conditions.

To demonstrate the conclusion which can be drawn from these relations, a series of cases will be calculated. First, consider the effect of speed on the ability of a planing bottom to carry load and the associated resistance. Take:

$$\theta_p = 10° \qquad AR = 0.2 \qquad C_f = 0.003 \text{ (friction coefficient)}$$

V		$\dfrac{Lift}{S}$	$\dfrac{R_i}{S}$	$\dfrac{R_f}{S}$	$\dfrac{R_f+R_i}{S}$	$\dfrac{Lift}{R_f+R_i}$
ft/sec	knots	lb/ft²	lb/ft²	lb/ft²	lb/ft²	
10	5·9	8·3	1·46	0·286	1·74	4·76
20	11·9	33·2	5·85	1·01	6·86	4·84
40	23·7	132·8	23·3	3·63	26·9	4·94
80	47·5	531·2	93·5	13·0	106·5	4·98

Next consider the effect of changing AR. For this case take:

$$V = 40 \text{ ft/sec} \qquad \theta_p = 10°$$

AR	$\dfrac{Lift}{S}$	$\dfrac{R_i}{S}$	$\dfrac{R_f}{S}$	$\dfrac{R_f+R_i}{S}$	$\dfrac{Lift}{R_f+R_i}$
	lb/ft²	lb/ft²	lb/ft²	lb/ft²	
0·1	101	17·8	3·63	21·4	4·72
0·2	132·8	23·2	3·63	26·8	4·94
0·4	169	29·8	3·63	33·4	5·06
1·0	248	43·7	3·63	47·3	5·25

For the third case consider the effect of θ_p keeping:

$$AR = 0\cdot2 \qquad V = 40 \text{ ft/sec}$$

θ_p	$\dfrac{Lift}{S}$	$\dfrac{R_i}{S}$	$\dfrac{R_f}{S}$	$\dfrac{R_f+R_i}{S}$	$\dfrac{Lift}{R_f+R_i}$
0°	0	0	3·63	3·63	0
5°	35·8	3·12	3·63	6·75	5·31
10°	132·8	23·2	3·63	26·8	4·96
15°	230·0	61·5	3·63	65·1	3·53
20°	337·0	115·5	3·63	119·1	2·83

The maximum value of $Lift/R_f+R_i$ occurs where $R_f=R_i$ for both the above examples.

For the last example, consider a boat requiring a lift of 100 lb/ft^2 and $AR=0\cdot2$ and find its velocity and resistance at different trim angles.

θ_p	V	$\dfrac{R_i}{S}$ lb/ft^2	$\dfrac{R_f}{S}$ lb/ft^2	$\dfrac{R_f+R_i}{S}$ lb/ft^2	$\dfrac{L}{R_f+R_i}$	$\dfrac{Power}{S}$ hp/ft^2
20°	21·8	36·4	1·18	37·6	2·66	1·49
15°	26·4	26·8	1·66	28·5	3·50	1·37
10°	34·8	17·7	3·16	20·9	4·78	1·32
5°	66·0	8·74	9·14	17·8	5·62	2·14

The power decreases as the speed increases until the power to overcome skin friction starts to predominate. The calculations show that the trim angle reduces as the speed increases but that planing is possible over a wide speed range.

The maximum values of lift to resistance ratio found in any case of these examples is 5 or a little better. This result shows that a planing boat is never highly efficient relative to other means of transportation. It may also be concluded that long-range planing craft are not practical because of their inability to carry sufficient fuel.

It is interesting to compare this result with the high-speed displacement boat. The boat shown in Figure 4.5 gives a wave drag coefficient of 0·0035 at Fr=1·0. Using a friction coefficient of 0·003 a lift/resistance ratio of 6·5 is found, which is as good or better than a planing boat. In many ways, however, the long narrow hull of the displacement boat is not as convenient as the short wide planing boat hull.

4.7.3   STANDARD SERIES OF PLANING BOAT HULLS

One means of predicting the performance of planing boat hulls is to test a series of hulls and apply the results to similar hulls. This procedure has been carried out for a family of hulls of the type shown in Figure 4.12.[9] These sections are for a hull consisting of developable surfaces which have been found to give favorable performance. The hull is straight from section 5 aft with a deadrise angle of $12\frac{1}{2}°$. A series of hulls of various length to beam ratios can be formed by changing the spacing between sections. It has been found that the performances of all these hulls can be expressed in terms of four parameters:

R/D resistance/displacement ratio
C_{Lb} lift coefficient based on beam
L_{cp}/b aspect ratio: the distance from center of gravity to the stern divided by the beam
D gross weight

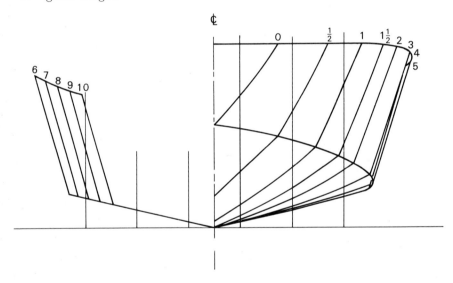

4.12   Standard series planing hull design

A series of curves as shown in Figure 4.13 can be used to express the resistance to displacement or weight ratio as a function of other parameters. The gross weight at a given lift coefficient is really a measure of the size or Reynolds number of the hull for a restricted family of this type. The resistance decreases with increasing weight because of the decrease in skin friction with Reynolds number.

   An example of how these curves can be used to determine the performance of a given boat will now be given. Consider a 15 000 lb boat with a beam of 10·9 ft and a center of gravity 15·3 ft forward of the transom. Then $L_{cp}/b = 1·4$. Assume $C_{Lb} = 0·030$ then from Figure 4.13, $R/D = 0·195$ and $R = 2925$ lb. The speed is then found from the relation

$$V_b = \sqrt{\frac{D}{C_{Lb}b^2}} = 64·93 \text{ ft/sec} = 38·47 \text{ knots}$$

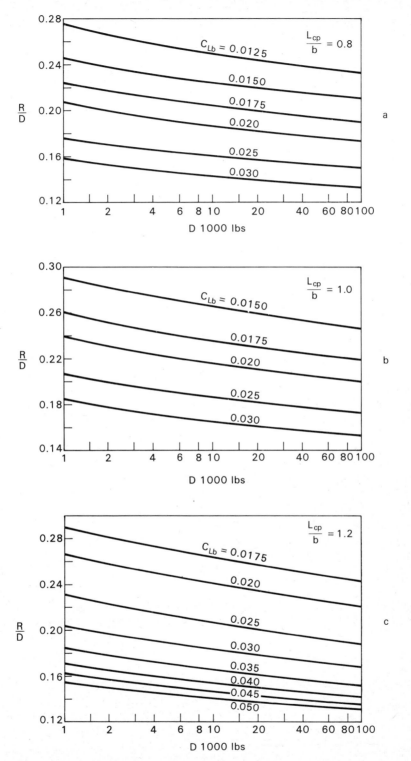

4.13a   Resistance to weight ratio for standard series hull for different lift coefficients and center of gravity locations

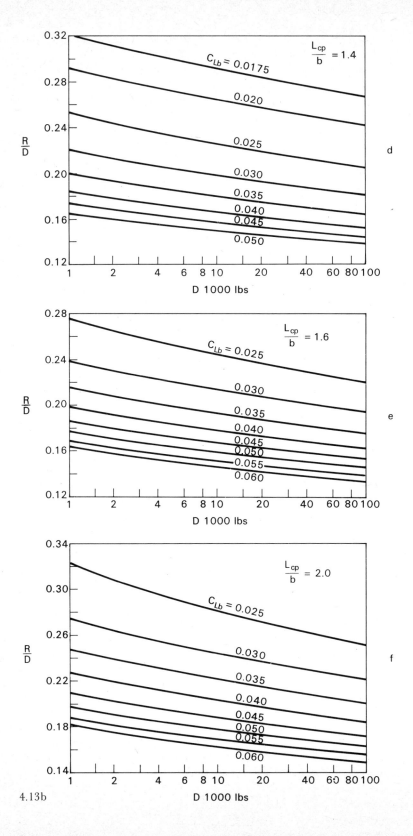

4.13b

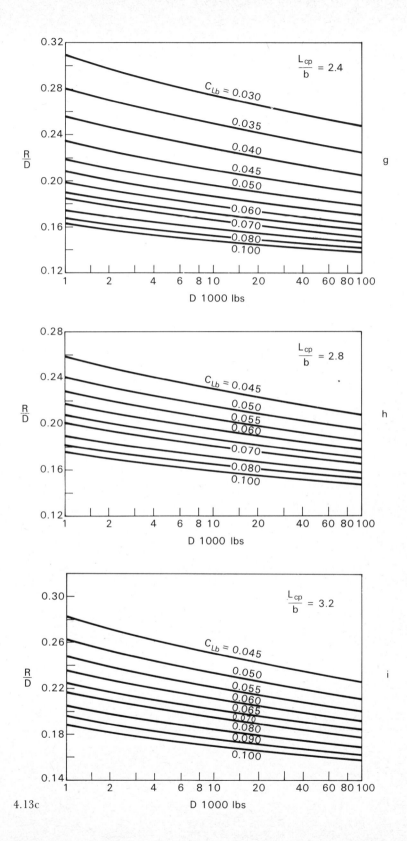

g

h

i

4.13c

While these curves apply only to the particular family of hull shapes tested, they do give results that can be considered a reasonable approximation for hulls of this same general shape. The results found for this family of hull shapes are reasonably consistent with those predicted by the simplified theory previously given. Both of these methods show that the resistance to weight ratios to be expected from planing hulls are high. In the chapter on power plants it will be shown that these high resistance to weight ratios limit the application of planing hull to relatively short range and duration.

4.7.4   STABILITY OF A PLANING BOAT

When a boat is planing its stability is usually considerably more than when the same hull is supported by buoyancy. A planing metacenter can be found as well as the displacement metacenter. Consider the situation shown in Figure 4.14 for a plane rectangular surface. The average pressure on each strip parallel to the hull should be about the same since each strip is at the same angle of trim but the length or area of each strip is different. The total lift over the dynamic pressure is:

$$\frac{\text{Lift}}{\frac{w_w}{2g} V^2} = 2 \int C_L \ dS = C_L A_w \tag{4.19}$$

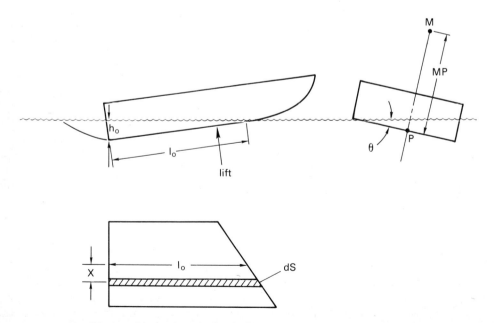

4.14   Diagram illustrating planing hull metacenter

The righting moment then is:

$$\frac{M}{\frac{w_w}{2g} V_b^2} = \int C_L y \, dS \tag{4.20}$$

But

$$dS = \left(1 + \frac{x \sin \theta_H}{h_0}\right) dS_0 \tag{4.21}$$

Therefore

$$\frac{M}{\frac{w_w}{2g} V_b^2} = C_L \int_{-b/2}^{+b/2} \left(x + \frac{x^2 \sin \theta_H}{h_0}\right) dS = \frac{C_L \sin \theta_H I}{h_0} \tag{4.22}$$

Define

$$MP = \frac{M}{L \sin \theta} = \frac{I}{h_0 A} \tag{4.23}$$

where P is the center of the planing forces on the bottom of the boat. Since, for the normal metacenter height $MB = I w_w/D$, D/w_w is the total stationary volumetric displacement of the boat and $h_0 S$ is twice the volumetric displacement of the boat when planing. Since when planing the actual volume of water displaced by the boat is much less than when stationary, the planing MP is much greater than the stationary MB. The result is that the boat is much more stable when planing than when stationary.

4.7.5   PLANING HULL DESIGNS

The discussion up to this point has been limited to simple planing surfaces. A planing hull must use a planing surface or surfaces in such a way to achieve good overall performance.

4.7.5.1   *Single surface hulls*
Hulls using only one planing surface are the most common. A common design uses a fairly sharp V section forward and a flatter section aft. Such a design seeks to achieve the advantage of a sharp V section forward to avoid pounding and the efficiency of a flat load-carrying surface aft. However, in such a design the buttock lines along the center of the hull are at a lower angle of incidence to the water than those away from the centerline. The result is that the water pressure along the

centerline of the hull is lower than away from the centerline and the whole bottom is not working at maximum efficiency. Under some conditions, a negative pressure can even be achieved under the central portion. To avoid this difficulty, the monohedron hull has been developed in which the buttock lines throughout the planing section are about parallel. If a V section is to be used forward then it must be carried all the way aft. Many seagoing planing hulls are of this deep-V monohedron design.

It has already been shown how a single planning hull can adjust to changes in speed and center of gravity locations, but the wetted surface and angle of trim will be affected by these changes and optimum conditions can be obtained at only one center of gravity position for each speed. To maintain the hull at near its optimum trim angle the center of gravity must be forward at low planing speeds and then move aft as the speed increases.

4.7.5.2   *Step and multi-point suspension hulls*

The step and multi-point suspension hull is designed to overcome this difficulty of change in trim with speed and center of gravity change. By using a step, two separate planing surfaces are obtained, one forward and the other aft. If the center of gravity is located between these two surfaces, then both must be in contact with the water and possible trim variations under planing conditions are quite limited. Variations in load between the two surfaces are accomplished by a change in wetted area of the surfaces. Since the depth of submergence of either surface is small compared with the distance between the surfaces, a change in wetted area is accomplished with only a small change in trim. The wetted surface adjusts to changes in speed while staying near the optimum trim angle.

In a two-point suspension hull, both planing surfaces completely span the hull, and the after surface is in the wake of the forward surface. Hulls of this type experience difficulty with ventilation behind the step. Ventilation is particularly a problem when operating in waves and make step designs impractical for seagoing hulls. Some of these difficulties are alleviated by a three-point hull in which the forward planing surface is split in two and located in sponsons on either side of the hull. The problem of ventilation behind the forward planing surface is reduced with this arrangement since it is completely open to the air and the after planing surface no longer runs in the wake of the forward planing surface. The three-point hull has shown considerable improvement over the two-point hull.

4.7.5.3   *Tunnel hulls*

Another type of planing hull is one incorporating one or more tunnels along the bottom. In the 1930s and '40s boats of this type were called sea sleds, but today they are also called catamarans and tunnel hulled boats. Such boats are usually without steps. Hulls of this type have generally been used in small sizes (less than 20 ft overall) and have shown considerable success as sea boats. An interesting feature of this design is that the spray from the bow is trapped in the tunnel and the boat then rides over this cushion of air and foam. While good quantitative tests of such designs appear to be lacking, one is led to speculate that a layer of air or foam may be formed between the hull and water and act as a lubricant to reduce the skin friction. If the skin friction were reduced the need to reduce wetted surface at higher speeds would be less important. A layer of air and foam might also act to cushion pounding and provide better performance in waves. While a good quantitative explanation of the performance of boats of this type is not available, their demonstrated performance makes them competitive with other planing hulls.

Chapter Five
Hydrofoil and Air Cushion Boats

5.1 Hydrofoil boats

Hydrofoil boats are similar to planing boats in that they obtain lift from the inertia forces of the water. The lifting surfaces are separate from the hull so that they can be designed strictly for this application and do not have to play the dual role of hull and lifting surface as is required of the hull of a planing boat. Another feature is that hydrofoils operate submerged in the medium as airfoils do and therefore do not sense the surface of the water.

This last feature leads to the most important advantage and also one of the major difficulties of hydrofoil craft. If the foils do not sense the surface a smooth ride over waves may be obtained. The boat, however, cannot be entirely free of a surface sensing ability since the hydrofoils must be prevented from surfacing and the hull cannot hit the water. Therefore some means must be provided to fly the boat at a given height above the surface. It cannot be done by a pilot as in an aircraft since the height must be regulated too closely; the hydrofoil boat must be designed to sense the surface. This can be accomplished in two ways: surface piercing foils can be used which do sense the surface, or a separate control system can be used.

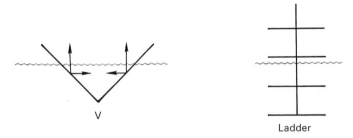

V   Ladder

5.1 Surface sensing hydrofoil configurations

5.1.1 SURFACE SENSING

Surface piercing foils are of two types, V or ladder, as shown in Figure 5.1. The surface sensing principle is the same for both in that the area of the foils changes as the depth of submergence changes. As the foil rises, some of the area rises above the surface, thereby reducing the area of lifting surface. Both types have the disadvantage that their efficiency is less than a simple hydrofoil. In the V type only the vertical component of the lift is useful and the horizontal components cancel each other. In the ladder type the foils interfere with each other and with the strut so that full efficiency is not realized. Both types must operate near the surface where cavitation and ventilation may be serious limitations. The V type is mechanically fairly simple while the ladder type is more complicated.

The surface piercing foil restores the boat's ability to sense the surface and consequently its reactions to waves. The change in the lift forces for a given change in submergence depends upon the foil design so the stiffness of the boat with respect to the position of the surface can be varied. This stiffness should be adjusted so that the boat's response is supercritical for small waves which it can easily pass over and subcritical with respect to the larger waves. The response is generally much softer than that of a planing boat so that an easier ride is provided. For surface piercing foils this response characteristic is determined by the draft of the foils which is considerably greater than the draft of a planing boat.

Fully submerged foils can be used only with some other means of sensing the surface. A surface piercing foil in front and a submerged foil behind makes a workable combination since the bow will be positioned relative to the surface by the forward foil and the resulting change in angle of attack on the after foil with pitch is stable.

A ski which rides on the surface has been used to mechanically adjust a flap on a submerged foil. This leads to greater mechanical complications and some form of non-mechanical sensor has been found desirable on naval hydrofoils. The output of such a sensor can be processed appropriately so that the characteristics of the boat can be modified to suit the existing sea conditions. Such a system is suitable for a relatively large naval craft but probably too complicated and expensive for a private boat.

5.1.2 LOAD-CARRYING ABILITY

The load-carrying ability for similar geometries is proportional to

$$\frac{w_w}{2g} V^2 S$$

Similarly to planing craft, $V^2 \sim gL$ (since $D \sim L^3$ and $S \sim L^2$) is required for similarity among boats of different sizes. Thus a larger boat would be expected to go faster before lifting onto the hydrofoils. Unfortunately, the cavitation limit does not scale in the same way so large hydrofoils are penalized by the scaling laws.

5.1.3 CAVITATION AND VENTILATION

When the pressure around a hydrofoil drops below the pressure of an available vapour or gas, that vapour is likely to fill the low pressure area and form a cavity. The available vapours are steam, at a vapour pressure which depends upon the water temperature, and air at a pressure of one atmosphere. The vapour pressure of water at the usual sea water temperatures is quite low and for our present purposes may be considered fairly near zero on the absolute pressure scale.

The formation of a cavity filled with steam will be called cavitation and one filled with air will be called ventilation. Since a cavity filled with steam can collapse violently when the steam condenses, cavitation can cause damage to the structural parts. Ventilation is a more gentle process and not as likely to cause structural damage.

A measure of the conditions under which cavitation and ventilation are expected to occur is given by the cavitation or ventilation number.

$$\text{Cavitation number} = \frac{p-p_v}{q} \approx \frac{p_a+w_wd}{q} \tag{5.1}$$

$$\text{Ventilation number} = \frac{p-p_a}{q} = \frac{w_wd}{q} \tag{5.2}$$

where $q = w_w/(2g)V^2$, $d =$ depth of submergence, $p_a =$ atmospheric pressure, $p_v =$ vapour pressure. Since q is a measure of the negative pressures that are created about a hydrofoil, these numbers represent the ratio of the pressures above the available gas or vapour pressures to the dynamic pressure q.

Ventilation can only occur when a passage is provided from the surface to the low pressure area so it is dependent on design features other than the hydrofoil itself. Since, for similarity, $V^2 \approx gL$, cavitation number $\approx (w_wd+p_a)/gL$ and ventilation number $\approx w_wd/gL$.

For similar boats of different sizes d/L would be a constant but p_a/L would not, so the cavitation number depends on size while the ventilation number does not. Critical cavitation numbers for hydrofoils are in the range of 0·5 to 1·5 depending on the conditions of operation. To obtain a feeling for the kinds of velocity which could cause cavitation it is useful to note that $q = 1$ atmosphere occurs at about $V = 46$ ft/sec.

A calculation of the value of d/L for which the cavitation and ventilation numbers are 1 at various values of Fr is also informative.

$\dfrac{V}{\sqrt{gL}}$	Ventilation number = 1 d/L	Cavitation number = 1 (L = 30 ft) d/L
0·8	0·32	0·68
1·6	1·28	0·28
3·2	5·12	4·12

As L becomes very large the d/L value for which the cavitation number = 1 will approach that for which the ventilation number = 1. Excessive submergence depths are required to obtain a ventilation number of 1 at a reasonably high Fr, but not for the cavitation number if L is not too large. This effect may limit the maximum size of hydrofoil boats. However, at high Fr ventilation is always a problem.

Another way of looking at this cavitation problem for large hydrofoil boats is to consider that the maximum speed is fixed by the cavitation limit and the Fr decreases as the boat size increases. As the Fr decreases the hydrofoil must become larger to carry the load and an impractically large foil results.

Hydrofoils are not limited to subcavitating conditions, and operations under supercavitating conditions are possible but have performance disadvantages. A subcavitating foil is completely surrounded by water. A supercavitating foil forms a vapour pocket on the upper or low pressure surface that extends well behind the foil before it collapses. If the vapour pocket collapses on the foil then severe damage to the foil surfaces may result. Except for the fact that sub-atmospheric pressure may exist around the foil, the cavity formed by cavitation has many similarities to the cavity formed behind a high-speed planing hull.

5.1.4   EFFICIENCY OF HYDROFOILS

The efficiency of hydrofoils is best described in terms of the lift to drag ratio. Reasonable values for this parameter are:

$$\frac{\text{Lift}}{\text{Drag}} = 8 \text{ at } C_L = 0\cdot6 \quad \text{for subcavitating}$$

and

$$\frac{\text{Lift}}{\text{Drag}} = 5 \text{ at } C_L = 0\cdot4 \quad \text{for supercavitating}$$

The subcavitating hydrofoil gives a better efficiency than a planing hull while the supercavitating is about the same. The action of a supercavitating foil is similar to a planing surface since the upper side is exposed to a vapour or gas in both cases.

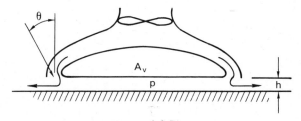

5.2   Air cushion vehicle configuration

5.2   Air cushion vehicle

The air cushion vehicle (ACV) is also known as a ground effect machine (GEM) when used on land, and as a Hovercraft. It is not really a boat, but its application is so similar to hydrofoils or planing craft that it seems useful to consider it briefly at this time. A simple analysis of this vehicle can be made which gives a reasonable understanding of its operation.

Figure 5.2 shows a simple schematic diagram of an ACV. As the name implies it rides on a cushion of air formed by air being blown under the vehicle by the blower provided. It may be propelled either by tipping the vehicle or by a separate propulsion system.

Using the terminology shown in Figure 5.2, the lift may be written as:

$$L = \dot{m}_a V_j \cos \theta + p A_v \tag{5.3}$$

The pressure in the cushion region turns the flow outward. This outflow of air can be related to the cushion pressure by the relation:

$$phC = \dot{m}_a V_j - \dot{m}_a V_j \sin \theta \tag{5.4}$$

The cushion pressure as determined by this expression can now be put into the expression for lift to give:

$$L = \dot{m}_a V_j [\cos \theta + (1 + \sin \theta)] \frac{A_v}{hC} \tag{5.5}$$

The power required to pump the air is $\dot{m}_a V_j^2 / 2$ therefore:

$$\frac{L}{P} = \frac{2}{V_j} \left[\cos \theta + (1 + \sin \theta) \frac{A_v}{hC} \right] \tag{5.6}$$

For a circular vehicle: $A_v/hC = D/4h$.

If the cushion is to be preserved as the vehicle moves forward the maximum vehicle velocity must be proportional to the jet velocity ($V_b \sim V_j$).

Therefore since $L/A_v \sim \dot{m}_a V_j \sim V_j^2$, then for similar vehicles of different size $V_j^2 \sim L$ so that $V_b^2 \sim L$. This results in the same Froude number velocity size scaling as for all other boats.

It is useful to calculate an example by selecting specific values of the parameters. Take $V_b/V_j = 2$ and a circular vehicle with $D/h = 10$ and $\theta = 0°$. Then

$$\frac{LV_b}{P} = 2 \frac{V_b}{V_j} \cos \theta + (1 + \sin \theta) \frac{A_v}{hC} = 3{\cdot}5 \tag{5.7}$$

The quantity LV_b/P is equivalent to L/D for hydrofoils. This number is on the low side but was found by rather crude assumptions. Actually, successful ACVs use a flexible skirt to partly seal the edges of the air cushions to increase the values of effective D/h. When this is done, values of LV_b/P of the order of 10 appear to be obtainable.

Another form of the air cushion vehicle is the trapped air bubble configuration. In this case the ship consists of two side walls which actually extend into the water with an air bubble trapped in between. Various ingeneous means are used to control the escape of the bubble or reduce the air loss either in the forward or aft directions from between the two side walls. With this configuration, it appears to be possible to maintain the air cushion with less expenditure of power than for the more conventional air cushion arrangement.

5.3   Wave resistance

Both the hydrofoil and air cushion vehicle cause waves on the surface of the water and as a consequence must overcome a resistance which can be related to these waves. For the planing boat, the resistance component of the pressure force on the bottom of the boat was shown to be related to the wave resistance. For an air cushion vehicle, the situation is very similar. The cushion pressure will cause a depression in the water under the vehicle. If the vehicle is traveling at high Froude number, the shape of the depression will be distorted so that the vehicle must be continually climbing a wave similarly to the planing boat. For a hydrofoil the situation is somewhat more complex; however, the surface is distorted into a depression which trails behind the boat. The distorted surface causes a modification of the flow about the hydrofoil so that the force vector is rotated aft causing a larger drag component.

While the air cushion vehicle and the hydrofoil do not escape from wave resistance they do have a considerable reduction in frictional resistance. The hydrofoil has very low wetted area, and the air cushion vehicle has no wetted area or can be thought of as imposing a layer of lubricating air between the vehicle and the water.

Chapter Six
Sailboat Performance

While sailboats represent one of the oldest means of transportation, it is only in modern times that aerodynamic and hydrodynamic theory has developed to the point that a quantitative understanding of the mechanics involved has become possible. In its original concept, and up until modern times, sails and hulls were thought of as drag devices, producing forces only along the directions of relative fluid motion (the concept is appropriate for a boat going downwind). In later years, the concept of both the sail and hull as lifting devices was understood along with the concept of sailing to weather. The lift force is the force developed at right angles to the direction of fluid motion. The study of aerodynamics has shown that it is possible to develop a lift force considerably greater than the drag force so that the resulting force is almost at right angles to the relative fluid motion.

A major step in putting the prediction of sailboat performance on a quantitative basis was taken in the 1930s by K S M Davidson at the Stevens Institute of Technology in Hoboken, New Jersey.[6] Davidson's measurements of the performance of the 6 Meter boat *Gimcrack* both full scale under actual sailing conditions and in a towing tank, provided a set of engineering measurements which formed a basis for understanding sailboat performance. The resulting measurements are referred to as the '*Gimcrack* coefficients' and even today are one of the few results available in the literature. Since that time the Davidson Towing Basin at Stevens and other towing tanks have developed methods of predicting the performance of sailboats from model tests so that it is becoming a fairly exact science. Unfortunately, the wealth of data gathered on various hull configurations is a rather closely guarded secret of individual naval architects and the many variations of hull designs make good correlation of such data difficult. There are no tests of standard series such as for ships and planing hulls, but only a few spot data points.

6.1   Sailboat performance predictions

The prediction of the performance of a sailboat may be broken down into consideration of the propulsive effects of the sails and the resistance and stability of the hull. It is convenient to consider the sail forces with respect to the wind direction and the hull forces with respect to the direction of motion instead of the boat's heading. These references make it possible to carry out the analysis without considering either the actual trim of the sails or the leeway of the hull.

The direction and strength of the wind relative to the boat's course in the plane perpendicular to the mast involves the ratio of the wind's velocity to the boat's velocity, the angle between the boat's course and the wind's direction, and the angle of heel of the boat. The effect of the angle of heel on the direction of the relative wind requires some consideration. While the actual relations will be given in a later section, the effect can be understood if it is realized that the direction of the relative wind must be from directly ahead or behind when the angle of heel is 90°.

The hull's reaction to the sail forces is to heel and to move ahead. The pitch caused by the sail forces is small and will not be considered. The resistance to motion of the hull is conveniently broken into several separate resistances. These are (1) wave resistance, (2) friction resistance, (3) side force or induced resistance, and (4) heel resistance. The first two are the usual ones involved in powerboat design for which considerable data is available. Under most conditions these are the principal drag terms for sailboats also. The side force resistance is that caused by the requirement that the boat must develop a force perpendicular to its direction of motion to balance the side force of the sails. The boat must have some leeway to cause this side force, which increases the resistance to forward motion. It is equivalent to the drag due to lift as used in aerodynamics. The resistance due to heel is the increase in resistance caused by the inclined position which the boat assumes because of the side force of the wind. This might be either positive or negative. These last two resistances are relatively unimportant except when closehauled. Under this condition the resistance due to side force can become quite large and is important in limiting how close to the relative wind the boat may be sailed.

The wave resistance is a relatively well known function of the specific speed $V_b/\sqrt{L}$ and the hull shape parameters such as displacement/length ratio and prismatic coefficient. This data has been presented in Chapter 4 for standard ship hulls, but data specifically for hulls with long overhang ratios, often found in sailboats, is less available. The ship results are presented on the basis of waterline length, but for hulls with large overhang ratios some corrected waterline length, between the waterline and the overall length, is probably the correct one to use. The overhang ratio could also have an effect on the change in resistance when the boat is heeled because the effective waterline may change.

The analysis presented here will be limited to the case of displacement hulls with no shifting ballast. The boat must be large enough so that the crew weight is negligible, a condition which will also rule out most planing hulls. The extensions to these cases are obvious but will not be included.

6.1.1   SCALING EFFECTS

As was previously discussed, there is no true scaling since wave-making and friction resistance do not scale in precisely the same way. However, the difference in the two laws is not large if small changes in scale are considered, and the laws are well known so that corrections can be made for larger changes. At the higher specific speeds, wave resistance predominates, so scaling according to the wave drag law gives fairly exact results.

By application of dimensional analysis, a set of parameters may be found to characterize a sailboat. If this list is to be limited to reasonable size discretion must be used to keep only the most important parameters. Once these parameters are chosen, the conditions necessary for scaling are determined. The following list of parameters will be chosen as the most appropriate for the purposes of this analysis.

$V_b/\sqrt{L}$ specific speed of the boat

V_w/V_b wind/speed ratio

A_sL/D specific sail area ft^3/ton
$D/(L/100)^3$ displacement/length ratio $ton/(100\ ft)^3$
σ prismatic coefficient
A_wL/D specific wetted surface ft^3/ton
h_{cp}/h_m stability ratio
A_b/A_s hull lateral area ratio
AR hull lateral aspect ratio
ε arc tan of lift/drag ratio of sails
C_N force coefficient of sails

Some of these parameters have dimensions. They can all be made dimensionless by the use of the acceleration of gravity or the specific weight of water used appropriately. This has not been done since they traditionally appear in the units used and the factors left out are constants. For present purposes they may be considered to represent the dimensionless parameters. These parameters are not sufficient to fix all the characteristics of a boat, but they are the ones which specify the first order effects. For instance, the hull form is specified by the displacement/length ratio and the prismatic coefficient. While the value of these parameters is the same for many different hull shapes, all these shapes should have about the same resistance to motion if they are of the general family acceptable for hulls. The details of the sail plan are summed up in the force coefficient and the lift/drag ratio. In this way the hull performance can be considered independent of detailed considerations of the sails. The aerodynamics of the sails will be considered in a later section.

If these parameters are held constant, boats of different sizes will be similar to each other except for the error introduced by the scaling of the skin friction (Reynolds number effect). In the remaining discussion, this limitation should be understood. The significant feature brought out by consideration of the scaling law is that all parameters are constant for geometrically similar boats if the wind/speed ratio is also constant. Similarity cannot be achieved unless the wind velocity scales as $\sqrt{L}$. This means that larger boats need stronger winds to perform similarly to smaller boats. No real similarity can be achieved without this condition. It is required by the fact that a similar wave pattern requires the same specific speed and that a similar wind velocity triangle requires the same wind/speed ratio. Since the wind speed is not at the discretion of the yacht designer and is constant regardless of boat size, it can be seen that it is more difficult to make a larger boat perform at the same specific speed as a small boat and more difficult to make a small boat stand up to high wind conditions. Since, in general, larger boats which are expected to perform extended voyages are subject to stronger winds than the smaller craft which sail in protected harbors, this condition is fortunate. However, the same specific speed should not be expected of the larger boat as the smaller one in average wind conditions. While it would not be unreasonable to expect a small yacht of, say, 25 ft effective waterline length to reach a specific speed of one under normal wind conditions, it would be unreasonable to expect a truly large sailing vessel, of say 1000 ft effective waterline—the size of a large ocean liner, to approach such a specific speed in normal wind conditions. For normal yacht designs a wind/speed ratio of about 2 is required for a specific speed of 1 which, for the small yacht, means $V_b = 5k$ and $V_w = 10k$ but for the large vessel means $V_b = 31 \cdot 6k$ and $V_w = 63 \cdot 2k$. If such wind speeds were common, the sailing vessel might still rule the seas.

Another effect of this scaling is that stability increases with size. A better point of view is that the stability of the boat is the same when operating under the similarity conditions but the larger boat may be expected to operate under relatively lighter wind conditions. For this reason the larger boat can be designed with less stability.

It is also interesting to note that these same similarity parameters apply to the planing type craft. Since SL/D will be a constant for this similarity law, the ratio of lifting force to displacement will remain constant. Similar boats would plane at the same specific speed which would require very strong winds for the larger boats. It is also difficult to provide in large boats the comparable amount of movable ballast provided by the crew in small planing boats.

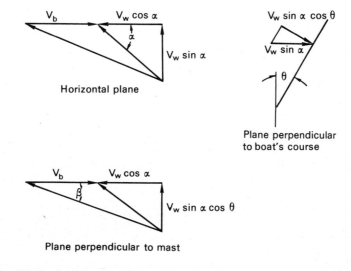

6.1   Wind velocity vector diagram for sailboat

6.1.2   SPEED CALCULATIONS

Having established the similarity parameters, it is necessary to specify the actual relations between them. In order to do this on the basis of available data, a certain degree of approximation is required. Once the parameters that describe the boat are chosen and the desired angle α between the boat's and wind's direction fixed, the velocity triangle is fixed (Figure 6.1). The complicating feature is that when the boat is heeled a three-dimensional problem is introduced. The wind that influences the sails is that in the plane perpendicular to the mast. An examination of Figure 6.1

demonstrates these relations. The magnitude and directions of the apparent wind are both affected by the angle of heel. The appropriate relations are:

$$\tan \beta = \frac{\dfrac{V_w}{V_b} \sin \alpha \cos \theta}{\dfrac{V_w}{V_b} \cos \alpha + 1} \tag{6.1}$$

$$\frac{V_a}{V_b} = \sqrt{\left(\frac{V_w}{V_b} \sin \alpha \cos \theta\right)^2 + \left(\frac{V_w}{V_b} \cos \alpha + 1\right)^2} \tag{6.2}$$

As θ increases, β decreases so that the apparent wind comes from more directly ahead. Plots of the variations of β, θ and V_a/V_b with α and V_w/V_b are shown in Figure 6.3.

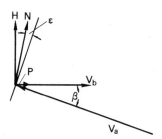

6.2   Propulsive force diagram for sailboat

Once the direction and magnitude of the apparent wind are known, the forces on the sail can be calculated. The total force is taken to act at angle ε behind the direction perpendicular to the apparent wind. This rule is followed as the wind moves aft until the force so found is in the same direction as the direction of motion of the boat. After this point the force direction is kept in alignment with the direction of motion of the boat. This is a somewhat simplified representation but adequate for a first approximation. The forces which drive the boat are illustrated in Figure 6.2 and the appropriate relations for these forces are given by a heeling force coefficient:

$$C_H = \left(\frac{V_a}{V_b}\right)^2 \cos(\beta - \varepsilon) \tag{6.3}$$

and a propulsive force coefficient:

$$C_p = \left(\frac{V_a}{V_b}\right)^2 \sin(\beta - \varepsilon)$$

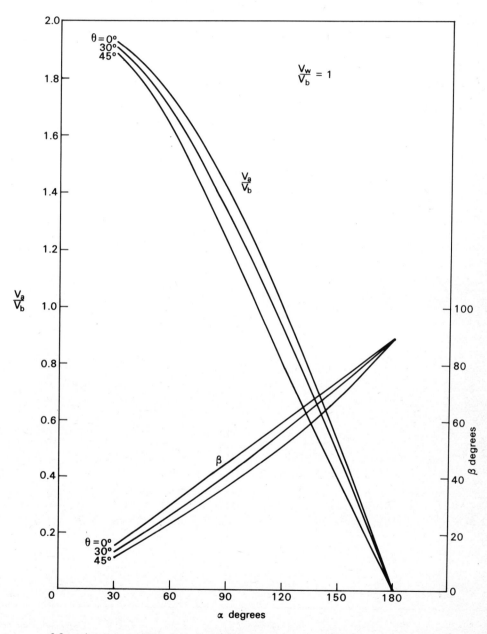

6.3a Apparent wind velocity and direction as function of boat speed and course

6.3b

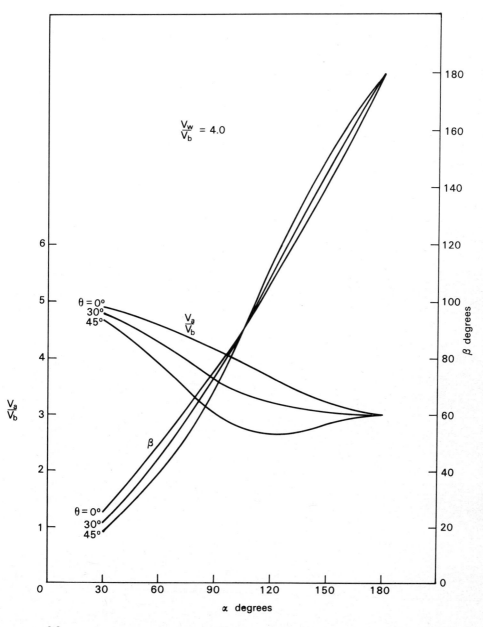

6.3c

where

$$C_H = \frac{H}{\frac{1}{2}\frac{w_a}{g}V_b^2 C_N A_S}$$

and

$$C_p = \frac{P}{\frac{1}{2}\frac{w_a}{g}V_b^2 C_N A_S}$$

These relations are appropriate for the geometric relations and the coefficients C_N and ε give the performance of the sails. The values of C_N and ε are functions of β and the details of the boat's rig. For purposes of calculation, the values measured by Davidson for the 6 Meter boat *Gimcrack* will be used.

For sailing closehauled ε equals $10°$ and C_N equals $0\cdot8$. For the calculations presented here, C_N is kept as $0\cdot8$ and ε as $10°$ for $\beta<100°$, the point where the heeling force becomes zero. After that point it is unnecessary to define ε, and C_N is kept constant at $0\cdot8$. Plots of C_H and C_p for various values of α, θ and V_w/V_b are presented in Figure 6.4. C_H is almost zero for all values of $\alpha>120°$ so it is not shown; also only the curves for $\theta=0°$ are shown for $\alpha>90°$ since side forces are too small to create an appreciable heeling moment. C_H and C_p give the driving and heeling force on the hull. The effects of these sail forces on the hull will be considered next. The resistance force will be divided into four separate resistances; wave resistance, friction resistance, resistance due to side force, and resistance due to heel. The first two are common to all boats while the last two are peculiar to sailboats; these last two will be considered first.

The drag due to side force is the increase in drag caused by the leeway of the hull moving at an angle of attack. The lifting line theory of aerodynamics provides a way of calculating this force for high aspect ratio wings. This formula was developed for large aspect ratios but is reasonably accurate at small aspect ratios. It was applied by Davidson to *Gimcrack* with some success. The correct definition of the aspect ratio to use in this formula is not clear because of the presence of the free surface; however, the aspect ratio will be taken as the cross-sectional area of the hull divided by the draft squared. The formula for the drag is:

$$R_H = \frac{H^2}{\frac{\pi}{2}\frac{w_w}{g}V_b^2 AR A_b} \tag{6.4}$$

which can be written in terms of dimensionless parameters as

$$\frac{R_H L}{D V_b^2} = \frac{1}{2\pi}\frac{w_a^2}{g w_w}\frac{C_N^2}{AR}C_H^2\frac{A_s}{A_b}\frac{A_s L}{D} \tag{6.5}$$

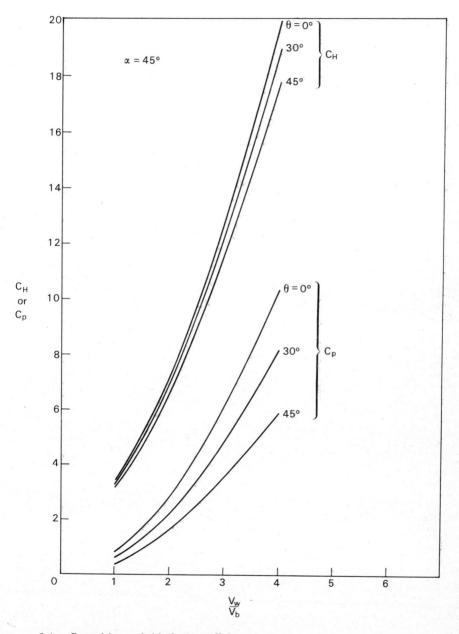

6.4a   Propulsive and side force coefficients

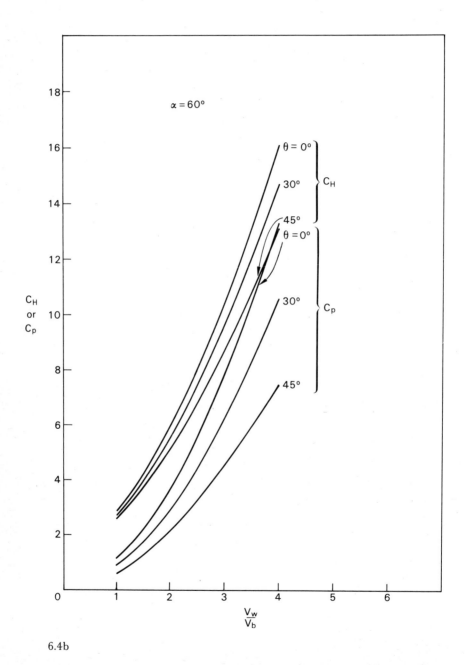

6.4b

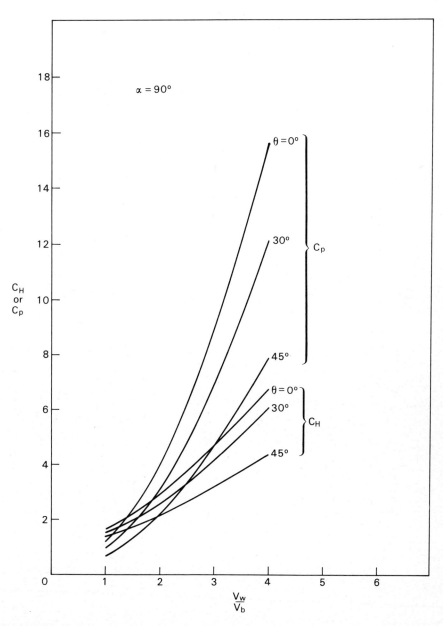

6.4c

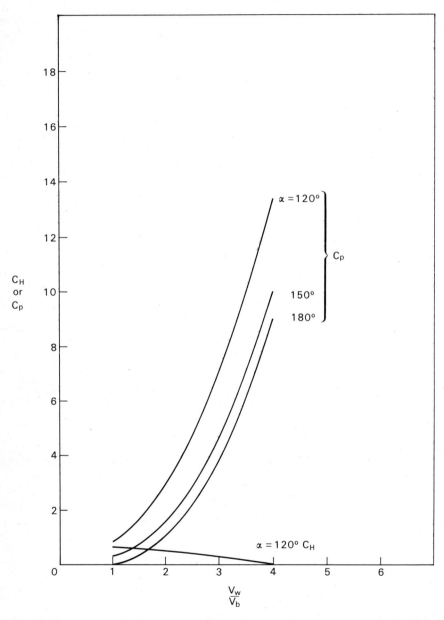

6.4d

The resistance due to the angle of heel is more difficult to calculate. This resistance will depend on the exact shape of the hull form and may be either positive or negative. It is probably also a function of speed since it has an effect on both the wetted surface and waterline length. Because of the lack of better information, a derivative of the form $d(R/D)(L/V_b^2)/d\theta$ will be introduced which will be assumed to be independent of speed and angle of heel. For calculating purposes it will be taken as

$$\frac{d\left(\dfrac{R}{D}\dfrac{L}{V_b^2}\right)}{d\theta} = 1 \cdot 79(10)^{-5}\ \frac{ft}{k^2\ degrees} \tag{6.6}$$

based on the value measured for the *Gimcrack* at $\theta = 20°$. Fortunately, the contribution of this term to the total resistance is not large, so important errors may not be introduced by these crude assumptions.

The major resistances to motion under most conditions are the skin friction and wave resistance. Both of these terms are important in ship design and are known with fair accuracy. The skin friction is given by the relation

$$R_f = \tfrac{1}{2}\frac{W_w}{g}V_b^2 C_f A_w$$

or

$$\frac{R_f}{D}\frac{L}{V_b^2} = \frac{W_w}{2g}C_f\frac{A_w L}{D} \tag{6.7}$$

where C_f is given in Figure 4.1 as a function of Reynolds number and roughness. The wave drag depends principally on $V_b/\sqrt{L}$, $D/(L/100)^3$ and σ. Figure 4.6 shows this relation based on the Taylor standard series tests; Figure 6.5 is a set of such curves to which the friction resistance has been added. This has been done for a smooth surface and a length of 35 ft and for the optimum prismatic coefficient of about $\sigma = 0 \cdot 55$. While these curves are for a particular value of L, they change only slowly with L and are useful over a range of at least 10 to 100 ft.

The curves in Figure 6.5 have been drawn for different displacement/length ratios. Since the curves for $D/(L/100)^3 > 200$ are all about the same, none greater than this value are shown. It should be realized, however, that it will be easier to obtain a low value of $A_w L/D$ for large $D/(L/100)^3$. In this respect, the resistance does change with displacement/length ratio for $D/(L/100)^3 > 200$. At the lower values of displacement/length ratio, greater changes occur and different curves have been shown. The shapes of the curves of Figure 6.5 show that initially the resistance coefficient decreases with increased speed and rises rapidly as wave resistance takes over.

The sum of the four resistance terms may now be equated to the propulsive force. For each particular value of V_w/V_b and θ the value of $V_b/\sqrt{L}$ can be found. If it is desired to calculate the boat's speed for a given $V_w/\sqrt{L}$, then different values

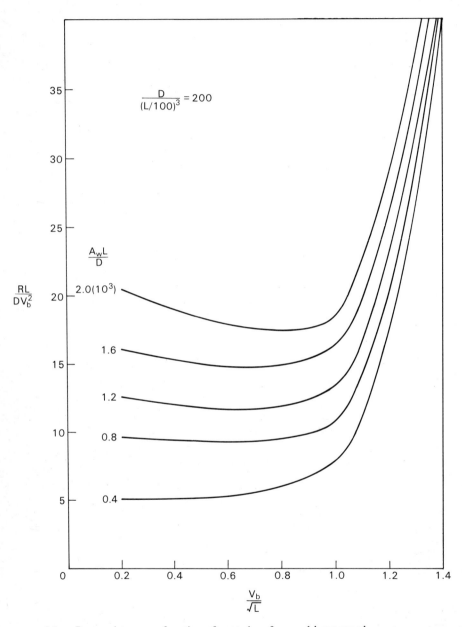

6.5a   Boat resistance as function of wetted surface and boat speed

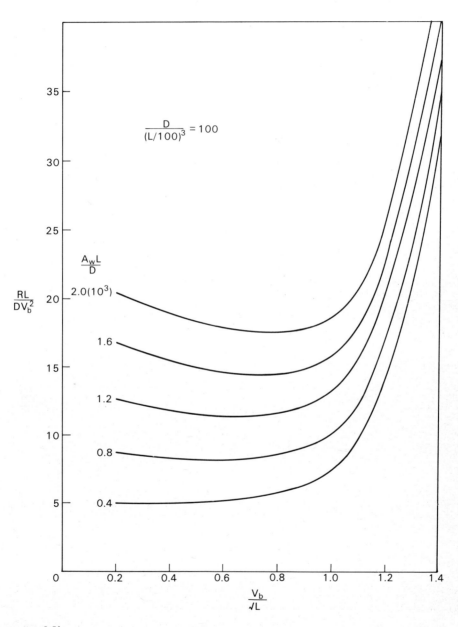

6.5b

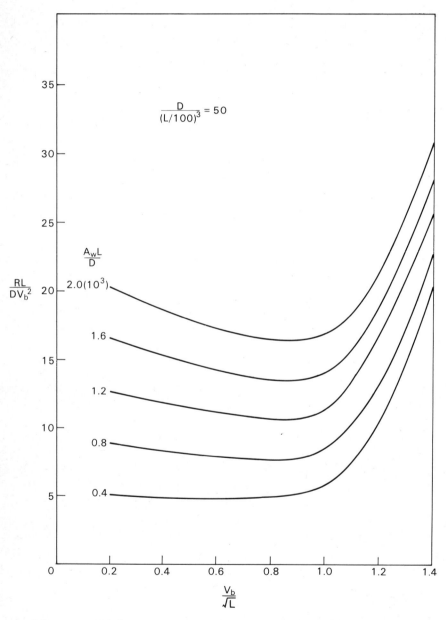

6.5c

of V_w/V_b must be chosen until the desired $V_w/\sqrt{L}$ results. The relation between the hull characteristics and the heeling angle must also be considered. The relation may be derived by equating the heeling and righting moments.

$$\sin \theta = 1\cdot46(10^{-6})C_N C_H \frac{h_{cp}}{h_m} \frac{V_b^2}{L} \frac{A_w L}{D} \tag{6.8}$$

The stability of the boat is characterized by h_{cp}/h_m which is the ratio of the height of the center of the pressure of the sails above the center of lateral resistance of the hull to the height of the metacenter above the center of gravity. To a first approximation, the centers of pressure can be taken as the geometric centers of the sail and lateral plane of the boat. The metacenter can be considered constant, but it is better to use the righting moment curve as a function of angle of heel.

An iterative procedure is required to solve these equations for a given stability parameter. The angle of heel must be assumed to find C_H and V_b^2/L which are required to compute θ, so the computation must be repeated to define the correct θ. Fortunately, a little experience allows θ to be estimated quite accurately and small changes in θ introduce only small changes in C_H and $V_b/\sqrt{L}$.

With these relations, we are now able to calculate the speed of a sailboat. While the relations are not known as accurately as might be desired, they are still useful in an absolute, and especially in a relative, sense. Several results for $V_b/\sqrt{L}$ at different values of α and variations of several of the parameters are shown in Figure 6.6; the parameters for the cases shown are listed in Table 6.1 on page 150. The values of the parameters chosen are typical of sailboats of about 25 ft LWL and have been varied to bring out certain specific effects. The first set of results, cases 1–3, are an attempt to explore the effect of different wind speeds. The curves of speed at different sailing directions are shown in Figure 6.6a. Although the wind speed increases by a factor of 2, the speed of the boat never varies by so large a factor. As the wind speed increases the course for maximum speed moves further off the wind. For the light wind condition, maximum speed occurs at about 80° from the actual wind, where the apparent wind would be about 50° from the bow. The α for maximum speed increases at the strongest wind condition to 100° and an apparent wind direction of 85°. The speed before the wind is most affected by change of wind speed and that closehauled the least. Actually the speed closehauled at $V_w/\sqrt{L}$ of 2·82 is less than that at $V_w/\sqrt{L}$ of 2. This reduction is caused by the rapid increase in resistance due to side force. Qualitatively the curves shown are correct, but exact quantitative results cannot be expected unless more exact hull characteristics derived from tests of a particular configuration are used.

The next set of comparison curves are those of cases 2, 4, 5, 6, in Figure 6.6b. These cases are designed to show the effects on increased wetted surface and decreased displacement. In general, if length is kept constant and the displacement varied by decreasing the midship section, the wetted surface ratio should be expected to go up as displacement decreases. In this sense, cases 2 and 5 might be considered comparable. The displacement/weight ratio of 50 is very light and unrealistic in a

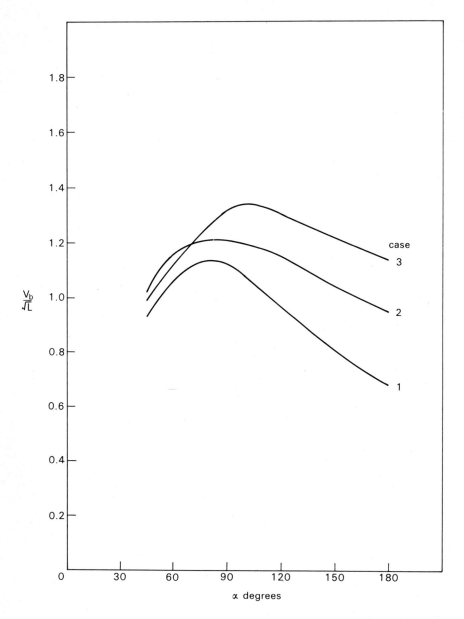

6.6a   Sailboat speed for different courses

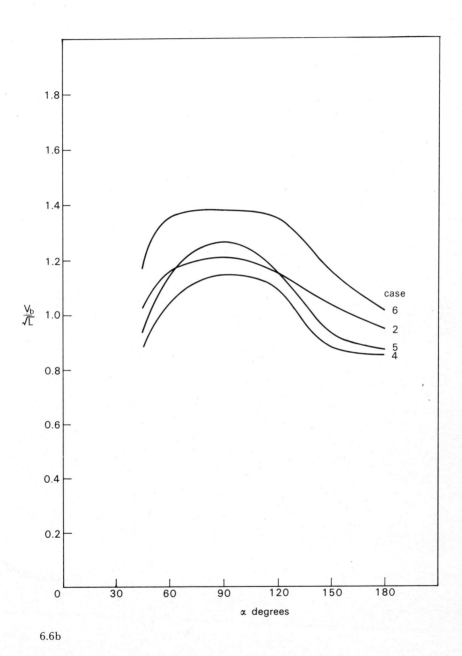

6.6b

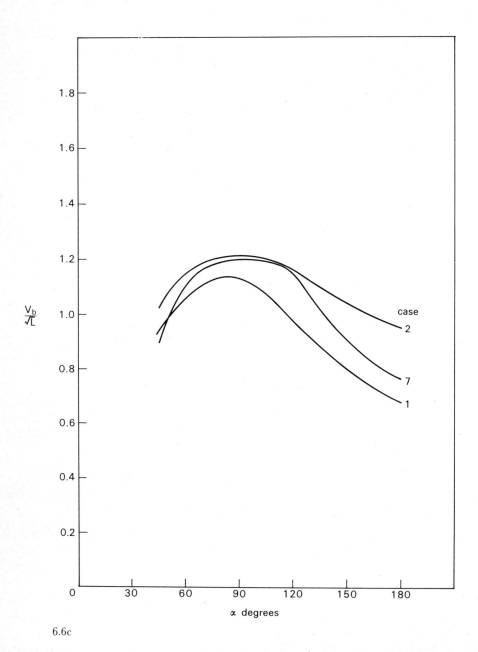

6.6c

cruising boat. These curves show that decreasing the displacement if it results in increased wetted surface is not beneficial for the wind speed considered except on a broad reach. At higher wind speeds it would probably be beneficial downwind. If the sail area ratio is increased as the wetted area ratio, the decreased displacement does lead to higher speeds.

The last comparison is between case 1, 2 and 7 in Figure 6.6c. This case is designed to demonstrate the effect of scaling on performance. Cases 1 and 2 may be considered as a comparison of similar boats different in length by a factor of 2. These curves show the difference in specific speed caused by the effect of scale in the same wind. Case 7 demonstrates what might be done if the larger boat was specifically designed for the same actual wind strength as the smaller one. The larger boat is designed to heel to the same angle in this same actual wind strength by decreasing the midships section. If this is done, the conditions shown in case 7 are one possible solution. The curve shows that this boat does perform better than case 1 and for conditions near a beam reach does almost as well as the smaller boat. However, for downwind conditions there is not much improvement as might be expected in these light winds.

At the lower speeds, $V_b/\sqrt{L} < 1$, the hull resistance is more than half friction. Under these conditions, a light displacement has no advantage and results in a lower specific speed if $A_s L/D$ is constant while $A_w L/D$ increases. At higher speeds, where wave drag predominates, the lighter displacement boat will actually result in higher specific speeds since the resistance per ton goes down. So far the comparison has been made on the basis of specific speed. However, if actual speed is considered, then the lighter displacement boat has considerable advantage and will be considerably faster for a given displacement. Whether a light displacement boat is faster depends on the conditions considered and the definition of speed.

For a given cross-sectional area h_m increases with beam and decreases with draft. For stability, the wide shallow boat is best and an analysis based on smooth water conditions will always lead to that conclusion. The wider beam would result in increased drag when going to windward against a head sea. Good practice in beam to length ratios should be considered as a guide on this point.

6.2   Optimum wind propulsion

The development of sailboats has taken place over many years which have seen the the gradual refinement of the concept. Sails were initially considered as a drag device but gradually through the centuries their potential as a lifting device was discovered and exploited. It seems natural to ask if there are other ways that the wind, the relative motion of the air over water, could be used to drive a boat, and what would be the limitations of such propulsion. Having considered the way in which a real sailboat is propelled it is useful to take a more general view of the problem.

For this purpose consider a general wind-driven vehicle. The restriction will be imposed that only devices mounted upon and moving with the vehicle will be allowed. An evaluation of these devices will be made by considering the power developed when the vehicle is moving at different directions and speeds relative to the wind velocity. It is assumed that if power is available it can be used to propel the vehicle. The power developed will determine the type and size of vehicle which can be driven at the assumed speed. This analysis will be carried out in an idealized way assuming perfect frictionless devices.

Since the analysis is limited to devices mounted on the vehicle, only the relative or apparent wind can be felt by the device. Because the wind velocity is a vector quantity it is possible to change its speed or direction (Figure 6.7). A device capable of changing the direction of the relative wind is an airfoil or sail, and a device capable of changing the magnitude of the relative wind is a windmill or rotating airfoil. A sail can also affect the magnitude of the velocity if used as a drag device.

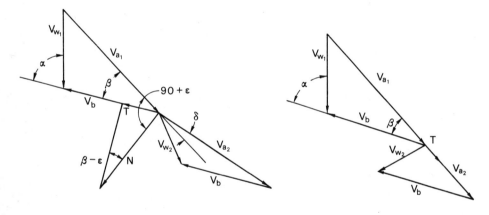

6.7   (a) Velocity diagram for velocity turning device—airfoil
       (b) Velocity diagram for velocity decreasing device—windmill

6.2.1   SAILS

If an ideal airfoil of finite length is used, the force which will be developed will depend upon the deflection of the relative wind. The force generated will lie at some small angle ε behind the perpendicular to the apparent wind direction. There is some loading value of this airfoil which will give the maximum force component in the vehicle's direction of motion for each heading of the vehicle.

The relation between the turning angle and the flow direction of the resulting force can be arrived at in two different ways. If a particular mass of air can be turned through a given constant angle (Figure 6.7) then momentum considerations show that the resulting force must bisect the angle between the resulting direction of the velocity vectors. The inadequacy of this simple model is in accurately predicting the mass of air affected and the resulting turning angle. If the airfoil is of infinite length the mass of air is always infinite and the resulting turning angle is zero. If, however, the airfoil is of finite length then the mass is not infinite and the turning angle is finite.

These same results can be developed based upon airfoil theory. For an elliptic lift distribution, the downwash angle is constant all along the span, and the resulting direction of the force is rotated back from the direction perpendicular to velocity ahead of the wing by this downwash angle. This constant downwash angle distribution also represents the minimum induced drag or average downwash angle. For a sail it is reasonable to apply this theory as if the sail were half a wing sealed against the vehicle. The usual relation is

$$\varepsilon = \frac{C_L}{\pi AR} = \frac{C_L A_s}{2\pi h^2} = \frac{C_L'}{4} \tag{6.9}$$

where

$$C_L' = \frac{L}{\frac{1}{2}\frac{w_a}{g} V_a^2 \left(\frac{1}{2}\pi h^2\right)} \quad \text{and } AR = \frac{2h^2}{A_s}$$

where h is the half span of the wing, A_s is the area of half span, and $\pi h^2/2$ represents an effective streamtube of cross-sectional area equal to a semicircle with the half-wing as a radius. The simple momentum model gives

$$C_N' = \frac{N}{\frac{1}{2}\dot{m}_a V_{a_1}} = 4 \sin \varepsilon = 4 \sin \frac{\delta}{2} \tag{6.10}$$

where ε is equal to the half-deflection angle and gives the direction of N. These two sets of relations are consistent if $\dot{m} = \frac{1}{2}\pi h^2 (w_a/g) V_a$ and ε is a small angle. To apply to large δ it seems most reasonable to use the above relation for C_N' keeping $\dot{m}$ constant at $\frac{1}{2}\pi h^2 (w_a/g) V_a$. The assumption that the apparent mass flux $\dot{m}$ remains constant at all turning angles is particularly questionable when turning angles greater than 90° are considered, so the results which will be presented should be questioned under these conditions.

6.2.2   WINDMILLS

The change of the magnitude of the velocity vector can be treated in a consistent way using the conventional propeller momentum theory. The propeller can be considered to be a rotating wing affecting a streamtube of size $\pi d^2/4$ and causing a decrease in velocity by an amount 2a, $V_{a_2} = V_{a_1}(1-2a)$ (Figure 6.7b). The relations for the power and thrust resulting from slowing down the air is thus

$$P_R = 4 \frac{\pi d^2}{4} \left(\frac{\frac{1}{2} w_a V_{a_1}^2}{g} \right) a(1-a)^2 \tag{6.11}$$

and

$$T = 4 \frac{\pi d^2}{4} \left(\frac{\frac{1}{2} w_a V_{a_1}^2}{g} \right) a(1-a) \tag{6.12}$$

and defining power and thrust coefficients

$$C_{pR} = \frac{P_R}{\frac{\pi d^2}{4} \frac{\frac{1}{2} w_a V_{a_1}^2}{g}} = 4a(1-a)^2 \tag{6.13}$$

and

$$C_T = \frac{T}{\frac{\pi d^2}{4} \left(\frac{\frac{1}{2} w_a V_{a_1}^2}{g} \right)} = 4a(1-a) \tag{6.14}$$

This change of velocity of the air through the propeller is similar to the turning of air by an airfoil. In both cases the magnitude of the velocity with respect to the airfoil is not reduced but the turning of the air results in a change in absolute velocity in both cases and, for the case of the propeller, a change in velocity relative to the propeller disc.

6.2.3 VEHICLE PROPULSION

Using these descriptions of the airfoil and the propeller, the application of such devices to driving a vehicle will be considered. These two idealized devices, representing a change in velocity and a change in magnitude of the relative wind vector, encompass all possible changes. If both the turning δ and the change in magnitude of velocity a are small, the effects become independent and the result will be the sum of the two effects. Therefore, the first order results for the potential of a combined device can be obtained by considering the effects independently.

First consider the sail or turning device. Figure 6.7a shows the appropriate vector diagram for calculating the power developed. The relative wind velocity is

$$V_a^2 = (V_w \cos \alpha + V_b)^2 + (V_w \sin \alpha)^2 \tag{6.15}$$

and the relative angle β is given by

$$\tan \beta = \frac{V_w \sin \alpha}{V_w \cos \alpha + V_b} \tag{6.16}$$

The value of β for different headings and vehicle/wind speed ratios is shown in Figure 6.8. The force developed by the turning of the relative velocity is

$$N = \frac{1}{2}\frac{w_a}{g}V_a^2\frac{\pi h^2}{2}4\sin\varepsilon \qquad (6.17)$$

and the component of this force in the direction of motion is

$$T = N\sin(\beta-\varepsilon) \qquad (6.18)$$

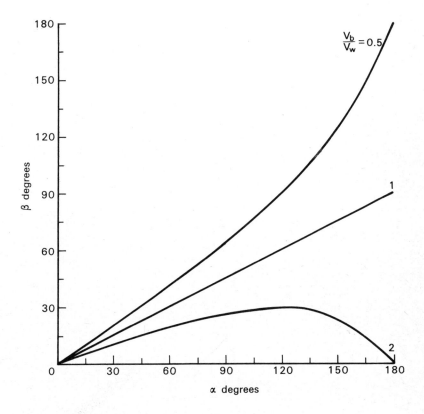

6.8   Apparent wind direction for different vehicle headings

The power developed written in coefficient form is then

$$C_p = \frac{P}{\dfrac{1}{2}\dfrac{w_a V_w^3}{g}\dfrac{\pi h^2}{2}} = 4\left(\frac{V_a}{V_w}\right)^2\left(\frac{V_b}{V_w}\right)\sin\varepsilon\sin(\beta-\varepsilon) \qquad (6.19)$$

This power coefficient is maximized by different values of ε at different values of β. If the power coefficient is differentiated with respect to ε and set equal to zero, an expression for the optimum ε which will give maximum power is obtained. The result is

$$\varepsilon_{opt} = \frac{\beta}{2} \qquad (6.20)$$

This result for $\varepsilon_{s\ opt}$ could probably have been deduced directly from the momentum model. The maximum thrust will be delivered to the vehicle if the relative wind is turned so that it leaves the boat in a direction opposite to the course of the boat. This value may be related to the usual value of force coefficient for a given aspect ratio.

$$C_N = \frac{N}{\dfrac{1}{2}\dfrac{w_a}{g}V_a^2 A_s} = \pi\, AR\, \sin \varepsilon \qquad (6.21)$$

Results for the optimum value of C_N for given values of AR are shown in Figure 6.9. It should be remembered that this is based on a very ideal airfoil which only has induced drag. If friction drag and the efficiency of the vehicle in resisting side forces and heeling moment are included the optimum loading will be changed. The present analysis, however, presents a simple limit which cannot be exceeded with any degree of cleverness in solving these other problems.

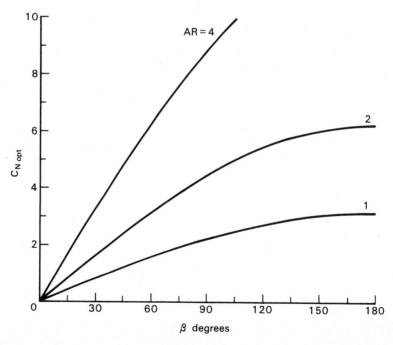

6.9   Optimum airfoil force coefficients

The maximum power coefficients can now be calculated for different values of the heading and vehicle/wind speed ratio (Figure 6.10). These curves show the power that can be developed on different courses. The maximum values occur with the wind on the beam and the minimum directly upwind and downwind. They also show that power can be developed at vehicle speeds which have downwind components greater than the wind speed. Whether a vehicle can actually be driven at these speeds depends on whether the required power is greater than the available power at the speed considered.

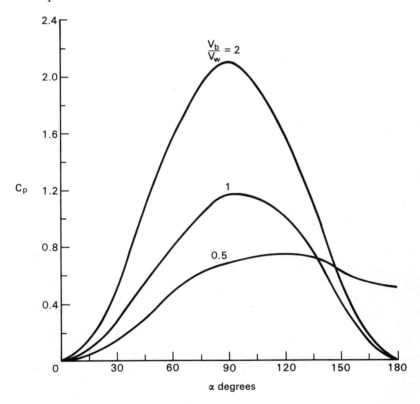

6.10   Power coefficients for airfoils

For the case of the propeller, or any device which changes the magnitude of the relative wind, the power developed when mounted upon a moving vehicle is derived from Figure 6.7b.

$$P = P_R - TV_b \cos \beta$$

$$C_p = \frac{P}{\frac{1}{2} \frac{w_a}{g} V_w^3 \frac{(\pi d^2)}{4}} = 4a(1-a) \left(\frac{V_a}{V_w}\right)^2 \left[(1-a)\frac{V_a}{V_w} - \frac{V_b}{V_w} \cos \beta\right] \qquad (6.22)$$

This expression can be maximized for a particular value of a which depends upon the course and the vehicle wind speed ratio. Differentiating C_p with respect to a, setting equal to 0, and solving for a gives

$$a_{\text{opt}} = \frac{\left(2\frac{V_a}{V_w} - \frac{V_b}{V_w}\cos\beta\right) \pm \sqrt{\left(2\frac{V_a}{V_w} - \frac{V_b}{V_w}\cos\beta\right)^2 - 3\frac{V_a}{V_w}\left(\frac{V_a}{V_w} - \frac{V_b}{V_w}\cos\beta\right)}}{3\frac{V_a}{V_w}} \qquad (6.23)$$

where the $-$ sign gives the optimum a. The values of a for maximum power are shown in Figure 6.11 as a function of course and vehicle/wind speed ratio. a is a loading parameter in the same sense as the turning angle for the airfoil, however, the two quantities are not numerically comparable.

The power coefficient can be calculated for the optimum value of a and is shown in Figure 6.12. For headings and vehicle/wind speed ratios such that the vehicle is proceeding downwind at a higher speed than the actual wind, the optimum values

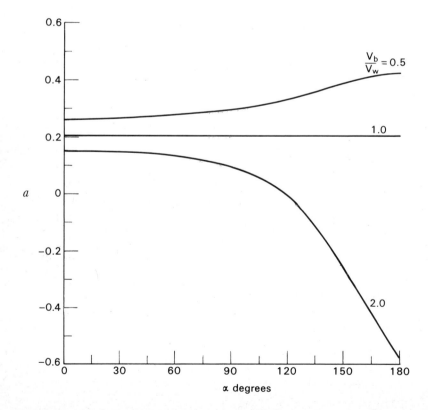

6.11   Optimum loading coefficients for windmills

of *a* are negative. This means that the velocity of the apparent wind through the propeller is increased and the propeller will produce a thrust in the direction of motion but require power to drive it. This power comes from the TV_b term and means that some of the power developed by the thrust will be required to drive the propeller just as some of the power developed by the propeller is required to overcome the thrust when the vehicle is going to windward and *a* is positive.

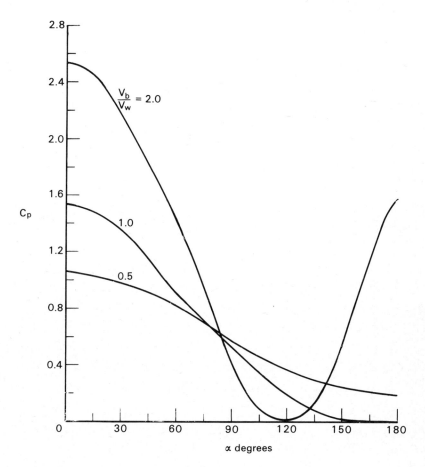

6.12   Power coefficients for windmills

A comparison between the power coefficients of the airfoil and propeller should be made. In making this comparison the difference in the definition of C_p should be properly considered. If the airfoil effectively seals against the surface on which the vehicle is operating, then h, the half span, may be considered to be the total height of the airfoil and the expression for the airfoil is correct. Notice that if h and d for the airfoil and propeller are equal, a given C_p results in twice the power for the airfoil as the propeller since the apparent mass is twice as large. If the flow is not restricted about the bottom of the airfoil then the apparent mass is reduced from $\pi h^2/2$ to $\pi h^2/4$ and the aspect ratio for the same height h is decreased from $2h^2/A_s$ to h^2/A_s. For this case the definitions of C_p for the airfoil and the propeller are the same.

A comparison of the power coefficients for the two devices shows that the propeller device has considerably better potential for driving the vehicle to windward. The airfoil becomes better for reaching headings and the propeller again becomes better for the dead downwind direction at high vehicle speed. The propeller produces surprisingly large amounts of power going directly to windward and performs best in this direction. For a given wind speed, the power produced by the propeller going to windward increases more rapidly than linearly with vehicle velocity, which means that a vehicle whose drag was independent of speed would accelerate indefinitely until some other effect became important.

An optimum propulsion system would involve a combination of these two systems; a magnitude of velocity change device for windward and downwind, and a direction of velocity changing device for reaching. Sails used as drag devices do decrease the magnitude of the relative velocity and fulfil the requirement when on a 180° heading at vehicle/wind speed ratios of less than 1. The practical limitations of providing such devices and the modification of the ideal results presented here by the actual performance of such devices will cause the true optimum to be different than the ideal. Nevertheless, the ideal analysis does show the potential performance of wind as a vehicle propulsive system and the means required to reach this potential.

6.2.4   FASTER THAN THE WIND

In Figure 6.12 it is shown that a propeller driven vehicle has the potential of going downwind at a speed greater than the wind. It also appears from this figure that no power is available when going downwind just at wind speed and, therefore, that the vehicle could not accelerate to a speed greater than wind speed. Actually, the condition of zero power when going at wind speed is a result of using only the minus sign in Equation 6.23. If Equation 6.23 is rewritten for the boat going downwind only and the quantity $v = aV_a$ used instead of a itself, which is more appropriate when V_a is near zero, the result is

$$a_{opt}\frac{V_a}{V_w} = \frac{v}{V_w} = \frac{2\frac{V_a}{V_w}+\frac{V_b}{V_w}\pm\sqrt{\left(2\frac{V_a}{V_w}+\frac{V_b}{V_w}\right)^2-3\frac{V_a}{V_w}\left(\frac{V_a}{V_w}+\frac{V_b}{V_w}\right)}}{3} \quad (6.24)$$

Both the plus and the minus sign give a useful result for $0 < V_b/V_w < 1$. The optimum values of v/V_w given by this relation are shown in Figure 6.13; the value of V_a/V_w is also shown for reference on this figure. For one of these curves the propeller is acting as a propeller, absorbing shaft power, and for the other as a windmill. Notice that

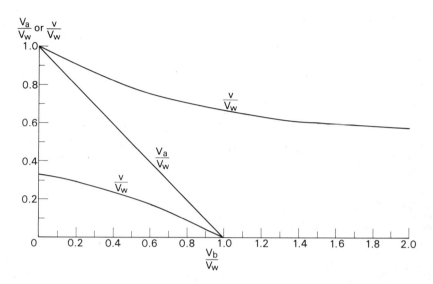

6.13   Optimum values of velocity change through propeller for maximum speed downwind

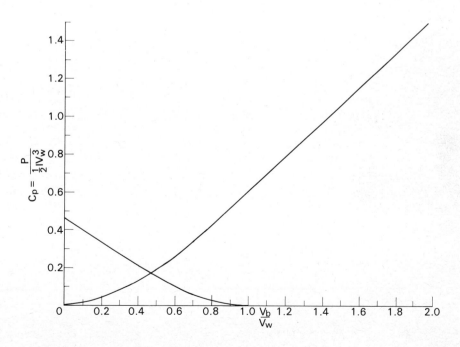

6.14   Maximum power coefficient for downwind operation

for the windmill curve $v < V_a$ so the velocity through the propeller disc $V_a - v$ is in the same direction as V_a while for the propeller curve $v > V_a$ gives the velocity through the propeller disc in the opposite direction from V_a. The power coefficient for both of these conditions is shown in Figure 6.14 as calculated from Equation 6.22. At low forward velocities, operating as a windmill gives greater power; however, as the vehicle velocity increases, the situation changes and operation as a propeller gives greater power. It is only by operating in the propeller mode that power can be obtained as the vehicle velocity approaches and exceeds wind speed. It is interesting that either mode of operation can be used when the vehicle speed is less than wind speed and that there are two optimum values.

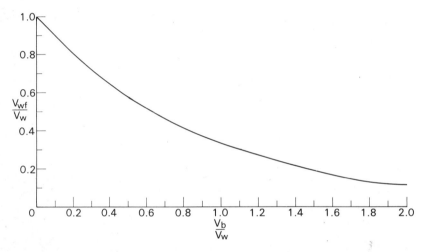

6.15   Decrease in absolute air velocity with respect to the ground plane caused by propeller

For operation as a windmill, it is rather obvious that power is extracted from the wind by decreasing the velocity of the wind and the shaft power of the windmill plus the drag force are both useful in driving the vehicle. When operating as a propeller, it is the difference between the thrust power of the propeller and the shaft power that is available to drive the vehicle. This power is extracted from the air, and results in a decrease in the wind velocity with respect to the water or ground plane. This is accomplished by the propeller which accelerates the air in the same direction as the relative velocity of the air with respect to the propeller disc but in the opposite direction from the velocity of the air with respect to the water or ground plane. Lest all this sounds like a violation of the principle of conservation of energy or a perpetual motion machine, Figure 6.15 shows the change in ratio of the air velocity with respect to the ground plane before and after being processed by the propeller. There is a decrease in air velocity and consequently a decrease in kinetic energy which is the energy available to drive the vehicle.

6.16 Windmill driven land yacht

The fact that a low-resistance boat such as an iceboat can tack downwind at a speed in excess of the wind speed has been demonstrated and is well accepted. That the propeller-driven vessel can do the same directly downwind is not nearly as well accepted. This idea may sound more reasonable if it is pointed out that the motion of the propeller blades with respect to the hull of the boat really results in the propeller blades tacking downwind while the hull does not. In an attempt to demonstrate that a real vehicle can perform in this way, the land yacht shown in Figure 6.16 was constructed. A tuft on the front of the vehicle was used to show the apparent wind direction. The vehicle went downwind fast enough so that the tuft indicated a head wind indicating that it was exceeding wind speed. The instrumentation used in this experiment may not be adequate to convince the skeptic that the vehicle is exceeding windspeed, but it is an interesting demonstration.

6.3   Sail area

The amount of sail which should be carried on a particular sailboat depends upon many factors. It is desirable to provide enough sail area to drive the boat satisfactorily but not too much so that it heels excessively. One useful guide to the sail area requirement is the practice which has developed over preceeding years. The resistance of a boat depends primarily on the wetted surface and displacement: therefore it is useful to consider the ratios of sail area to wetted area A_s/A_w, and sail area times length to displacement $A_s L/D$, or alternatively sail area to displacement to the $\frac{2}{3}$ power $A_s/D^{2/3}$. It was pointed out in Section 6.1.1 on scaling that it is not reasonable for large and small boats to have the same value of these parameters since similar conditions would then require that the wind speed vary as $\sqrt{L}$. The result in practice is that larger boats have larger values of these parameters. Figures 6.17–18 show typical values of these parameters as a function of waterline length.[4] These figures should be considered as guides to accepted practice. If it is desired to design a high performance boat, then it would be desirable to increase these sail area parameters. A high A_s/A_w will be particularly effective in producing a fast boat in light winds, while a high $A_s L/D$ is of importance in strong winds when the boat is sailing near hull speed.

The limiting factor on how much sail a boat can carry depends on its ability to carry sail without excessive heel. The heel angle of a boat is usually judged in two ways, by the Dallanbaugh angle or the wind pressure coefficient. The Dallanbaugh angle is defined as the angle of heel when the boat's sails are trimmed amidships and the sails are subjected to a pressure of 1 lb per sq ft. The wind pressure coefficient is the pressure on the sails in lb per sq ft necessary to cause a 20° angle of heel. Actually these quantities are different expressions for the same concept. Since the heel angle and the wind pressure can be related thus:

$$h_{cp} A_s (WPC) = (h_m) D \sin \theta \qquad (6.25)$$

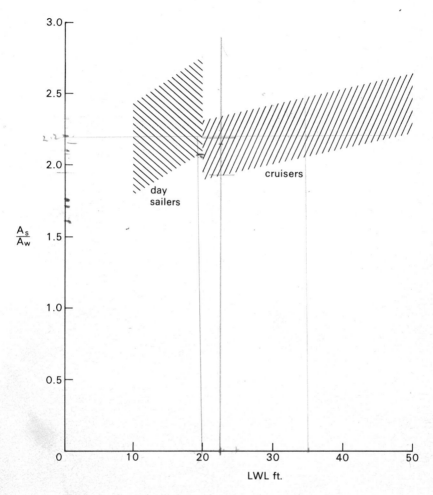

6.17   Typical values of sail area as function of wetted area

Then

$$\frac{WPC}{\sin \theta} = \frac{(h_m)D}{h_{cp}A_s} \tag{6.26}$$

The right-hand side of this relation contains the boat design parameters and typical values are shown as a function of boat length in Figure 6.19. This parameter is directly related to wind pressure coefficient by multiplying it by sin 20° and θ becomes the Dallanbaugh angle if WPC = 1 lb/ft². Figure 6.19 shows that the value of this parameter goes up with size. For similar boats it would rise directly as the length but this does not occur in practice since A_sL/D also increases as the size increases.

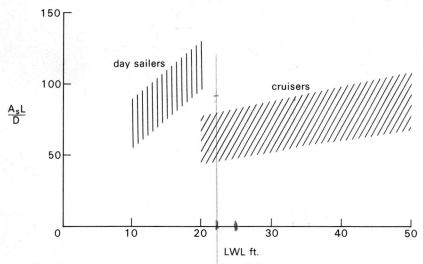

6.18   Typical values of sail area as function of displacement

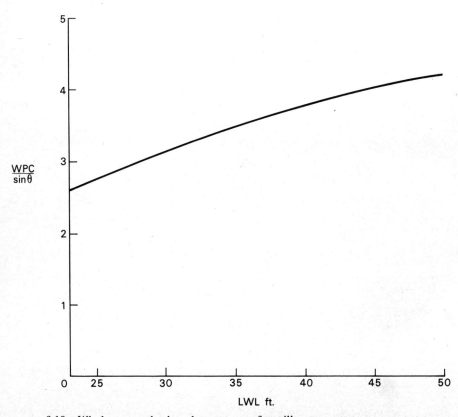

6.19   Wind pressure heel angle parameter for sailboats

6.4   Sails

Sails are the means used to convert wind energy to boat propulsion energy. In the previous sections the action of the sails has been considered from a rather general point of view. It is now useful to consider some of the more specific aspects. A sail or an airfoil can develop a force whose direction is somewhere between the wind direction and the perpendicular to the wind direction. The component of the force along the wind direction is called drag, and the component in the direction normal to the wind is called lift. By designing and trimming the sail in different ways the ratio between the magnitude of these two forces can be varied. The force can also be described by its magnitude N and its direction, in this case the angle ε measured from the direction perpendicular to the wind. Defined in this way

$$\tan \varepsilon = \frac{\text{drag}}{\text{lift}} \tag{6.27}$$

Figure 6.20 shows these force and wind vectors. It is possible to design and trim a sail so that the angle ε becomes small (tan ε≈0·1) and also so that ε=90° or any value in between. The magnitude of the force is best specified in terms of a coefficient C_N thus:

$$N = \frac{1}{2}\frac{w_a}{g}\, V_a^2 A_s C_N \tag{6.28}$$

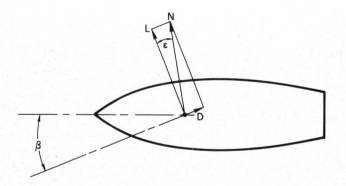

6.20   Sailboat wind vector triangle

The advantage of defining C_N in this way is that its value is essentially independent of wind speed. Typical curves for an airfoil as a function of angle of attack are shown in Figure 6.21. The lift force is zero when the airfoil is at zero angle of attack with respect to the wind, and the drag is small but finite. The lift force increases fairly linearly with angle of attack until a stall condition is reached at an angle of attack of around 13° for a symmetrical airfoil at a normal force coefficient of around 1·35. The meaning of stall is that the flow no longer smoothly follows the surface of the airfoil but separates from it in the manner illustrated in Figure 6.22. At higher angles of attack a separated area continues to exist behind the airfoil, and when the angle of attack is at 90° the lift is essentially zero. Another interesting feature is that before stall the force developed by the airfoil is located near the $\frac{1}{4}$ chord point. Once stall occurs the location of the force moves towards the trailing edge and is at approximately the mid-chord point at 90° angle of attack.

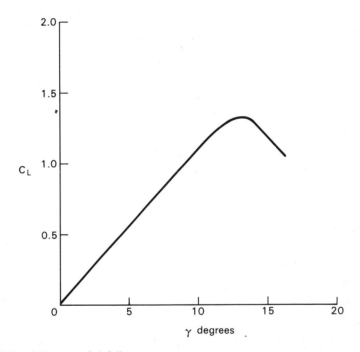

6.21   Lift curve of airfoil

For sailboat applications we are really interested in sails, not airfoils. The airfoil is simpler since the shape is fixed and does not change as load is applied. Another important difference between the airfoil and the sail is that the airfoil has a thick, rounded leading edge which is capable of operating over a reasonably broad angle of attack range while sails have a sharp leading edge (particularly sails set on stays), but can change their camber. To understand the significance of this feature, consider what happens to a thin, flat plate airfoil at different angles of attack. The flow about a flat plate at zero angle of attack is shown in Figure 6.23. At zero angle of attack a streamline divides at the leading edge and passes down each side of the plate. At angle of attack, the dividing streamline now stagnates along the bottom of the plate with the flow above this streamline reversing and passing around the leading edge. Actually the flow will not be able to pass smoothly around the sharp leading edge of the plate and consequently a flat plate at angle of attack is not a good

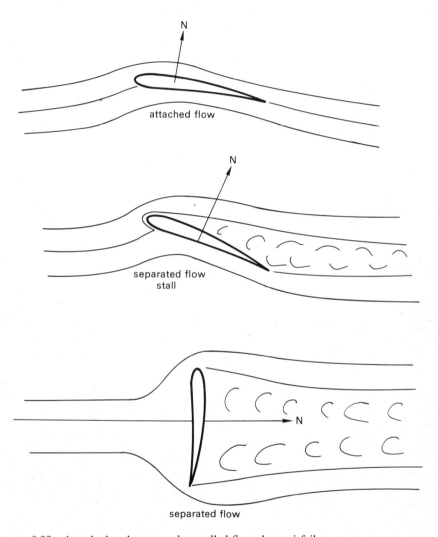

6.22   Attached and separated or stalled flow about airfoil

airfoil. If the leading edge is rounded, then the flow can follow the contour and a satisfactory airfoil is obtained. Another means of obtaining lift, which is the one used by a sail, is a cambered surface. With the proper amount of camber, the dividing streamline can be made to split at the leading edge of the airfoil. The usual technique of trimming a sail is to adjust it so that the flow is smoothly divided by the leading edge. However, this adjustment only provides a smooth entrance condition and does not determine the lift coefficient. If the sail had zero camber, this method of trimming would give zero lift. Once the leading edge is correctly adjusted, then the lift of the sail is set by adjusting the camber. In practice this second adjustment is made by moving the sheeting point and controlling the shape of the sail by halyard tension and other techniques.

For a mainsail or other sail set behind a mast, the mast provides a thickness to the leading edge which is beneficial but, in the usual arrangement, does not provide smooth transition to the sail. The flow usually separates behind the mast but then re-attaches to the sail. In both these ways the mast decreases the importance of the proper trim at the leading edge and allows a mainsail to have its angle of attack varied at a fixed camber without as strong an effect as for a jib or staysail.

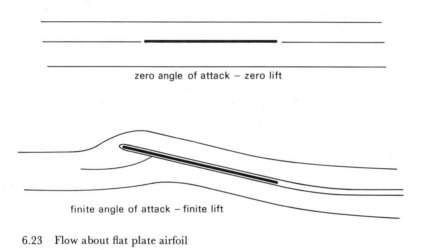

zero angle of attack − zero lift

finite angle of attack − finite lift

6.23   Flow about flat plate airfoil

6.4.1   PRESSURE DISTRIBUTION ABOUT SAILS

The air pressure on a sail is responsible for the lift force and part of the drag force. It is the pressure difference between the two sides of the sail that is important. Considerable discussion has occurred concerning whether the important cause of this pressure difference was the increase in pressure on the windward side of the sail or the decrease on the leeward side of the sail. From the standpoint of developing force, it really makes very little difference. For a sail or thin airfoil the amount of pressure increase is smaller than the pressure decrease (Figure 6.24). For a thick airfoil at zero angle of attack the pressure, except in the immediate area of the leading edge, is below atmospheric. When such an airfoil is at an angle of attack or cambered the pressures rise on the windward side and fall on the leeward side. The result is that the pressures on the leeward side are more negative and those on the windward less positive than for the thinner airfoil. This condition has led to the statement that it is the vacuum above the wing which lifts the airplane and not the pressure below.

Stall is caused by the inability of the low-velocity air close to the sail which has been slowed by friction (the boundary layer) to flow against an adverse pressure gradient.

The negative pressures on the leeward side of the airfoil must recover to atmospheric pressure at the trailing edge. If the pressure gradient to accomplish this increase in pressure is too large the low-velocity air along the surface of the sail which has been slowed down by friction will be unable to flow along the surface and will separate from it. When this separation occurs, the whole flow pattern about the sail changes and the lift decreases. For this reason, the smaller negative pressure along the lee side of a correctly trimmed thin airfoil requires less pressure recovery than for a thick airfoil and is advantageous.

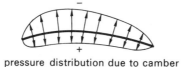

pressure distribution due to camber

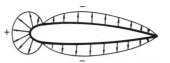

pressure distribution due to thickness

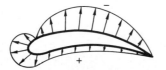

pressure distribution due to both
thickness and camber

6.24   Pressure distributions caused by camber and thickness

In this same connection, the porosity of the sail is important. Air leaking from the windward high pressure side of the sail to the leeward low pressure side is not important for normal sail porosities as far as the direct effect of reducing the lift by decreasing the high pressure and increasing the low pressure is concerned. The important effect is that the air which bleeds through the sail loses all its forward velocity. This low velocity air then augments the low speed friction boundary layer on the leeward side of the sail and decreases the pressure rise possible without separation. For this reason even a small porosity can be detrimental.

The center of pressure of an unstalled airfoil at an angle of attack is usually forward of the midpoint. For a symmetrical airfoil, it is only $\frac{1}{4}$ of the total distance from the leading edge. For positive camber (concave on the pressure side) it moves aft and for negative camber it moves forward. Just because the forces on the after part of the airfoil are smaller than on the forward part, the conclusion cannot be drawn that the after part is not useful and should be removed. If the airfoil chord is reduced to half its original size, the force will be reduced by half, the center of pressure will be moved forward, and the after part will be unloaded. The after part of the foil is just as important as the forward part even though the pressure loads on it may be less; it is essential to creating the higher pressures on the forward part.

6.4.2　SPECIAL FEATURES OF SAILS

Sails are a special type of airfoil. One important special feature is the thin leading edge which requires one particular angle of attack in order to achieve a smooth flow onto the sail. Analysis methods have been developed for airfoils which allow predictions of the characteristics of thin airfoils such as sails. These predictions will first be discussed for infinitely long airfoils so that the effects caused by the ends can be neglected.

It is found that in a first approximation the effects on angle of attack and camber can be separated. It is convenient to draw a reference line from the nose to the tail of the airfoil (Figure 6.25) and measure the angle of attack from this direction.

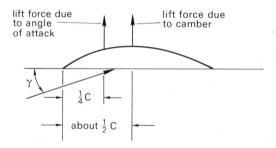

6.25　Lift force location caused by angle of attack and camber

For an uncambered airfoil zero lift occurs at zero angle of attack. For a cambered airfoil some lift occurs at zero angle of attack and this lift can be said to be caused by the camber. The amount of lift and the location of the lift force depend on the amount and distribution of the camber. For an airfoil with the maximum camber at the mid-chord point the lift force is also located near the mid-chord point. If an airfoil is at an angle of attack, a lift force is generated that is proportional to the angle of attack and given by the relation

$$C_L = 0.11\,\gamma \quad \text{where } \gamma \text{ is given in degrees}$$

The total lift on the airfoil is the sum of that due to angle of attack and camber. The lift force due to angle of attack is always located at the $\frac{1}{4}$ chord point. The location of the total lift force is then a weighted average between the location of the lift force due to camber and angle of attack.

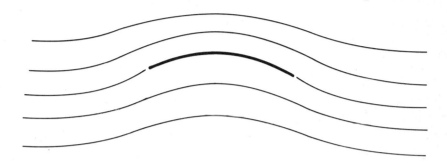

6.26   Streamline pattern about thin cambered airfoil at zero angle of attack

The angle of attack of a sail, however, must be selected so that the air flows smoothly at the leading edge. For an uncambered airfoil, this condition is obviously zero angle of attack and for a cambered airfoil it also occurs at zero angle of attack (measured from the line from luff to leech). A sketch of the streamlines at zero angle of attack is shown in Figure 6.26. The sail causes a flow pattern upstream that distorts the streamlines so that they flow smoothly onto the sail. The conclusion is that the sail operates at zero angle of attack and that only the lift due to camber is of importance. Figure 6.27 shows the lift coefficients of cambered airfoils at zero angle of attack for different cambers and different locations of maximum camber. Figure 6.28 shows the point of application of the lift force.

Experimental results for the characteristics of thin airfoils of different cambers are also available. Figure 6.27 shows the experimentally measured lift force at zero

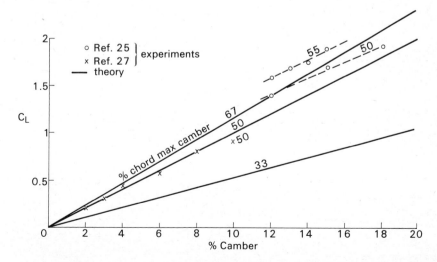

6.27   Lift coefficients of thin cambered airfoil at zero angle of attack showing theoretical and experimental results

angle of attack in comparison with the theoretical predictions and 6.28 the location
of the lift force. These experimental results bear out the predictions reasonably well
and give confidence in the predictions for other than the shapes tested. Figure 6.29
shows the lift coefficient as a function of angle of attack for 12% camber. The theoretical prediction is also shown. Since the theory does not consider separation, it should
be expected to be unreliable at other than zero angle of attack. A striking feature of
the experimental curve is the rapid change in lift with angle of attack near zero
angle of attack. A major drop-off occurs at a few degrees of negative angle of attack.
For a sail this effect should not be as severe as for the solid airfoil tested since the sail
will luff and change its shape at the leading edge so separation will be delayed.
The drag for the airfoil is shown in Figure 6.30. This drag is about a factor of 5
higher than typical values for a rounded nose airfoil. However, this is not really an
important factor since the induced drag that will be considered in a later section is
much larger. Measured lift/drag ratios for these airfoils were of the order of 20
or higher which is high enough so that the actual magnitude of the drag is not too
important.

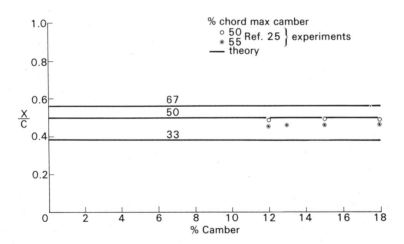

6.28   Location of lift force on thin cambered airfoil at zero angle of attack
showing theoretical and experimental results

6.4.3   ASPECT RATIO

The aspect ratio is a measure of the length of an airfoil perpendicular to the flow
direction compared with that in the flow direction. For a rectangular isolated airfoil
it is simply the span over the chord. For sails it is usually defined as

$$AR = \frac{2h^2}{A_s}$$

which assumes that the span is double the mast height since flow between the hull and sails is restricted. (This corresponds to the definition used for the half wing of an airplane). A high aspect ratio is important for an efficient airfoil since it reduces the amount of fluid which can flow around the end of the airfoil. In Figure 6.31 a sail is shown with high pressures on one side and low on the other viewed along the direction of flow. The tendency is for the air to flow from the high pressure to low pressure side around the tip. With higher aspect ratios, relatively less of the total flow goes around the tip and as a result the high aspect ratio increases the efficiency and lift to drag ratio of an airfoil.

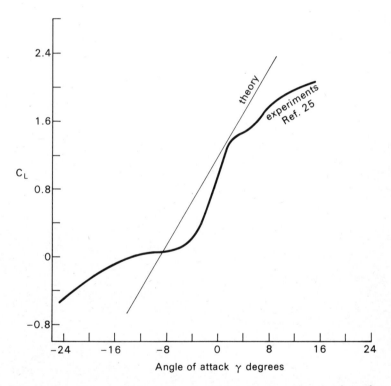

6.29   Lift coefficient of thin cambered airfoil as function of angle of attack showing theoretical and experimental results

The result of the flow around the tip of the airfoil is that a change in the direction of flow is caused near the airfoil. It is as if the flow direction far from the airfoil were changed by an angle ε in such a direction to decrease the angle of attack of the airfoil. The value of ε is related to the lift coefficient and the aspect ratio

$$\varepsilon = \frac{C_L}{\pi\,AR} \tag{6.29}$$

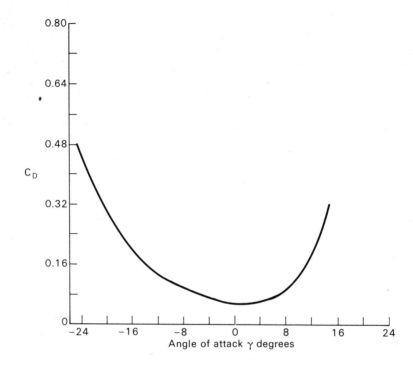

6.30   Drag coefficient of thin cambered airfoil as function of angle of attack

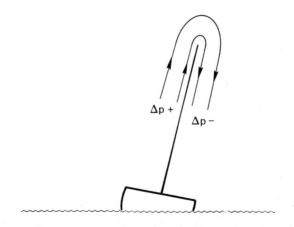

6.31   Flow about tip of airfoil or sail from high to low pressure side

The lift coefficient however is decreased by the change in flow direction

$$C_L = 0 \cdot 11 (\gamma - \varepsilon) \tag{6.30}$$

Therefore

$$C_L = \frac{0 \cdot 11 \, \gamma}{1 + \dfrac{2}{AR}} \tag{6.31}$$

and

$$\varepsilon = \frac{\gamma}{1 + \dfrac{AR}{2}} \tag{6.32}$$

Another result is that the direction of the force developed by the airfoil is rotated backward by the angle ε. The angle of attack must be increased by ε in order to achieve smooth flow onto the airfoil but the lift coefficient at this angle of proper trim is not changed. The magnitude of the angle ε increases as the lift increases and as the aspect ratio decreases.

6.4.4   SAIL PROPULSION FORCES

In sailing to windward the lift force on the sail causes the propulsive force and the drag force on the sail detracts from the propulsive force. The vector diagram of Figure 6.20 shows that the lift force's line of action lies at the angle β (the angle of the apparent wind) forward of the beam. Actually the direction of the line of action of the total sail force will be somewhat behind the direction perpendicular to the apparent wind because of two effects: the air flowing around the top of the sail causes the sail force to be rotated aft of the perpendicular to the apparent wind, and the friction of the air flowing along the sail causes a force along the apparent wind direction. This force causes an additional rotation of the resulting sail force further aft. The resulting propulsive force coefficient can be written

$$C_p = C_L \sin \left(\beta - \varepsilon - \frac{C_D}{C_L} \right) \tag{6.33}$$

In order to determine how the useful propulsive force varies with lift coefficient it is necessary to consider the side force generated by the sails and the increase of boat resistance caused by this side force. The side force is

$$C_H = C_L \cos \left(\beta - \varepsilon - \frac{C_D}{C_L} \right) \tag{6.34}$$

If a quantity Q is designated to represent the ratio of the increased hull drag caused by the side force to the side force, then

$$C_p^* = C_L \left[\sin\left(\beta - \varepsilon - \frac{C_D}{C_L} \right) - Q \cos\left(\beta - \varepsilon - \frac{C_D}{C_L} \right) \right] \qquad (6.35)$$

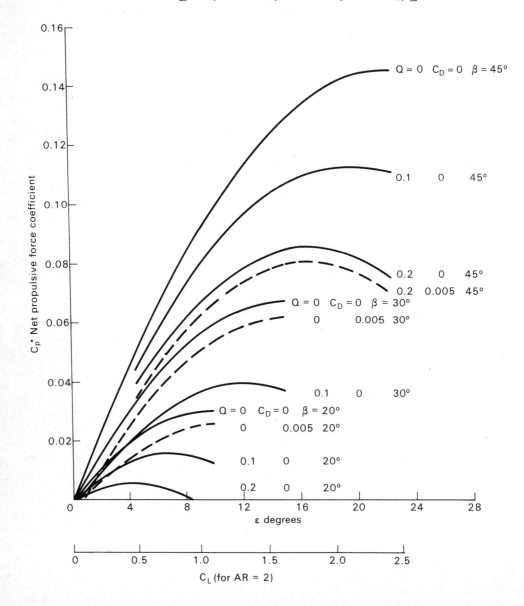

6.32   Net propulsive force coefficient as a function of wind turning angle

where C_p^* is the net propulsive force coefficient which is the difference between the propulsive force and the drag caused by the sail force.

In Section 6.2.3 it was shown that for the very idealized case of Q and $C_D=0$ the maximum propulsive force was obtained for $\varepsilon = \beta/2$ which means that the flow is turned by an amount 2ε to a direction parallel to the one in which the boat is moving. If Q and C_D are not zero, then the optimum turning angle is changed. The drag term has a small effect but the increase in resistance of the boat with the increased side force has a rather major one. Figure 6.32 shows the net propulsive force as a function of ε for $\beta = 20°$ to 45°. Values of Q of 0·1 and 0·2 cause effective reductions in the net propulsive force and in the optimum value of ε. The addition of a drag force on the sail of a realistic value has only a small additional effect.

The lift coefficient needed to achieve a given turning angle depends upon the aspect ratio; the larger the aspect ratio the larger the lift coefficient. An auxiliary scale on Figure 6.28 shows the lift coefficients corresponding to a given ε for AR = 2. The general conclusion is that it is difficult to achieve lift coefficients which exceed the optimum value. At $\beta = 30°$ and low aspect ratio rigs it may be possible to exceed the optimum values but it is not likely to occur at higher values of β. Figure 6.33 shows these same results as a function of lift coefficient and aspect ratio. At $\beta = 30°$ and AR = 2 the optimum lift coefficient occurs at a value less than 2. However, for $\beta = 45°$ and greater and AR = 4 or greater, $C_L = 2$ is always below the optimum. The importance of this optimum lift angle is only to know under what conditions the sails should not be trimmed for maximum lift but carried flatter and at a reduced angle of attack. These results show the advantage of high aspect ratio.

Figure 6.33 shows that at any lift coefficient an increase in propulsive coefficient can be obtained by an increase in aspect ratio. When heading close to the wind this effect is most pronounced. Under these conditions a high lift to drag ratio becomes of increasing importance and has a strong effect on the performance of the boat in going to windward. The high aspect ratio rig is only really useful when sailing closehauled, but it does have a pronounced benefit under those conditions.

Under strong wind conditions when side force must be reduced to limit heeling, the nature of the problem changes. A tall, high aspect ratio rig is no longer an advantage because of the heeling moment which it causes. Using Equation 6.35 the net propulsive force is

$$P^* = \frac{1}{2}\frac{w_a}{g} V_a^2 A_s C_p^* = \frac{1}{2}\frac{w_a}{g} V_a^2 A_s C_L \left[\sin (\beta - \varepsilon) - Q \cos [\beta - \varepsilon]\right] \qquad (6.36)$$

for $C_D = 0$.

The heeling moment is

$$HM = \frac{1}{2}\frac{w_a}{g} V_a^2 A_s C_L \cos (\beta - \varepsilon) h_{cp} \qquad (6.37)$$

If this last equation is used to eliminate C_L from Equation 6.36, then

$$P^* = (HM) \frac{\sin (\beta - \varepsilon) - Q \cos (\beta - \varepsilon)}{\cos (\beta - \varepsilon) h_{cp}} \qquad (6.38)$$

Using Equation 6.29

$$\varepsilon = \frac{C_L}{\pi AR} = \frac{C_L A_s}{2\pi h^2} = \frac{HM}{2\pi h^2 h_{cp} \cos(\beta - \varepsilon)} \tag{6.39}$$

Using 6.39 to eliminate C_L in 6.37 and replacing sin ε for ε

$$\left(\frac{h}{L}\right)^3 = \frac{1}{2\pi} \left(\frac{HM}{\frac{1}{2}w_a L^4}\right) \left(\frac{gL}{V_a^2}\right) \frac{h}{h_{cp}} \frac{1}{\cos(\beta - \varepsilon) \sin \varepsilon} \tag{6.40}$$

and

$$\frac{P*L}{HM} = \frac{\sin(\beta - \varepsilon) - Q \cos(\beta - \varepsilon)}{\left[\frac{1}{2\pi}\left(\frac{HM}{\frac{1}{2}w_a L^4}\right)\left(\frac{gL}{V_a^2}\right)\right]^{\frac{1}{3}} \left(\frac{h_{cp}}{h}\right)^{\frac{2}{3}} [\cos(\beta - \varepsilon)]^{\frac{4}{3}} (\sin \varepsilon)^{\frac{1}{3}}} \tag{6.41}$$

For fixed values of heeling moment, boat dimensions and wind strength a maximum propulsive force will be obtained at a value of ε which depends only on β. This

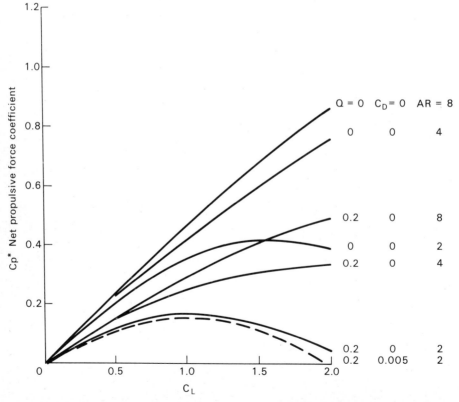

6.33a   Net propulsive force coefficient as function of lift coefficient.
(a) $\beta = 30°$, (b) $\beta = 45°$, (c) $\beta = 60°$

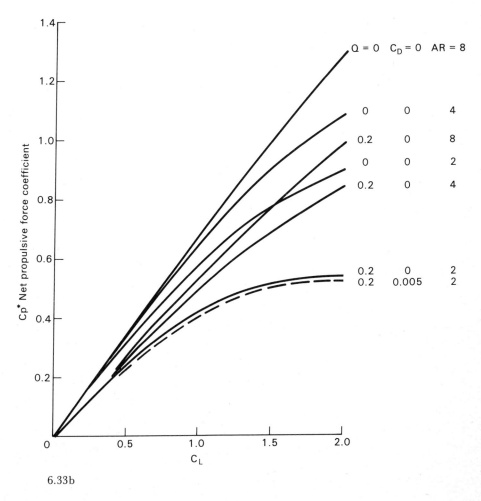

6.33b

value of ε is shown in Figure 6.34 for $Q=0$ and $0\cdot2$. The optimum value of ε reaches a maximum near $\beta=60°$. For values of β less than $60°$ a lower value of ε is desirable in order to increase the forward component of the sail force. At values of β greater than $60°$ smaller ε are desirable to decrease the side force and allow larger total sail forces while not increasing the heeling moment. The corresponding values of AR/C_L are also shown on the right hand side of this figure.

The mast height corresponding to these optimum conditions can now be obtained from Equation 6.40. Define a quantity M

$$M = \frac{1}{2\pi} \left(\frac{HM}{\frac{1}{2}w_aL^4} \right) \left(\frac{gL}{V_a^2} \right) \frac{h}{h_{cp}} \tag{6.42}$$

This parameter defines the stiffness of the boat relative to the wind strength in which it is sailing. The optimum mast height will be proportional to the cube root

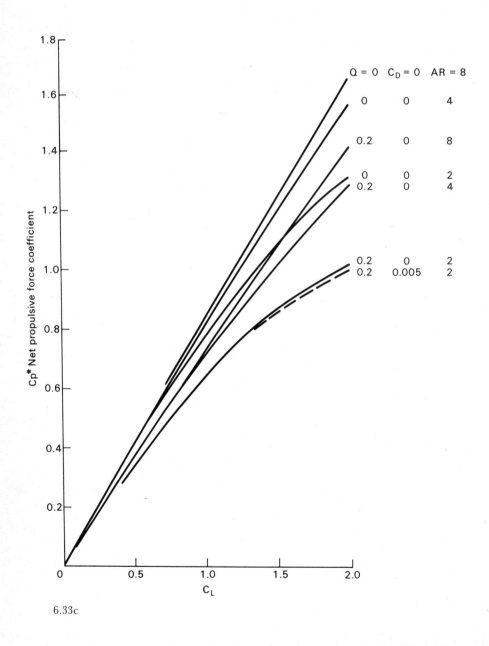

6.33c

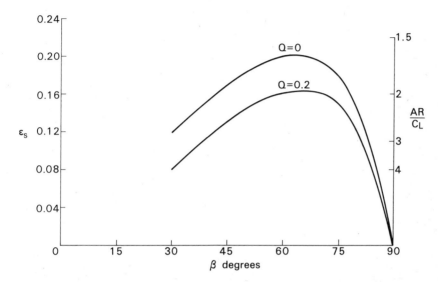

6.34   Optimum value of wind turning angle for maximum net propulsive force for heel angle limited conditions

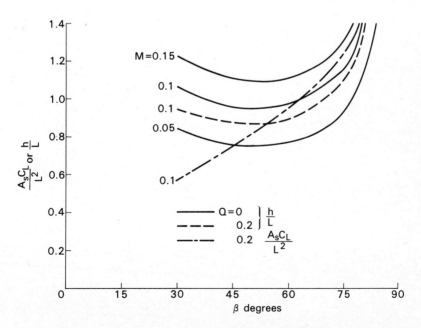

6.35   Optimum mast height for maximum net propulsion force for heel angle limited conditions as a function of stiffness parameter M

of this parameter. Figure 6.35 shows the optimum mast for different β and M values. These M values represent a reasonable range for normal sailing conditions. For instance a boat with a 25 ft waterline length, a displacement of 13 000 lb and a maximum righting moment of 26 000 ft lb sailing in a 20 knot wind with $h_{cp}/h = 0.3$ would have $M = 0.075$. Since $h/L \sim \sqrt[3]{M}$ changes in this parameter are not very effective in changing the optimum mast height. The rapid rise in mast height at $\beta > 75°$ is caused by the decrease in the heeling component of the force vector. At $\beta > 90°$ this analysis is no longer applicable since sails can be set to give no heeling moment and it is not the heeling moment but the ability to control the boat that sets the maximum mast height. Once the mast height has been determined the value of $C_L A_s$ can be found from

$$C_L A_s = 2\pi h^2 \varepsilon \qquad (6.43)$$

The desired sail area depends on how large a lift coefficient can be obtained. The value of $C_L A_s / L^2$ is also shown in Figure 6.35. For the 25 ft waterline length boat previously described this corresponds to a sail area of 300 to 400 sq ft for $\beta = 30°$ to 45° and $C_L = 1.25$.

The conclusion to be reached from this discussion is that when the amount of sail carried by a boat is limited by the heeling angle, the optimum value of the aspect ratio depends only on the relative wind angle β and the lift coefficient of the sails. The optimum mast height does depend upon the righting moment and wind strength. For conventional values of the righting moment, the mast height should be of the order of the length of the boat. These conclusions also relate to the best way to reduce sail. The conventional ways of reefing a mainsail result in keeping the aspect ratio constant; however, a smaller headsail may have a reduced foot or hoist. If a sail with a reduced foot is used, the aspect ratio of the sail plan will be increased and if a reduced hoist is used the aspect ratio will be reduced. When the amount of sail carried is not limited by the angle of heel, a high aspect ratio is desirable. If the yacht is designed with a high aspect ratio for this reason, it would be desirable to decrease the aspect ratio when reducing sail. However, if the aspect ratio is not large with the full sails, then the reduced sails should maintain the same aspect ratio. The decision whether the heavy weather sails should be of lower aspect ratio than the full sails depends only on the aspect ratio of the full sails and not on whether the boat is tender or stiff. The only effect of the magnitude of the righting moment is to determine at what wind strength the sail area must be reduced but not the aspect ratio of that reduced area.

6.4.5   INTERACTION BETWEEN SAILS

The problem of the interaction between jib and mainsail in a sloop rig or between main and mizzen in a ketch or yawl is a subject about which much has been written. Since sails interact with each other it is best not to think about the action of the individual sails but about the effect of the total sail plan. To ask whether the jib or the mainsail is more effective is not useful. It is useful to ask how the sail area should be distributed between the jib and the mainsail and if all the area should be concentrated in the jib or main alone. To compare the forces developed by two sails when both are used is not informative since the action of the after sail may be to increase the load on the forward sail with the result that the forward sail develops more force. This case, however, is no reason to say that the after sail is not useful.

There is no simple answer to the question of the best distribution of the area between jib and main. Apart from the question of sail measurement rules and their strong influence on design, different hull characteristics require different sail plans.

Probably the case of greatest interest is the combination of jib and mainsail on a sloop. The two sails acting together form a single system that performs very differently from the single sail alone. It is useful to look at the problem both as two airfoils interacting with each other and as a single airfoil with a slot. From this second point of view the problem of the relative size of the jib and main for the same total area becomes the question of the best location for the slot through the airfoil.

An airfoil with a slot makes it possible to achieve a higher lift coefficient than with a plane airfoil. The maximum lift coefficient that can be achieved by a sail or airfoil is set by the condition for which the low velocity fluid in the boundary layer can no longer flow against the imposed pressure gradient. For an airfoil with a slot, the boundary layer which starts at the leading edge only has to follow the surface of the airfoil for part of the length and achieve part of the pressure recovery. A new boundary layer then starts at the slot and sustains the rest of the pressure rise. Another way of thinking about this problem is in terms of two airfoils. The trailing edge of the forward airfoil is then in a low pressure area caused by the after airfoil. The forward airfoil can now be trimmed to achieve higher lifts than without the after airfoil present since the boundary layer need only return to a reduced pressure. Boundary layer separation or stall limits the lift coefficient that can be obtained and it is only by techniques that prevent this separation that higher lifts can be obtained.

An interesting calculation of the streamline pattern about a mainsail and a jib and mainsail is shown in Figure 6.36.[13] The dotted lines show the streamlines with the main alone and the dashed lines with the jib and main combined. While there have been many sketches of the streamline patterns about sails, this figure is unusual in that it represents a calculated and not a sketched result. It is possible to sketch a streamline pattern to illustrate almost any result desired, but the correct conclusions can only be drawn if the correct streamline pattern is used. An interesting point to note is that the dotted streamline marked H which passes through the position of the leading edge of the jib (when there is no jib) is considerably above the dashed streamline marked S which is the streamline separating the flow going on each side of the jib. The flow passing between the jib and mainsail, when the jib is used, is considerably less than the flow between the jib leading edge location and the main, when the jib is absent. This result is contrary to many of the suppositions which have been made. The pressure distributions about the main and jib both alone and together are shown in Figures 6.37 and 6.38. The mainsail causes a considerable

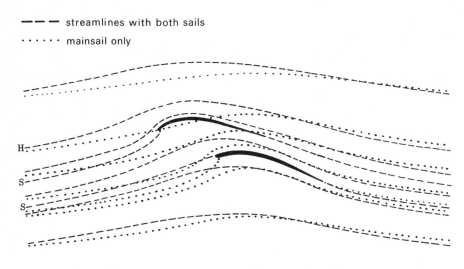

- - - streamlines with both sails
· · · · · · mainsail only

6.36   Streamline pattern caused by jib and mainsail. $\beta = 25°$

reduced pressure on the leeward side of the jib and a reduced pressure at the trailing edge. Figure 6.39 shows the difference between the pressure coefficients along the jib and at the trailing edge. The pressure recovery required along the leeward side both with the mainsail and without are almost the same. The effect on the main of the jib is to increase the pressures on the leeward side considerably reducing the lift. The pressure recovery required by the boundary layer on the leeward side of the main is considerably reduced showing that the main should be trimmed when the jib is hoisted. The lift coefficients for the sails operating both independently and in conjunction is shown in Table 6.2 on page 150. The lift coefficient for the main when used alone is unreasonably high and gives a strong adverse pressure gradient along the leeward side. The sail would probably be stalled under this condition, but these results are still useful to illustrate the interactions. The lift coefficient of the jib is considerably increased by the presence of the main, while that of the main is decreased by the jib (at the trim angle shown). With the untrimmed main, the lift coefficient for the two sails in conjunction is less than the sum for the two alone. However, if the main is trimmed in, its lift can be increased to approximately the value it had without the jib, giving a similar pressure recovery requirement along the leeward side.

6.4.6   SAIL INTERACTION BETWEEN BOATS

These same calculations give an interesting insight into the interaction between two sailboats. Figure 6.40 shows the wind pattern caused by the sail configurations considered in the previous section. Both the change in wind angle and speed is shown in the figure. It has been divided approximately horizontally by a line through

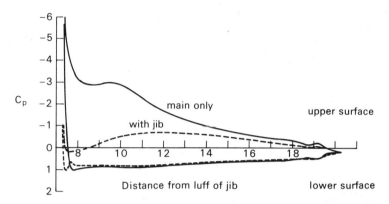

6.37   Pressure distribution on mainsail with and without jib. β = 25°

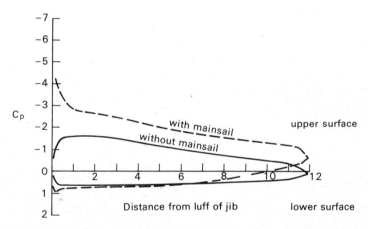

6.38   Pressure distribution on jib with and without mainsail. β = 25°, x measured from leading edge of jib

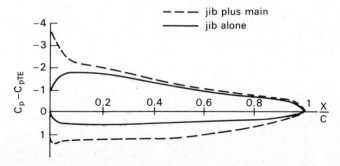

6.39   Pressure distribution on jib with and without mainsail relative to trailing edge pressure

the points where the wind is blowing at the undisturbed velocity of 10 knots; above this line the wind speeds are higher and below it lower. An approximately vertical line passes through the points where the wind direction is in the undisturbed direction; on the left hand side the wind speed is more favorable and on the right hand side less favorable. Another boat in the vicinity will be most favored in the upper left hand quadrant of this figure and least favored in the lower right hand quadrant. If another boat was located near this one the wind pattern would be that resulting from the combined effect of these two boats. A first estimate can be obtained by superimposing two diagrams of this type and adding together the deviations from the undisturbed condition. The result will be to increase the benefits of forward leeward position and the disadvantage of the trailing position.

This figure also suggests that passing a boat to leeward is favored. The overtaking boat should fall off as it pulls abeam and is headed by the wind shift, but it can then point up and pull ahead as it is lifted by the favorable wind shift ahead of the boat. During the entire process it will experience an increased wind velocity from the undisturbed value and will cause the windward boat to feel decreased velocities.

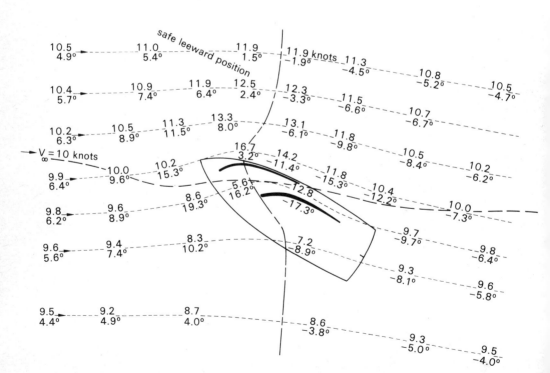

6.40   Streamlines about jib and mainsail showing local wind speeds and flow angles

6.4.7   SAIL PERFORMANCE CHARACTERISTICS

Some of the most used and best data on the performance of sails comes from the measurements made by Davidson on the yacht *Gimcrack* and published in 1936.[6] These were obtained from measuring the performance of an actual boat under sail and then deducing the sail forces from known characteristics of the hull such as resistance and stability. The resulting sail characteristics are usually referred to as the *Gimcrack* coefficients. Unfortunately only performance under the closehauled condition was determined. The tests were accomplished by sailing the boat to windward in various wind strengths at what the helmsman considered to be optimum and similar conditions, e.g. Davidson's statement 'the boat was sailed largely by the luff of the mainsail during the tests so that the angle of attack must have remained roughly constant.' If the apparent wind angle in the plane perpendicular to the mast is calculated using Equation 6.1 the angle is approximately 26° over the full range of wind speeds. It should be appreciated that each wind strength corresponds to a different angle of heel so that a constant apparent wind angle β in the plane perpendicular to the mast does not give a constant apparent wind angle in the horizontal plane but one which increases as the angle of heel increases.

From these data, the lift coefficient and the lift to drag ratio of the sails can be calculated. These calculations are based on the conditions in the plane perpendicular to the mast and employ the assumption that flow along the direction of the mast can be ignored. The data provide no check on this assumption since each angle of heel corresponds to only one wind velocity. The lift coefficient and lift drag ratio so obtained are shown in Figure 6.41 as a function of apparent wind velocity. The angles of heel that correspond to these wind velocities are also shown. This figure shows a definite decrease in lift coefficient with increasing wind velocity and also an increase in the lift/drag ratio. Equation 6.27 may be rewritten as

$$\frac{L}{D} = \frac{\pi AR}{C_L} \tag{6.44}$$

or

$$C_D = \frac{C_L^2}{\pi AR} \tag{6.45}$$

so that an increase in lift/drag ratio is to be expected with a decrease in lift coefficient. This relation suggests that if the drag is plotted against the lift coefficient squared, a straight line should be obtained. Figure 6.42 is just such a plot and a straight line is indeed obtained. The equation for this line is

$$C_D = 0{\cdot}038 + 0{\cdot}092 C_L^2 \tag{6.46}$$

which would correspond to an effective aspect ratio for the sails of 3·46. Davidson does not report the aspect ratio for the *Gimcrack's* sail plan but the value obtained

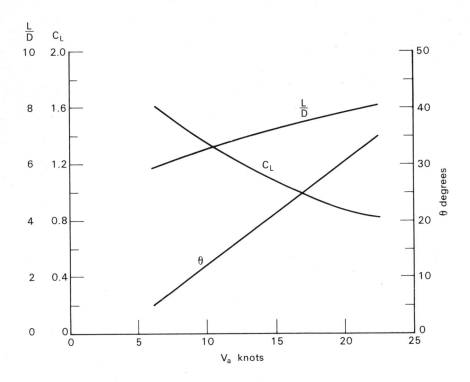

6.41   Lift coefficient, lift/drag ratio, and angle of heel from *Gimcrack* tests

appears to be a reasonable one. It is also obvious from Figure 6.42 that the induced drag (the drag caused by lift) is the important one and that the magnitude of the drag at zero lift is relatively unimportant.

The reason for the reduced lift coefficient with increased wind strength and angle of heel is not obvious. It has been shown in Section 6.4.2 that the lift on a properly trimmed sail depends chiefly on the camber of the sail. This fact would suggest that *Gimcrack's* sails were flattened as the wind strength increased. There would appear to be no inherent effect of either wind strength or heel angle which would cause this reduction in lift coefficient unless it involves a change in sail shape. However, it is important to determine whether lift coefficient can be maintained as wind strength and heel angle increases, and what measures have to be taken to do so.

The data for the sail performance off the wind are not nearly as well established as in the closehauled condition. A reliable set of tests compatible with those for *Gimcrack* do not seem to exist for these other sets of conditions. For the purpose of calculating yacht performance off the wind a set of sail performance characteristics have been used by the Davidson Towing Basin with reasonable success.[30] For this purpose

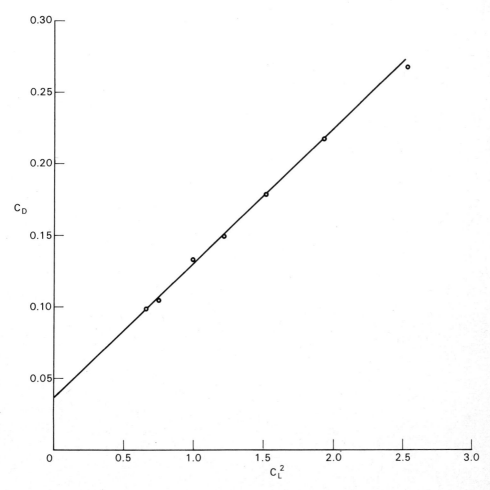

6.42   Drag as a function of lift squared showing straight-line relation for *Gimcrack* results

the value of the total force coefficient is assumed to be constant and ε to be a function of the angle of the relative wind. The relations used are as follows

$$C_N = 2{\cdot}0 \qquad\qquad (6.47)$$

and

$$\tan \varepsilon = 10{\cdot}0 + 0{\cdot}39\,\beta \qquad\qquad (6.48)$$

These relations are designed for reaching conditions. Unfortunately they do not smoothly match the closehauled *Gimcrack* coefficients either in the magnitude of

C_N or ε. While these coefficients have been used for performance predictions, it should be recognized that they have been adopted only in the absence of better data and should not be considered to be exact.

Table 6.1   The parameters of the cases shown in Figure 6.6, 'Sailboat speed for difficult causes'.

	$\dfrac{A_s L}{D}$	$\dfrac{A_w L}{D}$	$\dfrac{D}{(L/100)^3}$	$\dfrac{V_w}{\sqrt{L}}$	$\dfrac{A_s}{A_b}$	AR	$\dfrac{h_{cp}}{h_M}$	C_N	ε
Case									
1)	3000	800	200 or greater	1·41	10	·5	20	·8	10°
2)	3000	800	,,	2	10	·5	20	·8	10°
3)	,,	,,	,,	2·82	10	·5	20	·8	10°
4)	3000	1600	200	2	10	·5	20	·8	10°
5)	3000	1600	50	2	10	·5	20	·8	10°
6)	6000	1600	50	2	10	·5	10	·8	10°
7)	4770	1000	126	1·41	12·6	·4	20	·8	10°

Table 6.2   Lift coefficients for mainsail and jib

	C_L	
	Separately	*With other sail*
Jib	1·61	2·42
Main	2·04	0·995
Jib and main	1·83	1·67

Trim of sails is not changed when they are hoisted together.

Chapter Seven
Directional Control of a Sailboat

7.1   Directional stability

The directional control of a sailboat has become of greater importance to yachtsmen and designers in recent years. The real problems develop in sailing before the wind. The increased interest and participation in long-distance ocean racing, the design of higher performance light displacement boats with a higher ratio of sail area to displacement, and increased competition have all led to the increased emphasis on directional stability. Many ocean races, particularly those sailed on the West Coast of the USA, are primarily downwind races, the Trans-Pac Race from Los Angeles to Hawaii being the most notable example. The main limitation on the amount of sail which can be carried in such a race is the directional control which allows the helmsman to keep the boat on the desired course. Directional control is becoming one of the prime requirements for successful competition in major ocean racing events.

It is useful to consider three conditions which are important to the steering of a boat. First, the rudder must be able to develop enough force or moment to balance the moments developed by the sails and hull and allow the boat to be kept on course. The second and third considerations are static and dynamic directional stability. The requirement for static directional stability is that when the boat is properly balanced on its course, a small deviation from that course will cause a moment which will turn the boat back to course without any action by the helmsman. Dynamic directional stability is concerned with whether the oscillations about the desired course will increase or decrease. If a boat with static directional stability deviates from course it will then return to course; however, it may overshoot the desired course and the deviation may be larger or smaller than the original deviation. If the boat continues to oscillate about the desired course with increasing amplitude, then the boat is dynamically unstable.

A full analysis of stability characteristics of a sailboat is relatively complex if all possible motions and forces are considered. The study of the stability of airplanes provides a model of the way such a study can be performed. However, if done correctly it requires relatively complex mathematical procedures which are beyond the scope of this presentation. Luckily the most essential features of the problem can be relatively simply understood and the difference between directional stability when beating or running made clear.

When a boat is sailing at high speed the wave resistance is large and the important balance is between sail and hull forces. The inertia forces caused by accelerations are smaller and a useful and simplified analysis can be performed without considering the acceleration terms. Neglect of these terms greatly simplifies the analysis but also excludes the study of dynamic instabilities. Fortunately the actual performance of boats shows that dynamic instabilities are not of primary importance.

Figure 7.1 shows the force diagram applicable to a sailboat; α is the angle between the course and the actual wind and β between the course and the apparent wind. F is the force which the sails exert on the hull and R the force exerted by the water on the hull. If the boat is not accelerating these forces must be balanced. This

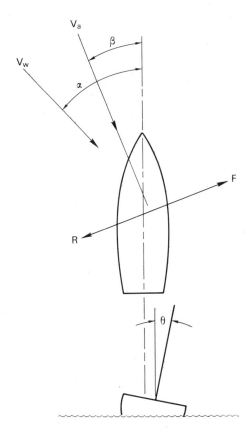

7.1   Sailboat force diagram

balance of forces is necessary and is created by the proper position of the helm. The question of stability which we wish to investigate concerns what happens when the heading of the boat relative to the wind direction changes. Does this change in heading cause a moment which will turn the boat back to the original heading or does it cause a moment which will turn the boat further away from the original heading? In the first case the boat is stable and the helmsman need not move the helm, and in the second case he must move the helm and must move it in a way which anticipates the turning of the boat in order to steer a straight course. When the boat's course changes relative to the wind direction the course with respect to the relative wind also changes and the force on the sails change. The lateral component of this force and the lateral force on the hull cause a turning moment. The lateral force also causes the boat to heel so that an additional turning moment is caused by the water forces on the asymetric hull; but, of greater importance, the line of action of the forward component of this sail force and rearward component of the resistance force are now moved relative to each other to cause a turning moment.

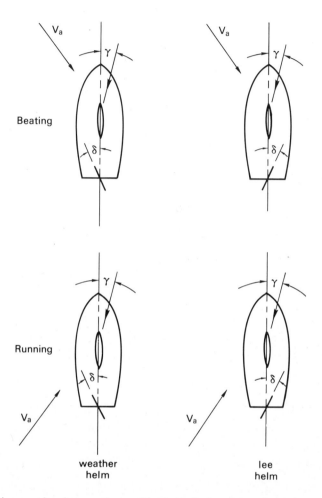

Beating

Running

weather
helm

lee
helm

7.2   Diagram showing weather and lee helm for beating and running

First, consider the direct action of the lateral force in creating a turning moment. This affect is most easily understood if a fin keel spade rudder configuration is considered (Figure 7.2). The boat may have either weather or lee helm. An increase in the side force of the wind means that the lateral resistance of the hull must also increase, which requires an increase in leeway angle γ. For a symetrical hydrofoil the lift force may be considered directly proportional to the angle of attack, which is γ for the keel and $\gamma+\delta$ for the rudder. Now if the leeway angle increases to $\gamma+d\gamma$ then the fractional increase in the angle of attack of the keel and rudder is $1+d\gamma/\gamma$ for the keel and $1+d\gamma/(\gamma+\delta)$ for the rudder. Since the forces on the two hydrofoils will be proportional to the angle of attack, the distribution of the side force between the keel and rudder will change. If the boat has a weather helm, δ is positive and an increase in side force will cause a greater increase in the force on the keel than the rudder ($d\gamma/\gamma$ is greater than $d\gamma/(\gamma+\delta)$; δ positive). The result will be that the turning moment will change in a way to cause the boat to turn to weather. For the case of a lee helm, δ is negative and the result is a change to leeward in turning moment.

Now consider the effect of an increase in side force on increasing the angle of heel. The change in heel increases the distance between the forward component of the sail force and the hull resistance force resulting in an increased turning moment to weather.

The relation between the side force and the boat's heading depends on the relative angle of the apparent wind. If the boat is closehauled a heading change to windward will decrease the side force, but if the boat is running, the opposite will be true. The conditions for a boat on both a closehauled and running course are shown in Table 7.1. This table shows the changes for a boat which has suffered a small course

Table 7.1   Directional stability summary

	Beating		Running	
Turn to windward	Apparent wind shifts away from beam		Apparent wind shifts toward beam	
Sail side force	Decreases		Increases	
Angle of heel	Decreases		Increases	
Rounding up moment (Thrust-forward resistance couple)	Decreases		Increases	
Effect	Stable		Unstable	
Leeway angle	Decreases		Increases	
	Weather Helm	Lee Helm	Weather Helm	Lee Helm
Ratio of keel to rudder side force	Decreases	Increases	Increases	Decreases
Rounding up moment	Decreases	Increases	Increases	Decreases
Effect	Stable	Unstable	Unstable	Stable

change to windward. The change in side force and the relation to the turning moment caused by the change in heel and keel rudder side force ratio is shown as well as the effects of both of these on directional stability. For a sailboat with a weather helm, both effects are stable when beating. That is, the boat will return to the course it was following before the disturbance with no motion of the rudder assuming that it was properly balanced on this initial course. If the boat is running, both effects are unstable. If the rudder is not moved, the boat will continue to turn from the initial course as the result of a small initial change. A lee helm will make the effect of the keel/rudder side force ratio unstable for a boat which is beating and stable for one running.

Only for the case of a very stiff boat, such as a catamaran, is it likely that this keel rudder side force effect is more important than the heel effect which is always stable in beating and unstable in running. The importance of the keel rudder side force term is increased when the helm necessary to balance the boat is large. On a well balanced boat this effect is minimal. The lee helm desirable for downwind stability can be achieved by moving the center of effort of the sails forward. It is probably intuitively obvious that carrying only headsails increases the running directional stability.

This discussion has been presented with respect to the fin keel with spade rudder configuration. The effects are similar for all other keel/rudder configurations but is simplest to understand in the case of the separate rudder.

7.2   Directional disturbances

In addition to the directional stability there are other effects which have an important influence on the steering of a sailboat. The sea is a major source of disturbances. Waves effect the boat through the surface currents which they generate as well as through rolling the boat. Another important effect is the aerodynamic instability of a sail which can behave as a rolling engine when running. All of these effects are most severe when running and will be discussed in that context.

The effect of the turning moment caused by roll is probably the most important. Roll would not occur if the boat was sailing dead before the waves but the more usual case is with the waves on the windward quarter. When the boat is on the forward face of a wave it will be rolled to leeward and a rounding up or broaching moment will be caused as previously discussed.

In Chapter 2, in which wave motion was discussed, it was pointed out that water particles perform a circular motion which results in an oscillatory surface current. This current reaches a maximum in the direction of the wave motion on the crest of the wave and in the reverse direction in the trough. The forward face of the wave is a region in which the water is accelerating in the direction of wave motion. If the boat is on the forward face of the wave the relative velocity between the boat and the water will be greater at the bow of the boat than at the stern. Figure 7.3 shows the appropriate vector diagram; it can be seen that the relative velocity between the boat and the water at the bow is different from that at the stern and that the velocity at the stern is more from the windward side than at the bow. The result is a turning moment to windward and a tendency towards broaching.

It is easy to write a quantitative expression for change in relative flow angle along the hull. The velocities on the forward face of the wave are

$$u = \sqrt{\frac{\pi}{2} g \frac{H^2}{\lambda}} \cos \frac{2\pi x}{\lambda}$$

where H is the wave height and λ the wave length.

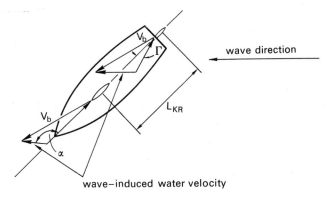

wave direction

L_{KR}

V_b

V_b

Γ

α

wave−induced water velocity

7.3   Wave motion direction stability diagram

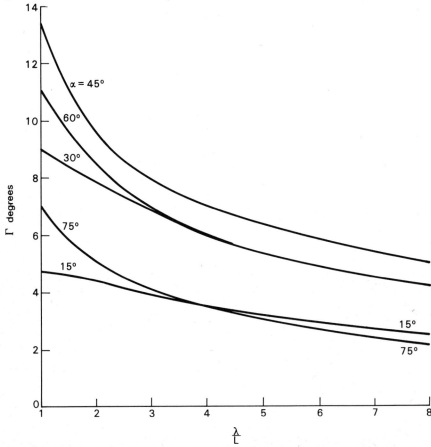

$\alpha = 45°$

60°

30°

75°

15°

15°

75°

Γ degrees

$\dfrac{\lambda}{L}$

7.4   Angular difference between rudder and keel caused by wave action for
boat moving at hull speed with the distance between rudder and keel equal to
$\frac{1}{2}$ the length, and wave height to length ratio of 0·05

If the distance between the keel and rudder is L_{KR} then the difference in velocity of the wave-induced current at these two stations is

$$u_1 - u_2 = \sqrt{\frac{\pi}{2} g \frac{H^2}{\lambda}} \left[\cos \frac{2\pi\left(x - \dfrac{L_{KR}}{2} \cos \alpha\right)}{\lambda} - \cos \frac{2\pi\left(x + \dfrac{L_{KR}}{2} \cos \alpha\right)}{\lambda} \right] \quad (7.1)$$

The change of flow angle is then

$$\sin \Gamma = \frac{\sqrt{\dfrac{\pi}{2} g \dfrac{H^2}{\lambda}} \sin \alpha}{V_b} \left[\cos \frac{2\pi\left(x - \dfrac{L_{KR}}{2} \cos \alpha\right)}{\lambda} - \cos \frac{2\pi\left(x + \dfrac{L_{KR}}{2} \cos \alpha\right)}{\lambda} \right] \quad (7.2)$$

A better understanding of the physical significance of this effect can be obtained if the boat is assumed to be running at approximately hull speed with respect to the water. The resulting expression is

$$\sin \Gamma = \pi \sqrt{\frac{H^2}{\lambda L}} \sin \alpha \left[\cos \frac{2\pi\left(x - \dfrac{L_{KR}}{2} \cos \alpha\right)}{\lambda} - \cos \frac{2\pi\left(x + \dfrac{L_{KR}}{2} \cos \alpha\right)}{\lambda} \right] \quad (7.3)$$

$$\sin \Gamma = 2\pi \sqrt{\frac{H^2}{\lambda L}} \sin \alpha \sin \frac{2\pi x}{\lambda} \sin \frac{\pi L_{KR} \cos \alpha}{\lambda} \quad (7.4)$$

Figure 7.4 shows a plot of this relation based on the condition that the keel to rudder distance is $\frac{1}{2}$ of the effective waterline length, and wave height to length ratio is 0·05. The figure shows the values when $\sin 2\pi x/\lambda = 1$ which corresponds to the boat being at the maximum slope of the wave. The plot shows that this change in angle reaches a maximum when the boat's course is 45° from the wave direction and that the longer the waves the smaller the effect. Angles of the order of 7°–9° occur for waves 2 to 4 times the boat's length. The turning moment induced by this change in angle depends on the boat's characteristics, but the change in rudder angle required to maintain a straight course is approximately equal to this angle for a spade rudder configuration and larger for other rudder configurations. The effect lasts for a shorter time for the shorter waves so the disturbance to the boat may be less for short waves even though the angle is greater.

The effect of surfing on the forward face of the wave can also have a tendency to turn the boat. If surfing did not occur and the boat's velocity remained constant but decreased relative to the water then the forward water motion would cause an increase in leeway angle which would make the boat tend to round up if sailing with a windward helm. This case probably never occurs even for a heavy displacement boat sailing at low speed and is not a particularly important one.

The more interesting and far more thrilling case is that for which the boat surfs down the forward face of the waves at greater relative speeds through the water than its average speed. If the effect of inertia terms can still be neglected, which seems more questionable under these circumstances, then the horizontal water forces must continue to balance the sail forces. The increased boat speed will rotate the apparent wind forward but also decrease its velocity. The side force can be increased or decreased depending upon the wind angle and boat/wind speed ratio. The effect of a change in the side force has been covered in the previous discussions. If the side force remains constant the increase in relative water velocity will result in a decrease in the leeway angle. For a weather helm, the result will be a bearing-away moment since the proportional decrease in keel angle of attack would be greater than for the rudder.

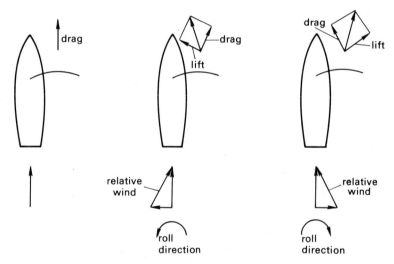

7.5   Rolling action of sail showing how roll develops a force in the direction of roll when the boat is running

Another important effect in downwind sailing is the rolling action of the sails. Any sail may produce such an effect but a spinnaker is particularly susceptible. If the boat starts to roll, the forces on the sail can couple with the rolling motion to increase the rolling. Since a heeling angle causes a turning moment, this rolling action has a serious effect on the steering of the boat. The cause of the rolling effect is illustrated in Figure 7.5. The diagram (a) shows a boat sailing before the wind without rolling. The wind is perpendicular to the sail and a pure drag force is generated in the same direction as the wind. Now assume the boat rolls to port (diagram (b)). Because of the rolling motion, the apparent wind is over the port quarter and a force on the sail is now generated with both lift and drag components. The lift component acts towards the port side which is the direction of roll. If the lift/drag ratio is sufficiently large, the resulting force acts in the direction of roll and increases the energy in the rolling motion. At some angle of heel, the righting moment will overcome the rolling moment and the boat will stop rolling. The boat will then start to roll to starboard and cause the same effect in the opposite direction (Figure 7.5c). The rolling motion will build up until the energy added to the rolling motion by the sail is equal to that damped out by the hull.

7.3   Rudder design

Sailboat rudders are of two general types, attached to the keel and separate from it (Figure 7.6). The attached rudder has been more common in the past but the separate rudder is gaining popularity. The separate rudder has been used extensively in small boats of the centerboard type. The separate rudder may be a spade rudder in which the whole rudder configuration is moved, or it may be a rudder attached

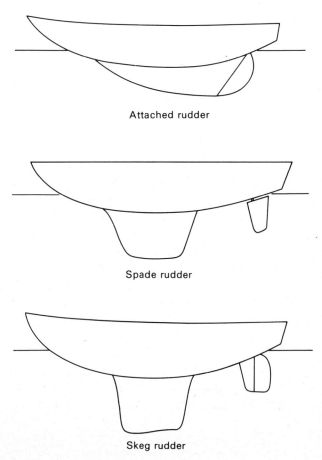

Attached rudder

Spade rudder

Skeg rudder

7.6   Sailboat rudder configurations

to a skeg in which the forward section is fixed and only the after part is movable. Another arrangement which has been used is the combination of both an attached and separate rudder. The attached rudder may be used as a trim tab on the keel and the steering done with the separate rudder, or they may both be used for steering.

In order to understand these different rudder configurations, it is worth reviewing some basic performance data for hydrofoils. In particular, it is useful to look at both the effects of aspect ratio and flaps.

7.3.1   HYDROFOIL CHARACTERISTICS

A simple symetrical hydrofoil has the characteristic that the lift and angle of attack can be related approximately by the formula

$$C_L = c(\gamma - \gamma_0)$$

(7.5)

$$c = \frac{0 \cdot 11}{1 + \dfrac{2}{AR}}$$

where γ is in degrees and

$$F_R = \frac{1}{2} \frac{w_w}{g} V_b^2 A_R C_L$$

The lift curve slope is steepest for the infinite aspect ratio foil and becomes flatter as the aspect ratio is reduced.

The resistance of the hydrofoil is the sum of the friction drag, which depends on the wetted area, and the skin friction coefficient, and the induced resistance, which depends on the lift.

$$C_{D_i} = \frac{C_L^2}{\pi AR}$$

(7.6)

If disturbances of the surface of the water are neglected, the aspect ratio may be considered to be twice the geometric value.

For a symmetrical airfoil the lift force acts through a point at a distance behind the leading edge equal to $\frac{1}{4}$ of the distance from the leading edge to the trailing edge. Typical characteristics of a symmetrical hydrofoil are shown in Figure 7.7.

The effect of a deflected flap is to change the angle of attack for zero lift and to move the center of pressure towards the rear of the foil. The flap deflection changes the whole pressure distribution about the foil and does not simply change the pressure on the flap. The total lift coefficients will be increased if the flap is deflected towards the pressure or windward side of the foil and decreased if towards the leeward side.

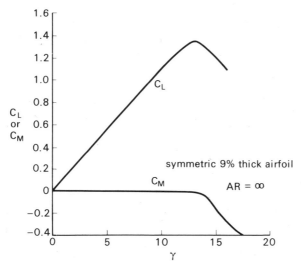

7.7   Lift and moment coefficient about $\frac{1}{4}$ chord point for symmetrical 9% thick hydrofoil of infinite aspect ratio

The angular deflection of the flap will be larger than the change in zero lift angle of attack. The zero lift angle of attack is given by the relation

$$\gamma_0 = -\beta\delta \qquad (7.7)$$

The value of β for different ratios of the chord of the flap to total hydrofoil chord C_F/C is shown in Figure 7.8. The parameter β can be considered to be the effectiveness of the flap deflection. It is seen that β varies from 0 to 1 for C_F/C from 0 to 1, but non-linearly so that the flap effectiveness is always greater than C_F/C.

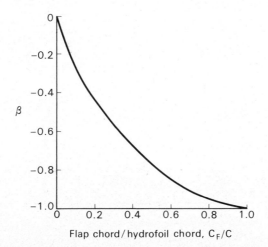

Flap chord/hydrofoil chord, C_F/C

7.8   Variation of lift effectiveness parameter with flap/chord ratio

The location of the lift force on the foil is also of importance. On a simple symetrical foil this force is applied at the quarter chord point, one-quarter of the way from the leading edge to the trailing edge. If the foil has a flap the center of pressure is moved aft. A rough estimate of the change in center of pressure can be obtained from the expression

$$\frac{L_{cp}}{C} = 0 \cdot 25 + \frac{8 \cdot 3 \, \dfrac{C_F}{C}}{1 + \dfrac{\gamma}{\delta}} \tag{7.8}$$

which is most accurate for $C_F/C \approx 0 \cdot 20$.

7.3.2   RUDDER TORQUE AND WORK

The torque on the rudder stock needed to deflect the rudder is an important consideration. For an attached or skeg rudder configuration the torque is given by the relation

$$C_H = \frac{T_R}{\dfrac{1}{2} \dfrac{w_w}{g} V^2 A_R C_F} = \frac{C_{H\gamma}\gamma + C_{H\delta}\delta}{1 + \dfrac{2}{AR}} \tag{7.9}$$

where $C_{H\gamma}$ and $C_{H\delta}$ are given in Figure 7.9. This torque depends both on the angle of attack and rudder deflection angle. The coefficients $C_{H\gamma}$ and $C_{H\delta}$ depend upon the flap to hydrofoil chord ratio as shown.

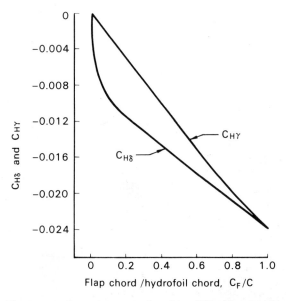

7.9   Flap hinge moment parameter as function of flap/chord ratio

A rudder torque coefficient can be defined as the rudder torque divided by the total side force on the keel and rudder times the boat's length.

$$C_{TR} = \frac{T_R}{HL} \tag{7.10}$$

For an attached or skeg rudder this torque coefficient is

$$C_{TR} = \frac{C_{H\gamma} + C_{H\delta} \dfrac{\delta}{\gamma}}{0 \cdot 11} \frac{A_{RF}}{A_b} \frac{C_F}{L} \tag{7.11}$$

For a spade rudder, the torque depends upon the amount the rudder post is displaced from the center of pressure of the hydrofoil. If this amount divided by the rudder chord is d/C then

$$C_H = \frac{T_R}{\dfrac{1}{2} \dfrac{w_w}{g} V_b^2 A_R C} = C_L \frac{d}{C}$$

and

$$C_{TR} = \left(1 + \frac{\delta}{\gamma}\right) \frac{d}{C} \frac{A_R}{A_b} \frac{C}{L} \tag{7.12}$$

The actual torque is obtained by multiplying by the side force on the boat and the length of the boat.

Another important consideration in determining the feel of the boat to the helmsman is the angular deflection and the work (torque times angular deflection) required to achieve a given change in lateral center of pressure. The rudder work coefficient is defined as

$$C_{WR} = C_{TR} \frac{\delta}{\gamma} \tag{7.13}$$

The work required is a more fundamental requirement than the torque since the actual force required by the helmsman on a tiller or wheel depends not only on the torque but the tiller length or wheel gearing ratio. The required work is fixed unless a power boost system is to be considered. At the present time, sailboat handling quantities are very poorly defined; however, it seems clear that there must exist a range of force and deflection values for tillers or wheels which give good steering ability. The optimum conditions will vary for individual helmsmen, but a range must exist to which most helmsmen can easily adapt. This range must also be affected by the speed of response required which depends upon the size of the boat and other characteristics.

7.3.3　CHARACTERISTICS OF DIFFERENT KEEL/RUDDER CONFIGURATIONS

Consider the three different rudder keel configurations in Figure 7.6: an attached rudder, a separate spade rudder, and a separate skeg rudder. The design criterion for the keel/rudder combination may be expressed either as a turning moment or as a shift in the lateral center of pressure. When considering the requirements needed to balance the sail forces, the latter method is probably more meaningful. Set an arbitrary but reasonable criterion for a change in center of pressure by 10% of the load waterline from the position with an undeflected rudder. Choose the lengths of the keel and rudder for the attached rudder configuration to be 0·8 of the load waterline, then the center of pressure will have to be shifted by 0·125 of the chord of the foil (keel plus rudder). Equation 7.8 can be solved for the ratio of rudder deflection to angle of attack to obtain a given change in L_{cp}/C.

$$\frac{\delta}{\gamma} = \frac{\Delta \dfrac{L_{cp}}{C}}{8 \cdot 3 \dfrac{C_F}{C} - \Delta \dfrac{L_{cp}}{C}} \tag{7.14}$$

For

$$\frac{C_F}{C} = 0 \cdot 20 \quad \text{and} \quad \Delta \frac{L_{cp}}{C} = 0 \cdot 125$$

then

$$\frac{\delta}{\gamma} = 3$$

For the separate rudder configurations, the distance between the rudder and the keel and the relative size of rudder and keel are important parameters. By taking moments about the center of pressure of the keel it is easily shown that

$$\frac{F_R}{F_K} = \frac{\dfrac{\Delta L_{cp}}{L}}{\dfrac{L_{KR}}{L} - \dfrac{\Delta L_{cp}}{L}} \tag{7.15}$$

and that

$$\frac{\gamma_R}{\gamma_K} = \frac{F_R}{F_K} \frac{A_K}{A_R} \frac{c_R}{c_K} \tag{7.16}$$

For a spade rudder the angle of deflection is

$$\frac{\delta}{\gamma_K} = \frac{\gamma_R}{\gamma_K} - 1 \tag{7.17}$$

For a skeg configuration the deflection angle must be divided by the rudder deflection coefficient β (Equation 7.7). For the skeg rudder

$$\frac{\delta}{\gamma_K} = \frac{1}{\beta}\left(\frac{\gamma_R}{\gamma_K} - 1\right) \tag{7.18}$$

Using the same example as for the attached rudder and taking

$$\frac{L_{KR}}{L} = 0.6, \frac{A_R}{A_K} = 0.1 \text{ and } \frac{C}{L} = 0.1$$

and $(AR)_R = (AR)_K$ then $c_R = c_K$,

$$\frac{F_R}{F_K} = 0.2 \quad \text{and} \quad \frac{\gamma_R}{\gamma_K} = 2$$

For the spade rudder $\delta/\gamma_K = 1$. For the skeg rudder with a flap to hydrofoil chord ratio of 0.5, $\delta/\gamma_K = 1.28$. The rudder post torque for these three rudders can also be calculated. For the attached rudder with 20% flap, the values are $C_{H\gamma} = 0.005$ and $C_{H\delta} = 0.0115$ (Figure 7.8). When substituted in Equation 7.11 the result is $C_{TR} = 0.0115$. The skeg rudder can be treated in a similar way; $C_{H\delta} = 0.016$ and $C_{H\gamma} = 0.0125$ for a 50% flap giving $C_{TR} = 0.00068$. For the spade rudder, Equations 7.12 must be used and the value of $d/C = 0.025$ has been selected for this example. For this value $C_{TR} = 0.00046$.

The value of C_{WR} (the rudder work coefficient) will also be calculated for these various examples using Equation 7.14. The results are

Attached rudder $C_{WR} = 0.0345$
Skeg rudder $C_{WR} = 0.000875$
Spade rudder $C_{WR} = 0.00046$

The different rudders chosen for this example are meant to be typical but many variations of the parameters are possible. The rudder torque for the spade rudder is particularly sensitive to the point of rudder post attachment. It must be very near the center of pressure if a small rudder torque is to be achieved. The spade rudder requires the least deflection which tends to give it a proportionally smaller C_{WR} than C_{TR}.

7.3.4   TURNING RADIUS

The turning radius of a boat depends upon the size and design. For boats of different sizes but similar design this turning radius is proportional to the length. The rate of turning is therefore proportional to the velocity over the length V_b/L and the time constant for turning is proportional to the reciprocal of this value or L/V_b. Since V_b is proportional to $\sqrt{gL}$ the time constant can also be expressed as $\tau = \sqrt{L/g}$ which is also the appropriate time constant for roll and pitch motions. Since roll has a direct coupling to directional characteristics, the time constants for these two motions should be compatible.

The effect of underbody configurations on turning rate and directional time constant is more difficult to determine. A first order estimate can be obtained by considering the rate of turn which causes the turning moment on the keel rudder combination to be zero. For the separate rudder configurations this is relatively easily done by determining the turning radius that gives zero lift force on the rudder. If it is assumed that the keel is at zero angle of attack, then as shown in Figure 7.10 the angle of attack relative to the centerline of the boat at the rudder will be L_{KR}/R where R is the radius of the turn. For a spade rudder, the deflection angle δ must be equal to this angle. The turning radius is then

$$R = \frac{L_{KR}}{\tan \delta} \tag{7.19}$$

For a skeg rudder arrangement, similar relations hold. In this case, the rudder deflection angle must be such that the change in zero lift angle of attack is equal to the change in flow angle at the rudder relative to the boat's centerline. Therefore

$$R = \frac{L_{KR}}{\tan (\delta\beta)} \tag{7.20}$$

where β depends upon the flap to chord ratio (Figure 7.8).

The spade rudder provides the shortest turning radius for a given deflection of the rudder. The skeg configuration will always require a larger rudder angle than the spade rudder for the same L_{KR}.

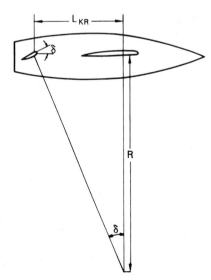

7.10   Turning radius diagram

For the attached rudder, the problem is more difficult. The length of the keel relative to the change in flow direction must be considered. A quantitative relation for this case is not easily obtained.

The ability to keep a boat on a straight course is no doubt related to the turning radius. It is commonly accepted that a long straight keel with an attached rudder configuration is easier to hold on a straight course than a short keel. The long keel certainly gives a longer turning radius. A comparison between the spade rudder and the skeg rudder can be made for both rudder fixed and rudder free conditions. For rudder fixed conditions, the spade rudder and skeg rudder are identical with respect to the moment required to achieve a given rate of turn if the total rudder or rudder skeg area is the same. However, for the rudder free condition, the spade rudder will give no lift force. It will weathervane at zero angle of attack. The flap of the skeg rudder will weathervane but there will be some resulting force. δ/γ can be found by setting $C_{TR} = 0$ in Equation 7.11. For a 50% chord flap the result is $\delta/\gamma = -0.78$. For this rudder $\beta = 0.77$ so, by Equation 7.7, $\gamma_0 = 0.6\gamma$. Therefore $\gamma - \gamma_0 = 0.4\gamma$. The effect of the rudder is reduced by 60% for the tiller free condition compared with the tiller fixed but not to zero as occurs for the spade rudder.

For the rudder free condition, the external turning moment needed to achieve a given turning rate will be much less with the spade rudder than the skeg rudder. This effect plus the sensitivity of the spade rudder to small angles of rudder deflection leads to a decreased feel of directional stability with this configuration.

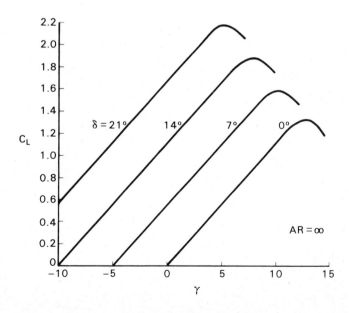

7.11   Variation of lift curve with deflection of 20% flap

7.3.5   RUDDER OPERATING CONDITIONS

In steering a boat a rudder must operate under a variety of conditions. It must turn the boat and it must also maintain the boat on a straight course when turning moments are imposed from other causes. Consider first the skeg rudder configuration. In turning the boat, it is necessary to create a force towards the side of the rudder from which the flow is approaching (Figure 7.12a). The rudder is operating at a negative angle of attack. Another case of interest (b) occurs when the boat is being held on a straight course through the water against the action of an external turning moment. Under this condition the rudder will be at zero or a small angle of attack which is the same as the keel. A third case (c) is when the boat is being held on a straight course under sea conditions which are pushing the stern and rudder to the side. In this case, the rudder must be developing a force towards the side from which the water flow is approaching. These three cases are the most common and correspond to the rudder operating at near zero or negative angle of attack. For the spade rudder, all these situations will be very similar since the rudder will be turned a different amount in each situation, but always enough to be at positive angle of attack.

Figure 7.11, which shows the characteristics of a hydrofoil with a 20% chord flap, can be used to illustrate the relative behavior of a skeg and spade rudder. The spade rudder, given by the curve for zero flap deflection, can go to a maximum

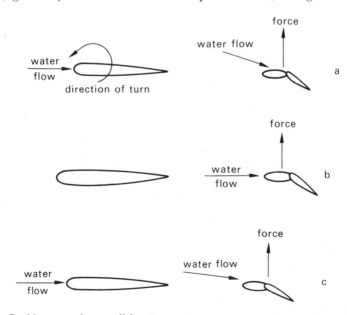

7.12   Rudder operating conditions:
   (a) Boat turning to port
   (b) Rudder balancing external moment
   (c) Rudder counteracting wave turning effect

lift coefficient of 1·35 at 13° angle of attack. However, with the flap deflected to 21° the maximum lift coefficient is 2·2, a considerable increase over that for the undeflected flap. It is very doubtful if this foil used as a skeg rudder would ever be used at the angle of attack and flap deflection to reach this maximum lift coefficient. For case (b) operating at essentially zero angle of attack, a lift coefficient of only 1·65 can be achieved with a 21° flap deflection. For cases (a) or (c) the rudder is at negative angle of attack. For −5° angle of attack the maximum lift coefficient is only 1·1 and for −10° angle of attack, 0·55 for a 21° flap deflection angle. The conclusion is that while the skeg rudder has the higher potential lift coefficient, the maximum that can be obtained under usual operating conditions may be more or less than for the spade rudder. It is also important to note that the skeg rudder is much more difficult to stall under these conditions than the spade rudder. The skeg rudder seems to be less advantageous in resisting the turning effects caused by seas than by sail forces. The former condition is most pronounced when running before a quartering sea.

It might be considered that an ideal rudder design would take advantage of both the changing angle of attack feature of the spade rudder as well as the deflecting flap of the skeg rudder. A spade rudder with a flap would accomplish this result but would be considerably more complicated mechanically (Figure 7.13a). A skeg

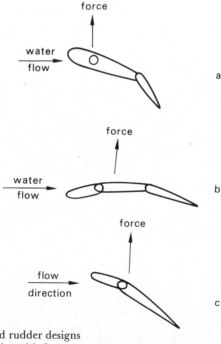

7.13   Articulated rudder designs
   (a) Spade rudder with flap
   (b) Skeg with leading and trailing flaps
   (c) Double flap rudder

rudder with both a leading edge and trailing flap has been tried with both flaps deflected to the same side by the action of the helm (Figure 7·13b). This arrangement appears to augment the negative angle of attack feature of the skeg rudder under usual operating conditions. The arrangement shown in Figure 7·13c is a modification of this leading and trailing flap arrangement which is similar to the spade rudder with a flap, but mechanically simpler. In order to achieve a weathervaning characteristic when the helm is released, the leading flap must only be about $\frac{1}{4}$ of the total chord and the trailing flap about $\frac{3}{4}$. However, these more complicated rudders do not seem to be justified.

7.3.6   RUDDER DRAG

The drag caused by the rudder is a large enough part of the total drag of the boat to bear consideration. Both the drag of the rudder at zero lift and when providing lift are important. At zero lift the most important parameter is the size of the rudder. Since the rudder must be capable of producing a given side force, the size of the rudder is inversely proportional to the maximum lift coefficient obtainable. The drag coefficient at zero lift of the skeg rudder configuration should be somewhat larger than the spade rudder. The increase is caused by the roughness at the hinge in the skeg rudder. The drag can be made to approach that of the spade rudder if a well fitted hinge is constructed. Since the skeg rudder will probably require a somewhat larger area than the spade rudder and have a larger drag coefficient, it will probably have a higher drag at zero lift. At large lift coefficient, the induced drag is the major part of the total drag. Since the induced drag depends chiefly on aspect ratio and plan form, the two rudder configurations should have the same induced drag if they have the same aspect ratio and plan form. Any gap between the flap and stationary part of the rudder which might exist in the skeg rudder configuration would increase the drag somewhat since water could pass through from the high to the low pressure side of the rudder.

Since the induced drag depends on the lift coefficient, the rudder size should be determined both by the maximum load to which it will be subject and the normal operating steady load at different points of sail. It should be large enough so that the lift coefficients are not too large for the normal operating conditions so that the induced drag does not become too large.

7.3.7   RUDDER POST ANGLE

For an attached rudder the rudder post commonly slants forward under the boat. For spade rudders the slant is often aft so that the rudder post is perpendicular to the hull at the point of attachment. As long as the angle is not large and the boat is not heeled excessively the affect of this rudder post angle is small. However, at large angle of heel there can be a noticeable affect. It is easiest to understand this effect if the boat is assumed to be heeled a full 90° and the rudder is still submerged. If the boat is heeled to leeward and making headway through the water, a rudder on a post which slants forward will turn the boat to leeward no matter which way it is deflected. The opposite is true of an aftslanting post. If the boat is running and is knocked down in a broach, then the forward-slanting post will provide a more effective rudder for turning the boat downwind again. The rudder on the forward-slanting post would be less effective in turning the boat into the wind if closehauled when the knockdown occurred. Since turning to windward is much less a problem than squaring off before the wind, the forward-slanting post is advantageous. However, this effect is only important for large angles of rudder post slant and high angles of heel.

7.3.8   RUDDER VENTILATION AND CAVITATION

The lift coefficients that have been discussed in this chapter are those that can be achieved in the absence of cavitation and ventilation of the rudder. At high speeds, the higher lift coefficients will result in low pressures on the rudder which can cause cavitation or ventilation. The phenomena was discussed in Chapter 5 and that discussion also applies to hydrofoils used as rudders.

7.3.9   RUDDER STOCK

The rudder stock must support and turn the rudder. On an attached or skeg rudder the torque is the main requirement. The torque causes a shear within the rudder stock by the amount

$$\tau = \frac{T_R d_{RS}}{2J_{RS}} \tag{7.21}$$

where J_{RS} is the polar moment of inertia of the rudder stock. For a round shaft,

$$J_{RS} = \frac{\pi(d_{RS}^4 - d_{RSi}^4)}{64} \tag{7.22}$$

The rudder torque is given by Equation 7.9 for an attached or skeg rudder and by Equation 7.12 for a spade rudder.

The bending load on the rudder stock must also be considered for spade rudders and determines the design of the rudder stock. The bending moment is given by the relation

$$M = F_R d_{Rcp} \tag{7.23}$$

where F_R is given by Equation 7.5 and d_{Rcp} is the distance to the center of pressure. The stress in the rudder stock is

$$\sigma = \frac{M_b d_{RS}}{2I_{RS}}$$

where

$$I_{RS} = \frac{\pi(d_{RS}^4 - d_{RSi}^4)}{32} \tag{7.24}$$

Again, consider the example of a 50% flap skeg rudder and a spade rudder for $d/C = 0.025$. Take the size of both rudders as 4 ft deep with a chord of 2 ft, giving a flap chord for the spade rudder of 1 ft and a boat speed of 10 K or 17 ft/sec. The effective aspect ratio is 4. The spade rudder gives a maximum lift coefficient at 13° angle of attack (Figure 7.7). The torque on the rudder at this angle of attack is given by Equations 7.12 and 7.5.

$$T_R = \frac{1}{2}\frac{w_w}{g}V_b^2 A_R C \frac{0.11\gamma}{1+2/AR}\frac{d}{C}$$

$$= \frac{1}{2}\frac{64}{32}(17)^2(8)(2)\frac{(0.11)(13)}{1+2/4}(.025) = 110 \text{ ft lb}$$

The total side force is given by Equation 7.5

$$F_R = \frac{1}{2}\frac{w_w}{g}V_b^2 A_R \frac{0.11\gamma}{1+2/AR}$$

$$= \frac{1}{2}\frac{64}{32}(17)^2(8)\frac{(0.11)(13)}{1+2/4} = 2200 \text{ lb}$$

If the skeg rudder is used and the keel is at zero angle of attack, the rudder must be deflected more than 13° to achieve the same side force. Equation 7.7 gives the angle of deflection δ and β is obtained from Figure 7.8. For a 50% flap

$$\delta = -\frac{\gamma_0}{\beta} = -\frac{13}{0.78} = -16.6°$$

The rudder torque is given by Equation 7.9. Figure 7.9 gives $C_{H\delta} = 0.016$. Therefore, since $\gamma = 0$

$$T_R = \frac{1}{2}\frac{w_w}{g}V_b^2 A_R C_F \frac{C_{H\delta}\delta}{1+2/AR}$$

$$= \frac{1}{2}\frac{64}{32}(17)^2(8)(1)\frac{0.016(16.6)}{1+2/4} = 410 \text{ ft lb}$$

A $1\frac{1}{2}$ in diameter solid rudder stock is adequate for the skeg rudder. Using Equations 7.21 and 7.22

$$J_{RS} = \frac{\pi d_{RS}^4}{32} = \frac{\pi(1.25)^4}{32} = 0.24 \text{ in}^4$$

$$\tau = \frac{T_R d_{RS}}{2J_{RS}} = \frac{410(12)(1.25)}{2(0.24)} = 12\,800 \text{ lb/in}^2$$

This same size rudder stock could easily carry the torque of the spade rudder. However, the rudder stock of the spade rudder is designed by the bending not the torque load. The bending moment given by Equation 7.23 is

$$M = F_R d_{Rcp} = (2200)(2) = 4400 \text{ ft lb}$$

For a rudder stock consisting of a tube of 4 in outside diameter and 3.5 in inside diameter

$$I_{RS} = \frac{\pi(d_{RS}^4 - d_{RSi}^4)}{32} = 10\cdot6 \text{ in.}^4$$

$$\sigma = \frac{M d_{RS}}{2 I_{RS}} = \frac{(4400)(12)(4)}{2(10\cdot6)} = 9900 \text{ lb/in}^2$$

The magnitude of this bending load is surprisingly large, requiring a large rudder stock for a spade rudder installation.

Chapter Eight
High Speed Sailboats

The secret to achieving a high speed sailboat is the obvious one of increased propulsive force and decreased resistance. For high speed sailing, meaning high specific speed or high Froude number, the reduction of the high wave drag which often occurs at hull speed is essential. This reduction can be accomplished by reducing weight and using hulls of either a planing configuration or ones that are very long and narrow. At the same time heel stability must be maintained so that a large amount of sail can be carried and a large propulsive force achieved. There are two techniques that are generally used in achieving high stability; movable ballast and multihull configurations. Movable ballast is generally only allowed under current racing rules in the form of live crew so this technique is limited to small boats where the crew weight is a reasonably high percentage of the total weight. For the larger boats, the multihull configuration is the usual approach. In small boats, both techniques can be combined with advantage.

With any arrangement low displacement to propulsive force ratios, of the order of 1 to 10, are required to achieve speeds in excess of hull speeds. Planing hulls also require that they be sailed at small angles of heel. For a monohull configuration, the hull can provide only a small righting moment under such conditions and movable ballast must be depended upon to a large extent. Consider a somewhat typical planing monohull day sailer. (A set of parameters is given in Table 8.1.) The conditions under which a displacement to propulsive thrust ratio of 1 to 5 and 1 to 10 could be achieved are shown.

Table 8.1   Planing conditions for single hull sailboat

Hull weight		300 lb		
Crew weight		350 lb		
Total displacement		650 lb		
Center of gravity of crew in hiking position				
Helmsman		3ft from centerline		
Crew (in trapeze)		6ft from centerline		
Sail area		200 ft^2		
Height to center of effort		10 ft		
Displacement/propulsive force ratio	5/1		10/1	
Propulsive force	130 lb		65 lb	
Righting moment (due to crew)	1575 ft lb			
Side force	157·5 lb			
Propulsive/side force ratio	0·825		0·412	
Lift/drag ratio of sails	4	8	4	8
Apparent wind angle	54°	47°	37°	30°

8.1   Multihulls

There are three prominent types of multihull sailboats, catamarans (two hulls), trimarans (three hulls) and outriggers (two hulls, one principle and one secondary).

Multihull sailboats have the feature that they obtain a large metacentric height without a large hull frontal area. The narrow hulls give low wave drag and the large static stability allows them to carry a great deal of sail and obtain a large propulsive force.

Multihull craft date from ancient times. The most noted are those of the South Pacific where both outriggers and catamarans were developed and used successfully on long sea voyages. In the western world they have never been the dominant type. Since World War II, interest in these types has been increasing in both the day sailing category and larger cruising and ocean racers.

From the point of view of maximizing the roll righting moment, the catamaran is optimum if symmetry about the fore-and-aft centerline is required and stability in roll in either direction is to be equal. As will be discussed in a later section, there may be some advantage in not requiring such symmetry. For a fixed beam, the catamaran does not have the maximum metacentric height. A flat bottomed barge-like hull has a higher metacenter. The maximum righting moment for the catamaran is greater, but a greater angle of heel is needed to achieve the maximum. The maximum occurs when all the weight is on one hull and the other is just leaving the water. The righting moment curve for a catamaran is shown in Figure 1.12.

A trimaran can achieve the same righting moment as a catamaran with the same beam if one outrigger can support the entire weight of the craft. While it is difficult to make the outrigger large enough to do this by buoyancy alone, it may be possible to develop considerable dynamic lift on the outrigger float when sailing fast when the large righting moments are required. The righting moment for the trimaran is the same as for the catamaran if one float can support the entire weight of the craft.

The trimaran may have some advantages over the catamaran in that the hulls and outrigger floats have different purposes and can be designed to take advantage of these requirements. The main central hull provides the buoyancy and has less wetted surface than the two hulls of the catamaran. The outrigger floats can be smaller than the central hull and designed using dynamic planing action to carry the full weight of the craft. In general, however, catamarans have dominated the racing multihull designs and trimarans have found their principle popularity in crusing where the larger central hull is an advantage in providing space for accommodation.

With a multihull configuration it is possible to obtain displacement/propulsive force ratios of the order of 1 to 10 and 1 to 5 without movable ballast. The maximum righting moment is approximately one-half the beam times the displacement

$$RM = \tfrac{1}{2}bD \tag{8.1}$$

The heeling moment is the heeling force times the height of the center of pressure of the sail

$$HM = Hh_{cp} = P\frac{H}{P}h_{cp} \tag{8.2}$$

Therefore, equating the righting and heeling moments

$$\frac{P}{D} = \frac{1}{2} \frac{b}{h_{cp}} \frac{P}{H} \qquad (8.3)$$

Table 8.2 shows the apparent wind angles which could be achieved for reasonable values of the parameters. Higher L/D ratios make it possible to achieve the necessary propulsive/side force ratio on a course considerably closer to the apparent wind. The sail area/displacement ratio can also be determined. The total sail force required is

$$N = P\sqrt{1 + \left(\frac{H}{P}\right)^2} \qquad (8.4)$$

The force developed by the sail is

$$N = \frac{1}{2} \frac{w_a}{g} V_a^2 C_N A_s \qquad (8.5)$$

Therefore

$$\frac{A_s V_a^2}{D} = \frac{P}{D} \frac{\sqrt{1 + \left(\frac{H}{P}\right)^2}}{\frac{1}{2} \frac{w_a}{g} C_N} \qquad (8.6)$$

Values of this sail area displacement parameter are also given in Table 8.2. Comparison of Tables 8.1 and 8.2 shows the advantages of a multihull boat in obtaining high propulsive force/displacement ratios and the practicality to do so even without movable ballast.

Table 8.2   Planing conditions for catamarans

Height center of pressure over beam	$h_{cp}/b = 1$	
Displacement/propulsive force ratio	$D/P = 5/1$	10/1
Propulsive/side force ratio	$P/H = 0.4$	0.2
Lift/drag ratio of sails	8 4	8 4
Apparent wind angle	29° 36°	18° 25°
$\dfrac{A_s V_a^2}{D}\left(\dfrac{ft^4}{lb\ sec^2}\right)$ for $C_N = 1$	490	465

The secret of high speed in a multihull is high propulsive force to weight ratio which can be achieved only with large $A_s V_a^2/D$ ratios. Low displacement/length ratio is important to achieve the required values without an impractically large sail area for the length of the boat and also to avoid the large drag hump at hull speed.

Figure 4.6 shows that wave drag is considerably reduced at low displacement/length ratios. If dynamic lift (planing) is to be used to reduce the large wave drag at hull speed, the low displacement/length ratio is still required in order that sufficient lift can be developed by dynamic forces at speeds of the order of hull speed.

8.2   Unconventional sailboats

This section will discuss several unconventional sailboat designs that employ novel methods to counteract heeling moments or reduce resistance and thereby achieve high speed.

8.2.1   PROA

While the proa is unconventional by western standards it has seen extensive service in the South Pacific where it was a well established type. Its unconventional feature is that it substitutes fore-and-aft symmetry for athwartship symmetry. Anyone who has ever sailed closehauled in a strong wind is painfully aware of the lack of athwartship symmetry. But, since a boat is required to sail on either tack, it may seem necessary to preserve this symmetry, at least in the hull design. The proa is based on the concept that the wind will always be on the same side and the boat will change tacks by reversing the direction of travel, substituting the bow for the stern. This type of fore-and-aft symmetry is not completely foreign to other boats. The ferryboat is the most common example and double-enders have some degree of fore-and-aft symmetry. This type requires a rudder arrangement which is symmetrical or at least workable in either direction of motion. The South Sea islanders accomplished this by a steering paddle which could be transported to the other end of the proa. A sail plan is also required that allows the sails to be trimmed for sailing in either direction. A sail plan that is symmetrical about the athwartship line of symmetry fulfills this requirement just as sail plans on conventional boats are symmetrical about the fore-and-aft line of symmetry. The proa is an outrigger boat designed to sail with the outrigger always to leeward.

Once the possibility of this type of symmetry is recognized, many advantages suggest themselves. The hull can now be designed unsymmetrically since its windward side will always be the same. At the limit, it is possible to achieve a righting moment equal to twice that of the catamaran or trimaran without the use of movable ballast. To achieve this righting moment all the weight would have to be located in the hull and the outrigger float be located to leeward and capable of sustaining the full weight of the craft, an arrangement something like a trimaran with only one float. The potential doubling of the righting moment over the catamaran can double the possible propulsive to side force ratio and thereby double the propulsive force to displacement ratio allowing the boat to sail at high speed closer to the wind. This type appears to offer the ultimate in speed of any design that depends upon buoyancy and gravity forces (body forces) to achieve righting moment.

8.2.2   NON-HEELING SAIL PLANS

Conventional sail plans produce forces in the plane parallel to the deck or perpendicular to the mast. These forces produce heeling and pitching moments when coupled to opposing resistance forces in the hull. However, it is possible to conceive of a sail plan in which forces do not lie in this plane. For instance, the sail can be trimmed at an angle to the vertical so that it produces an upward force. If the sail force is so directed that its line of action passes through the intersection of the line of action of the lateral hull forces and of the buoyancy and weight forces, then no heeling moment is created by the sail (Figure 8.1). In a sense, the sail is acting like a kite with the string tied to the intersection of the lateral force and the gravity-buoyancy force lines of action. Such an arrangement has been suggested several times, but there does not appear to be any really practical application.

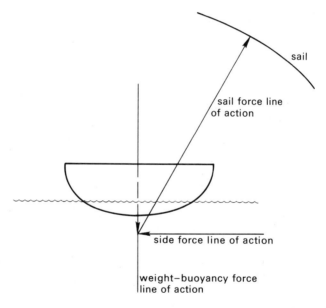

8.1   Sail design to prevent heeling moment by making the line of action of all forces cross at one point

8.2.3   HYDROFOIL SAILBOATS

The hydrofoil is a relatively new device in the marine environment and it is not surprising that it should be considered for application to sailboats. Actually sailboats have always used hydrofoils as keels and rudders, but what is new is the use of hydrofoils to support the weight of the boat. Their use in sailboats must combine the dual role of producing both vertical and lateral forces. Another possible use of hydrofoils is to increase the heeling stability by the use of dynamic forces to replace or supplement those of gravity and buoyancy. The use of dynamic forces offers a new degree of freedom in that the force may be in any direction instead of just up as for buoyancy and down for weight. Therefore, the use of hydrofoils in sailboats not only offers the possibilities of decreasing the resistance at high speed, but offers a new flexibility in balancing the aerodynamic sail forces. A serious disadvantage to the sailboat application is the unreliability of the wind. A sailboat designed both for foil-born and non-foil-born operation is necessarily a compromise that makes the design more difficult.

The principles by which hydrofoils may be made to sense and follow the surface of the water have been discussed in Chapter 5 and need not be repeated. The V and ladder type foils are suitable for surface following and supporting lateral side loads (the vertical strut must act as a hydrofoil in the ladder configuration). The V foil has the special characteristic that, if a lateral load is applied, the foil will

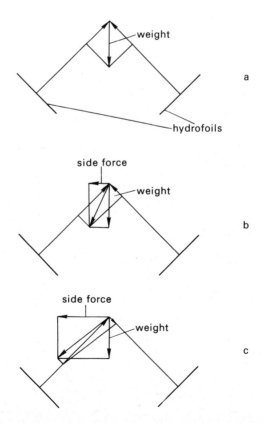

8.2   Hydrofoil design to prevent heel by causing line of action of hydrofoil forces to pass through intersection of line of action of side force and weight

develop a leeway angle which will change the angle of attack and lift force differentially on the two sides of the V. This characteristic seems to have useful applications in balancing heeling moments or creating righting moments. Figure 8.2 illustrates the point with two foils shown at such an angle that the line of action of the forces on the foils and that of the lateral sail force all meet at a point. In this condition the sail force causes no heeling moment. Figure 8.2a shows the case for no side force. In Figure 8.2b a side force exists and the line of action meets the intersection of the lines of action of the forces from the two hydrofoils. In order to balance the side force the angle of attack on the left hand foil must increase to increase the lift coefficient; the angle of attack and lift on the right hand foil must decrease. This change in angle of attack is accomplished by the boat assuming the proper leeway angle. In Figure 8.2c the side force is even larger so that the line of action of the resultant does not fall between the lines of action of the hydrofoil forces. The result is that the left hand hydrofoil angle of attack and lift must increase even further and the right hand hydrofoil will be at negative angle of attack and lift. Until the maximum lift coefficient of either hydrofoil is exceeded, the boat will remain level for all side forces. The optimum angle between the line of action of the hydrofoil forces depends upon the ratio of side force to weight. The minimum total lift force which the foils must supply occurs when the force on one foil is zero. For small side forces, the foils should be nearly horizontal and for large side forces at a much larger angle. As long as the force vector falls between the hydrofoils, the sum of the forces on the two foils is constant regardless of sail force. Once the force vector falls outside the foils, the one foil must be at negative lift and the sum of the absolute value of the lift forces must increase. The negative lift conditions are caused by the need for larger forces and result in higher drags.

While the heeling moment of a hydrofoil can be balanced by proper hydrofoil design, the pitching moment must be balanced by the foil forces and the weight. There must be sufficient spread between the forward and after hydrofoils to create the necessary pitching moment. A stable configuration is created by using surface sensing hydrofoils and different angles of attack.

Chapter Nine
Ship Propulsive Devices

There are numerous means which have been used to propel a boat by mechanical energy. All these devices work on the same common principle of creating a backward jet of fluid. The reaction force caused by this fluid jet pushes the boat forward. In most cases the fluid in which the jet is created is water, but air has also been used. The means for creating this fluid jet can either be external or internal but the external is the more common. The external devices fall into two classes, drag devices, where the force is in the direction of motion, and lift devices, where the force is perpendicular to the direction of motion of the propelling device. They may be listed as follows:

$$\text{Drag devices} \begin{cases} \text{paddles} \\ \text{oars} \\ \text{paddle wheels} \end{cases} \text{part of motion occurs out of water}$$

$$\text{Lift devices} \begin{cases} \text{sculling oar} \\ \text{propeller} \\ \text{rotating blade of} \\ \quad \text{cycloidal propeller} \end{cases} \text{continuously submerged}$$

The internal devices are pumps of one form or another and may well be propeller type pumps. A tunnel stern or shrouded propeller is intermediate between a completely external or internal device.

9.1   Momentum theory

A basic understanding of the action of all these devices can be obtained by considering the momentum and energy of the fluid in the jet. Consider a tube of fluid flowing through a propulsion device (Figure 9.1). This device is shown as a propeller in this figure but it may be any device which adds momentum to the water. For simplicity in this analysis, we will consider the device to be one which gives a sudden increase in the momentum to the fluid passing through it.

The velocities shown in the figure are all in a coordinate system stationary with respect to conditions far from the ship. The velocity ahead of the propeller is taken as V_1 and is the velocity given to the water by being dragged along by the boat.

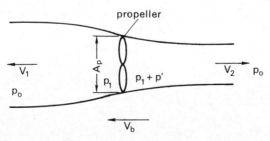

9.1   Propeller velocity diagram

The velocity V_b is the forward velocity of the boat. The velocity V_2 is the velocity of the jet far behind the propeller and V_{a_1} and V_{a_2} are the relative velocities between the water and propeller. The water undergoes an increase in pressure p' in passing through the propeller and the pressure p exists in front of the propeller. The pressure p_0 exists far ahead and far behind the propeller and is equal to the undisturbed water pressure. It is also useful to introduce the quantity a which is the fractional increase in relative velocity at the propeller disc.

By using the Bernouli equation, the conditions in front of the propeller may be related to each other and also those behind the propeller. In front of the propeller:

$$p_0 + \frac{1}{2}\frac{w_w}{g} V_{a_1}^2 = p_1 + \frac{1}{2}\frac{w_w}{g} V_{a_1}^2 (1+a)^2 \tag{9.1}$$

and behind the propeller:

$$p_1 + p' + \frac{1}{2}\frac{w_w}{g} V_{a_1}^2 (1+a)^2 = p_0 + \frac{1}{2}\frac{w_w}{g} V_{a_2}^2 \tag{9.2}$$

If these two relations are added together then:

$$p' = \frac{1}{2}\frac{w_w}{g}\left(V_{a_2}^2 - V_{a_1}^2\right) \tag{9.3}$$

The thrust developed by the propeller can be expressed in two ways, as the change in momentum caused by the propeller or as the change in pressure across the propeller. The change in momentum caused by the propeller is:

$$F = \frac{w_w}{g} A_p V_{a_1}(1+a)(V_{a_2} - V_{a_1}) \tag{9.4}$$

The change in pressure across the propeller gives:

$$F = A_p p' \tag{9.5}$$

By equating these two expressions for thrust and using the relation previously found for p', a relation for V_{a_2} can be obtained.

$$V_{a_2} = V_{a_1}(1+2a) \tag{9.6}$$

So the total change in velocity is twice that which takes place by the time the water passes through the propeller disc. The expression for thrust may now be written:

$$F = \frac{w_w}{g} A_p V_{a_1}^2 (1+a)2a \tag{9.7}$$

The power which the propeller delivers both to the boat and the water is the thrust times the boat's velocity plus the rate of kinetic energy deposited in the water.

$$P = \frac{w_w}{g} A_p V_{a_1}(1+a)\left(\frac{V_2^2}{2} - \frac{V_1^2}{2}\right) + FV_b$$

or

$$P = \frac{W_w}{g} A_p V_{a_1}^2 (1+a)\ (2a)\ \left(\frac{V_2 + V_1}{2}\right) + FV_b \qquad (9.8)$$

so:

$$P = F\left(V_{a_1} + \frac{V_2 + V_1}{2}\right) = FV_{a_1}(1+a) \qquad (9.9)$$

If the useful power is considered to be the energy delivered to the boat, then:

$$P_{useful} = FV_b$$

An efficiency η_w can now be defined so that:

$$\eta_w = \frac{P_{useful}}{P} = \frac{FV_b}{FV_{a_1}(1+a)} = \frac{1 + (V_1/V_{a_1})}{1+a} \qquad (9.10)$$

It now becomes useful to introduce a new quantity called slip, equal to the change in the velocity of the water through the propeller divided by the total velocity of of the water with respect to the boat far downstream.

$$S_w = \frac{2a}{1+2a} \qquad (9.11)$$

Using this definition in the expression for η_w gives:

$$\eta_w = \left(1 + \frac{V_1}{V_{a_1}}\right) \frac{2(1-S_w)}{2-S_w} \qquad (9.12)$$

η_w may be greater than 1 if V_1 is positive and S_w small. This condition is actually possible and means that the propeller is extracting part of the energy that was contained in the water moving with the velocity V_1. For an ideal propulsion device V_2 would be zero and there would be no wake. Actually, it usually is impossible to do so since the water, which is dragged along with the boat with velocity V_1, is spread out in a way so that the propeller can intercept only a small part of it; therefore, V_2 must be negative. Actually the net average velocity in the wake should be zero.

The expressions for thrust and power may now be rewritten in terms of the slip.

$$F = \frac{W_w}{g} A_p V_{a_1}^2\ (1+a)2a \qquad (9.13)$$

$$F = \frac{W_w}{g} A_p V_{a_1}^2 \frac{2 - S_w}{2(1-S_w)} \frac{S_w}{1-S_w} \qquad (9.14)$$

and power can be written:

$$P = FV_{a_1}(1+a) = \frac{W_w}{g} A_p V_{a_1}^3 \left[\frac{2-S_w}{2(1-S_w)}\right]^2 \left(\frac{S_w}{1-S_w}\right) \qquad (9.15)$$

In order to select a propeller for a given installation it is often more useful to express the area A_p in terms of the pitch/diameter ratio and the rotational speed. This can be done by introducing the propeller slip value

$$S = 1 - \frac{V_{a_1}}{pR} \tag{9.16}$$

which is similar but not identical to S_w. By using the pitch/diameter ratio

$$\frac{dR}{V_{a_1}} = \left(\frac{d}{p}\right)\left(\frac{1}{1-S}\right) \tag{9.17}$$

where dR/V_{a_1} is called the diameter factor. The expression for power can now be written:

$$\frac{g}{w_w}r^2 = \frac{PR^2 g}{w_w V_{a_1}^5} = \frac{\pi}{4}\left(\frac{d}{p}\right)^2\left(\frac{1}{1-S}\right)^2\left(\frac{S_w}{1-S_w}\right)\left[\frac{2-S_w}{2(1-S_w)}\right]^2 \tag{9.18}$$

where $\sqrt{PR^2/V_{a_1}^5}$ is called the power factor.

The quantities S and S_w are two different slip quantities, S defined by the geometry of the propeller and S_w by the motion of the slipstream, but as far as momentum theory goes these two slip quantities are the same.

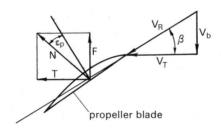

9.2   Propeller blade velocity and force diagram

9.2   Propeller blade effects

In the momentum analysis the propeller or other propulsion device has been considered as an actuator disc. It is useful to see how well an actual propeller might function in this way. To do this the action of an ideal blade section as shown in Figure 9.2 will be considered. The mean direction of the water relative to the blade is V_R, and the resulting force on the blade lags behind the normal to the velocity vector V_R by the angle ε_p which is related to the lift/drag ratio for the blade by the relation:

$$\cot \varepsilon_p = \frac{\text{lift}}{\text{drag}} \tag{9.19}$$

The power required to rotate the blade is the force times the velocity in the direction of that force (TV_T) and the power delivered to the water is $FV_{a_1}(1+a)$.

The ratio of these powers is the pumping efficiency of the propeller (η_p) and may be expressed in terms of β and ε.

$$\eta_p = \frac{FV_{a_1}}{TV_T}(1+a) = \frac{\sin\beta\,\cos(\beta+\varepsilon_p)}{\sin(\beta+\varepsilon_p)\,\cos\beta} = \frac{1-\tan\beta\,\tan\varepsilon_p}{1+\cot\beta\,\tan\varepsilon_p} \tag{9.20}$$

If ε_p is a small angle, then the maximum of η_p occurs near $\beta=45°$. The value of η_p at $\beta=45°$ is given by the expression:

$$\eta_p(\beta=45°) = \frac{1-\tan\varepsilon_p}{1+\tan\varepsilon_p} \tag{9.21}$$

and this value is near the maximum for η_p. The value of η_p for different angles is shown in Figure 9.3. The pitch/diameter ratio p/d is related to β by assuming that the specified value of β occurs at a mean diameter of $1/\sqrt{2}$ times the maximum diameter. The mean diameter of $1/\sqrt{2}$ of the tip diameter is chosen to divide the area of the propeller disc into parts of equal area.

The overall propeller efficiency would be a product of η_w and η_p.

$$\eta = \eta_w\eta_p \tag{9.22}$$

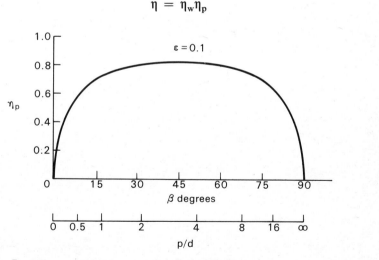

9.3   Propeller pump efficiency as function of blade angle

9.3   Propeller performance

Actual tests of propellers have been performed which allow a plot to be made relating these various parameters; Figure 9.4 is such a plot which shows the power factor plotted against the pitch ratio for various values of slip. The efficiency is

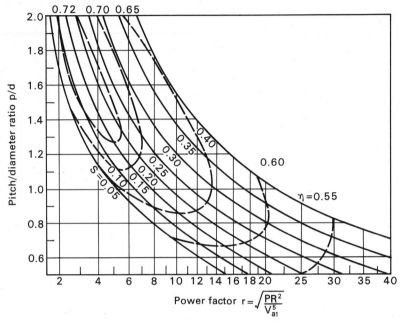

9.4   Propeller characteristics

also shown marked on this same figure. It is interesting to check the simplified formulas developed against this experimental data. This is done in the following table for the assumption that $S = S_w$. The quantities are expressed in terms of horsepower, rpm, and knots. The value of $\tan \varepsilon_p = 0 \cdot 1$ is used in this calculation:

	S	$\left(\dfrac{PR^2}{V_{a_1}^5}\right)^{\frac{1}{4}}$	$\left(\dfrac{PR^2}{V_{a_1}^5}\right)^{\frac{1}{4}}$ (Fig 9.4)	$\eta = \eta_w \eta_p$	η (Fig. 9.4)
	0·1	3·98	6·5	0·74	0·68
p/d = 1	0·2	8·05	9·5	0·69	0·68
	0·3	10·7	14	0·64	0·64
	0·4	16·4	21	0·59	0·59
	0·1	1·94	1·9	0·77	0·72
p/d = 2	0·2	3·94	2·8	0·72	0·72
	0·3	5·26	4·4	0·66	0·69
	0·4	8·03	6·6	0·607	0·64

The comparison seems reasonable considering the crudeness of the method and suggests that the most important phenomena have been considered.

The momentum analysis presented here is true with only minor modifications for all the propulsion devices considered. A different analysis should be used to replace the propeller blade analysis: one suitable to the particular device considered. Actually, the propeller blade analysis is suitable to all the lifting type devices and a different analysis should be made for drag devices. For internal devices the efficiency of the pump can be used for the value of η_p.

9.4 Examples of propeller design

In order to understand what is involved in actual propeller design, it is useful to work out a few examples. For a given power, the proper propeller size and speed of rotation depend very much on the speed of the boat. This fact is best illustrated by an example.

Consider a case of a rather good design point. Take $p/d = 1.1$ and $S = 0.2$. From Figure 9.4, $\eta = 0.69$ and $r = 8$. If $P = 100$ hp and different boat speeds are used, the following results are found for this design:

V_{a_1}	R	d	Tip speed
5k	44·8 rpm	12·8ft	1800 ft/min
10	254	4·56	3640
20	1430	1·61	7260
40	8100	0·57	14 500

For present day engines it is difficult to obtain the low speeds desired for a low speed boat and the high speeds desired for the fast boat.

Consider another similar example of the same engine power but fix $R = 1000$ rpm and pick the propeller to give the best efficiency.

V_w	r	s	η	p/d	d
5k	179	off chart (Figure 9.4)			
10	31·6	0·4	0·55	0·8	2·11ft
20	5·6	0·2	0·72	1·3	1·95
40	0·99	off chart (Figure 9.4)			

Only the 10 and 20 knot cases lead to reasonable designs. These two examples show the difficulty of using the same type of engine in boats of different speeds and the need for a wide range of reduction gear and step-up gear ratios.

Now consider a typical installation in an auxillary sailboat. An engine delivers 10 hp at a propeller speed of 1000 rpm and is expected to drive the boat at 6 knots

These values give a power factor $r = 35 \cdot 8$. From Figure 9.4, it can be seen that the best condition is:

$$S = 0 \cdot 4 \qquad p/d = 0 \cdot 75 \qquad \eta = 0 \cdot 53$$

giving $d = 1 \cdot 48$ ft and a thrust of 290 lb. If we consider these same conditions except that the propeller speed is reduced to 195 rpm, we get:

$$r = 7 \qquad S = 0 \cdot 2 \qquad p/d = 1 \cdot 2 \qquad \eta = 0 \cdot 71$$

giving $d = 3 \cdot 23$ ft and a thrust of 390 lbs. If this lower rotational speed could be used the thrust would be increased by about 35%.

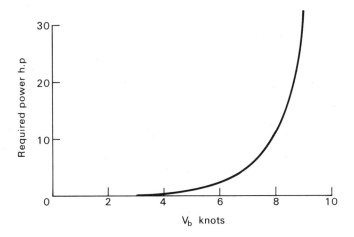

9.5   Typical propulsion power requirement as function of boat speed

It is interesting to examine how the performance of a particular engine propeller installation behaves as speed is reduced. Take the boat power required curve shown in Figure 9.5. The shape of this curve is typical and shows power requirements increasing rapidly as speed increases. The engine performance curve of maximum power at various speeds is also shown in Figure 9.6 using a $3:1$ reduction gear. Design the propeller for a speed of 600 rpm. To design the propeller, pick an expected boat speed by estimating the propeller efficiency and determining how fast the expected power available will drive the boat. If a propeller efficiency of 55% is chosen then 22 hp is available to drive the boat and a reasonable boat speed estimate would be 8·5 knots. Take $V_{a_1} = 0 \cdot 9 V_b$ as the relative velocity between the water and propeller. Then $r = 23 \cdot 4$ and Figure 9.4 gives:

$$p/d = 0 \cdot 9 \qquad S = 0 \cdot 40 \qquad \eta = 0 \cdot 58 \qquad d = 2 \cdot 32 \text{ ft}$$

as the best design condition.

To determine the performance at reduced power the process is as follows:

1. Choose the reduced engine speed to be considered.
2. Estimate the boat's speed.
3. Determine boat power required from the boat performance curve.
4. Estimate propeller efficiency for this condition.
5. Determine engine power from the boat power required divided by the efficiency.
6. Calculate r.
7. Determine S, η, d for the p/d of the propeller.
8. Check the value of η with estimated value and d with actual propeller diameter. If these do not check, repeat steps from (2) with better estimate of boat's speed and propeller efficiency.

Several trials will probably be necessary to determine the right condition. The following conditions were determined for the example.

Propeller speed	500	400 rpm
Boat's speed	8·1	7·2 knots
Engine power	20	10 h.p.
r	15·5	11·8
p/d	0·9	0·9
S	0·28	0·21
η	0·63	0·66
Boat power	12·6	6·6
Propeller diameter	2·28	2·32 ft

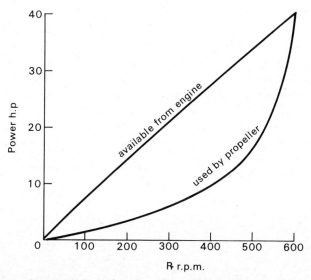

9.6   Power characteristics as function of propeller speed

The value of 2·28 ft was considered near enough to the actual value of 2·32 so that this value was accepted.

The actual required engine power is shown on Figure 9.6 and is seen to be considerably below the available engine power as speed is reduced. This means that a reduced throttle setting is needed to obtain this reduced speed. As the speed is reduced the engine is unloaded and the r value for the propeller is reduced. This reduction gives an increase in propeller efficiency. Since the maximum efficiency which can be obtained at reduced load depends on the pitch/diameter ratio, some consideration to choosing the best pitch/diameter ratio for partly loaded performance is worthwhile if the boat is expected to cruise at reduced power for long periods.

One other point to be noted is that if the design speed had been taken as higher than 600 rpm more engine power is available and a somewhat higher boat speed can be obtained. However, this would mean a lower propeller efficiency and that the engine would operate at a lower percentage of available power at reduced speed. The result would be a poorer reduced speed efficiency but an increase in maximum speed.

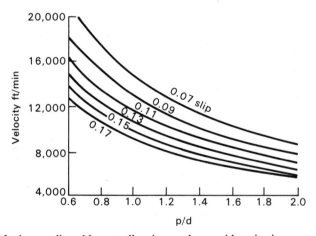

9.7   Maximum allowable propeller tip speed to avoid cavitation

9.5   Cavitation

Cavitation occurs when the pressure on the back side of the blade drops below the vapour pressure of the water and a bubble of steam is formed. The formation of the steam limits the minimum pressure which can be obtained on the blade, thereby decreasing thrust, and also causes damage to the blade when the bubble collapses. A rough estimate of the conditions under which cavitation is likely to be encountered can be obtained from Figure 9.7. In general, cavitation is a problem for high speed but not low speed boats.

9.6   Propulsion devices other than propellers

9.6.1   WATER JET PROPULSION

The same type of momentum analysis holds for water jets as for the propeller. In essence, the propeller acts as a pump similar to the pump in a jet system. The momentum analysis shows that it is best to handle a large amount of water at low velocities. It is hard to do so in a jet system where the water must be passed through passages within the hull of the boat. The result is that the jet system will tend to handle smaller masses of water at higher velocities than a propeller with resulting lower efficiencies. The pump used will probably be no more efficient than the propeller so that the whole system is less efficient. The jet system's advantage is the removal of the external propeller with decreased possibilities of fouling and greater safety for swimmers.

9.6.2   AIR PROPELLER

The analysis for air propellers is very similar to that for water propellers. Air, however, is about 850 times lighter than water so a much larger diameter propeller must be used. In order to handle the same mass flow of air at the same velocities, the air propeller would have to have its diameter increased by the square root of the density ratio if the same velocities were to be used. Therefore it would have to be about 29 times the diameter of the corresponding water propeller. In most cases this is impractical. It is only for high speed boats where the propeller diameters become small that an air propeller can be used with a reasonable efficiency.

9.7   Propeller drag resistance on sailboats

The drag of a propeller while sailing can be a noticeable resistance. Several approaches are used to reduce this resistance.

1. Small blade area. A two-bladed propeller is usually to be preferred to a three-bladed propeller in this respect. If a two-bladed propeller is placed in a cutout in the deadwood then the blades can be turned vertically behind the deadwood when the engine is stopped.
2. Low friction clutch. If a low friction clutch is placed between the engine and propeller then the propeller will rotate freely. Depending upon the pitch, this may or may not decrease the propeller resistance.
3. Feathering propellers. Feathering propellers have been developed which use the force of the water on the blades to hold them in a driving position when the engine is turning and in a feathered position when the shaft is stationary. An extra advantage of this arrangement is that the propeller can be designed

so that the same side of the blade is the pressure face in either ahead or astern operations. This feature makes the feathering propeller very good in reverse. The obvious disadvantages are high cost, reduced reliability, and greater upkeep.

4. Folding propellers. Folding propellers have also been developed in which the blades fold backwards when the shaft is not rotating. When the shaft is rotating, centrifugal force causes the blades to stand out. In ahead operation the water pressure on the blades pushes them forward against a stop. In astern operation only the centrifugal force holds the blades out resulting in rather poor astern performance. The folding propeller is less expensive than the feathering propeller but more than the fixed. It also requires less maintenance than the feathering propeller.

Cutting an aperture in the deadwood for a propeller increases the resistance of the boat. When the boat is sailing and the keel is developing a side force there is a difference in pressure across the deadwood, and cutting an aperture allows the water to pass through. In order to avoid this aperture, the propeller may be located behind the deadwood or to one side. The off-center location has the disadvantage that it involves an exposed propeller shaft and strut, and biases steering.

Some information on the drag caused by a propeller is contained in the change of rating given by the CCA rule. The drag is directly proportional to the propeller factor given in the following table.

Propeller factor	Type	Location
0·5	Folding	on centerline out of aperture
0·75	2-bladed feathering	on centerline out of aperture
1·0	2-bladed feathering	on centerline in aperture
1·0	3-bladed feathering	on centerline out of aperture
1·5	3-bladed feathering	on centerline in aperture
2·0	folding	off centerline out of aperture
2·0	2-bladed fixed	on centerline out of aperture
3·0	2-bladed feathering	off centerline out of aperture
3·0	2-bladed fixed	on centerline in aperture
4·0	3-bladed feathering	off centerline out of aperture

The advantage of a freely rotating propeller has been discussed for many years. If it seems obvious that free rotation reduces the drag, remember that a helicopter rotor must be left free to rotate, if the engine fails, to prevent a too rapid descent. In the ideal case of no shaft friction, the arrangement which gives the least resistance depends upon the pitch of the propeller. A relatively simple analysis can be performed to demonstrate the mechanism involved and estimate the conditions for least resistance.

The power required to pull a locked propeller through the water is

$$P_L = \frac{1}{2} \frac{w_w}{g} V_{a_1}^3 C_{DL} A \tag{9.23}$$

where C_{DL} is the drag coefficient for the locked blade and A is the blade area. The power used by the rotating propeller is:

$$P_R = \frac{1}{2} \frac{w_w}{g} V_{a_1}^3 C_{DO} \left(\frac{\pi d}{p}\right)^3 A \tag{9.24}$$

where C_{DO} is the drag coefficient for the blade moving at zero angle of attack through the water and $\pi d/p$ enters because of the greater speed of the water relative to the rotating blade. If the ratio of these powers is taken then:

$$\frac{P_L}{P_R} = \frac{C_{DL}}{C_{DO}\left(\dfrac{\pi d}{p}\right)^3} \tag{9.25}$$

and

$$\frac{P_L}{P_R} = 1 \qquad \text{when} \qquad \frac{C_{DL}}{C_{DO}} = \left(\frac{\pi d}{p}\right)^3$$

A reasonable value for C_{DL}/C_{DO} is 150, so for equal power $p/d = 0.6$ at the mean section. Shaft friction drag will increase the drag of the rotating propeller so higher pitch ratios will be required to give the rotating propeller reduced drag. The increased speed with which the rotating propeller blades meets the water is responsible for the higher drag possible with this arrangement at low pitch/diameter ratios.

9.8   Propeller shaft design

The purpose of the propeller shaft is to turn the propeller and push the boat. It transmits the engine torque to the propeller and the propeller thrust to the boat through the thrust bearing which is usually part of the engine for small boats. In addition to transmitting these loads, the shaft must be stiff enough not to whip or vibrate. No matter how stiff the shaft is, there will always be a speed of rotation which will cause whipping. If the shaft is not absolutely true, the center of gravity of the shaft at some station between the bearings will be displaced from the axis of rotation. A centrifugal force will be caused in a direction to increase the bend in the shaft. At a high enough speed, the centrifugal force will cause an appreciable bending and the shaft will whip. This speed is called the critical speed. The critical speed will depend upon the modulus of elasticity of the shaft, the size of the shaft, and the distance between shaft bearings.

Propeller shafts are made of corrosion-resistant materials which must also be strong, have a high modulus of elasticity, and be hard enough to resist wear in the bearings. Materials recommended for propeller shafts are monel, bronze and stainless steel. Monel is probably the best: it is very resistant to corrosion and wear. Bronze has good corrosion resistance, but is not as strong as monel and does not resist bearing wear nearly as well. Stainless steel is good in corrosion resistance but not as reliable as the other two. Its strength and wear resistance is between bronze and monel.

The shaft size required to transmit the engine torque is given in Figure 9.8 which is a nomogram for determining the shaft size for different materials, shaft speed, and power.[33] If the proper shaft speed and power are connected by a straight line the intersection with the third line gives the shaft diameter. Figure 9.9 is another nomogram which shows the relation between shaft speed, material, and bearing spacing. If a line connects the shaft material with the diameter it intersects the central line at a given point. If a line is now drawn through this point and the shaft speed, the intersection with the line on the right gives the bearing spacing required. The example shown in the figure will make this process clear. If the propeller shaft meets these two requirements it will usually be adequate and it will not be necessary to consider the thrust load.

The propeller is mounted on a taper on the end of the shaft and held in place with a nut. A key is used to transmit the torque from the shaft to the propeller. It is important to provide a radius in the corners of the keyway to prevent excessive stress concentrations at these points. Table 9.1 shows proper keyway sizes for different size shafts.

Table 9.1   Suggested radii for filleted keyways*

Approx. shaft diameter	Keyway fillet radius
$\frac{3}{4}$ to $1\frac{1}{8}$ in. incl.	$\frac{1}{32}$ in.
$1\frac{1}{4}$ to 2 incl.	$\frac{1}{16}$
$2\frac{1}{4}$ to 3 incl.	$\frac{3}{32}$
$3\frac{1}{4}$ to 4 incl.	$\frac{1}{8}$
$4\frac{1}{2}$	$\frac{5}{32}$
5 to $5\frac{1}{2}$ incl.	$\frac{3}{16}$
6 to $6\frac{1}{2}$ incl.	$\frac{7}{32}$
7 to 8 incl.	$\frac{1}{4}$

* As in 1950 *SAE Handbook* standards for marine propeller shaft ends and hubs.

9.9   Propeller shaft bearings

The propeller shaft requires at least a stern bearing and a stuffing box where it passes through the hull. If the propeller shaft is located in a deadwood the simplest

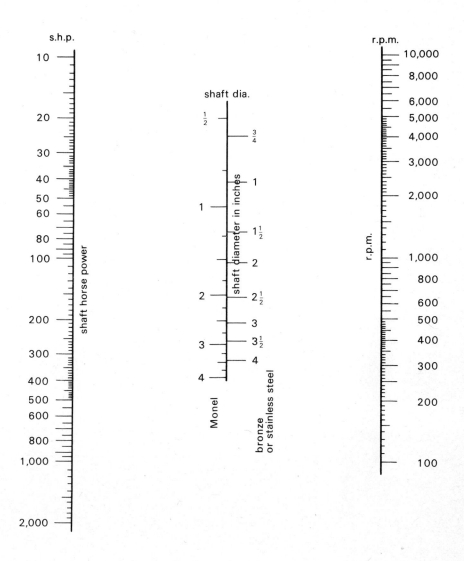

Chart published courtesy of Comdr. Paul G. Tomalin, U.S.C.G.

Instructions– Lay down a ruler to connect your horse power on the left
with your propeller r.p.m. on the right . Draw the line.
The point where it intersects the centre line shows the
size of shaft to use.

9.8   Propeller shaft size

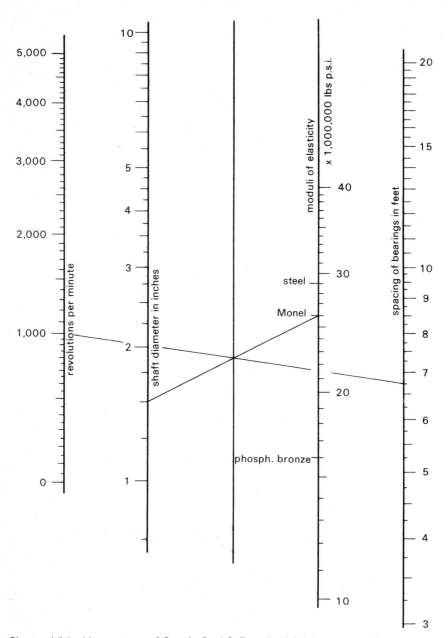

Chart published by courtesy of Comdr. Paul G. Tomalin U.S.C.G.

Instructions – Rule a line from shaft size in second scale to modulus in fourth scale
          Then rule a line from point of intersection on centre scale to connect
          the unsupported shaft length on right scale and extend the line to
          left scale to give maximum shaft speed.

9.9   Propeller shaft critical speed limitations

arrangement is a stuffing box at the after end of the deadwood. This can also be used as a shaft bearing where the shaft leaves the deadwood. With this arrangement only one bearing point is used and the alignment problem is minimal. The disadvantage is that the stuffing box is outside the boat and can only be serviced by hauling out or diving. A better arrangement is to locate the shaft bearing just ahead of the propeller and the stuffing box inside the hull at the forward end of the stern tube.

If a stern bearing is used it should be water lubricated. Rubber seems to be the best material for this bearing and is the most common. It is especially good where the water contains silt or sand. The soft rubber allows the sand to pass through the bearing without cutting the shaft. Stuffing boxes are usually packed with flax and are water lubricated. A very small seepage of water through the stuffing box is useful. The addition of grease to a stuffing box seems to be useful to increase the life of the packing. An ordinary grease cup can be used to advantage if mounted to force grease into the packing.

Chapter Ten
Marine Engines

Prime movers for marine propulsion systems are of several different types. The steam engine originally made mechanical propulsion of ships a reality and it has continued to be an important type of prime mover up to the present time. Steam engines were used in small power boats, but are no longer, except in a few special character boats. The internal combustion piston engine completely dominates the small boat field today with the gas turbine being used in a few cases where high power and light weight justifies the very high cost of this type of power plant. While the gas turbine is completely outside the price range for usual propulsion systems, it can be expected to become increasingly competitive in the large power sizes. A large scale commercial application of small gas turbines and the accompanying mass production would probably make competitive units available for the small boat field.

At the present time, the alternative is between gasoline (petrol) and diesel engines. The gasoline engine is by far the most common and cheapest form. In the gasoline engine a mixture of air and gasoline is taken into the cylinders where it is compressed through about a 6:1 to 10:1 volume ratio, ignited by a spark, burned, expanded and exhausted. This process can be carried out by a two or four-stroke cycle. The two-stroke gasoline engine is seldom seen today in the marine applications except for outboard motors. The two-stroke engine gives more power from a given engine size at a given speed of rotation, about 75% more than the four-stroke cycle. The fuel consumption tends to be higher than the four-stroke cycle since it is difficult to introduce the new charge of fuel and air into the cylinder at the same time that the burned exhaust gases are being expelled without having some mixing and some of the unburned mixture escaping with the exhaust products. Some form of blower, termed a scavenging blower, is required to blow the unburned mixture into the cylinder. In outboard motors the crankcase is usually used as the scavenging blower with the result that lubricating oil must be mixed with the gasoline to lubricate the crankshaft bearings. This practice results in a relatively high oil consumption and a smoky exhaust. If a separate scavenging blower were provided, as is usually done on a two-stroke diesel engine, then a conventional lubricating system can be used and lubricating oil need not be mixed with the fuel.

The diesel engine differs from the gasoline engine in that it burns a less volatile fuel. The fuel is not mixed with the air before entering the cylinder, but clean air is taken into the cylinder, compressed through about a 15:1 to 20:1 volume ratio, and then the fuel is injected into the hot compressed air. The air is hot enough so that the fuel ignites and burns without any other ignition systems. The burned gases are expanded and exhausted. Most of the smaller marine diesels are of the four-stroke type with the notable exception of the two-stroke engine manufactured by the General Motors Corp. However, many of the large diesels used in commercial vessels operate on the two-stroke cycle. The two-stroke diesel suffers no inherent loss in fuel economy since only air is blown into the cylinder and an excess may be provided to completely scavenge the cylinder and blow out the exhaust gases. The crankcase is seldom used as the scavenging blower, a separate blower being provided. There are many variations on the basic diesel engine and so-called semidiesels have been used. Most of these variations are an attempt to burn a heavier fuel oil than gasoline (petrol) without using a complicated fuel injector.

In the gas turbine, the whole compression process is accomplished in a turbo-compressor and the expansion in a turbine. A turbo machine is one which makes use of the inertia forces of the air to accomplish the compression or expansion. Since air is very light, the speed of the blades must be very high to accomplish the required pressure changes. The compressor is a very high speed fan and the turbine a high speed windmill. In a gas turbine the air is taken into the compressor, compressed and passed into a separate burner where the fuel is introduced. The burned mixture then expands through a turbine and is exhausted. The turbine uses part of the power it develops to drive the compressor and the rest is delivered for useful work.

10.1   Comparison of different engines

In the following table some of the important characteristics of gasoline and diesel engines are compared. The X is used to denote which type is superior in the particular characteristic being considered.

	Gasoline	*Diesel*
Weight	X	
Volume	X	
Low price	X	
Fuel consumption		X
Fire hazard		X
Reliability		X
Fuel cost		X
Cleanliness	X	
Smoothness (minimum vibration)	X	

The gas turbine can be compared with these two engines as follows:

Advantages
    light weight
    small volume
    burns light fuel oil
Disadvantages
    high cost
    high fuel consumption in small sizes
    high rotational speed

At the present time the high first cost is almost prohibitive so uses seem to be limited to naval services in craft such as hydrofoils.

A more detailed comparison of the gasoline and diesel engines can be made based upon current engine practice.

10.1.1   POWER OUTPUT

A good measure of the actual size of an engine is the displacement. The displacement of an engine is the volume swept out by all the pistons during one revolution. It is a measure of all the air or air and gasoline mixture which passes through the engine during one complete cycle (one revolution for two-stroke cycle or two revolutions for a four-stroke cycle). Since the engines of all manufacturers are basically similar, the amount of work from the same amount of air passing through the engine is similar. Once this basic concept is understood, it is easy to estimate the power which will be obtained from any given engine. For engines of different sizes to produce large differences in power, it is necessary to run them at considerably different speeds. Engines perform best when operated near their designed speed at which they are timed for proper operation. It is best not to buy a high speed engine to operate at low speed, and very poor practice to operate an engine above its design speed. For a given displacement a high speed engine will deliver more power, but, as a general rule, will wear out more rapidly than a low speed engine.

Figure 10.1 shows the horsepower per 100 cu in. of displacement, and 100 rpm speed of rotation, for both gasoline and diesel engines, two-stroke and four-stroke cycles of different displacements. This figure is based on manufacturers' specifica-

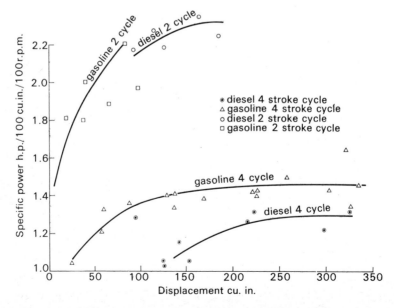

10.1   Specific engine power as a function of engine displacement

tions of typical engines. A diesel engine delivers about 15% less power for a given cylinder capacity and speed than a gasoline engine. This reduced power is caused by the fact that a diesel engine uses more air than is theoretically required to burn the fuel while a gasoline engine does not. As much heat cannot be released in the diesel engine cylinder as in the gasoline engine cylinder since the fuel/air ratio is leaner.

There seems to be a prevalent superstition that a diesel engine horsepower is worth several gasoline engine horsepower. The definition of horsepower is the same for both engines. Gasoline engines are usually rated at much higher speeds (rpm) than diesel engines and this high speed cannot be used in many installations. If a high speed gasoline engine is installed so that it can only run at half its rated rpm it will then produce roughly the same power as a similar displacement diesel engine rated to run at this same low rpm. The fact that the gasoline engine was rated at twice the power of the diesel, yet, in this installation, both do the same work, leads to the feeling that the diesel horsepower is larger. However, if the high speed gasoline engine were installed to run at its rated speed, it would produce considerably more power than the diesel engine.

Figure 10.1 also shows the effect that small engines with small cylinders produce somewhat less power than the larger engines. The points shown in this figure are numbers for actual engines, and indicate the type of variations that can be expected from the average curves.

The quantity hp per 100 in^3 per 100 rpm expresses the same concept as the 'break mean effective cylinder pressure, BMEP, which is often used in engineering textbooks. The BMEP is the average net pressure acting effectively on the piston during the power stroke. The formula that relates these two quantities is

$$\text{BMEP (lb/in)} = 80 \, \frac{\text{hp}}{(100 \text{ in}^3) \, (100 \text{ rpm})} \tag{10.1}$$

The difference in power between two- and four-stroke cycles is also clearly shown in Figure 10.1. The two-stroke gasoline engines shown are all of the outboard type. The increase over the four-stroke engines is only about 75% instead of the 100% which might have been expected based on doubling the number of power strokes.

10.1.2   WEIGHT

The weight of engines for a given power output also makes an interesting comparison. The same engines considered in Figure 10.1 are compared on the weight basis in Figure 10.2. The two-stroke gasoline outboard motors have been put on this figure even though the weight includes the underwater propulsion units and does not make a fair comparison. The curves show that the diesels are about 50% heavier than the corresponding size of gasoline engine. This difference is expected since the diesel must be built heavier to withstand the higher internal pressures caused by its high compression ratio. The two-stroke diesel is about the same weight as the four-

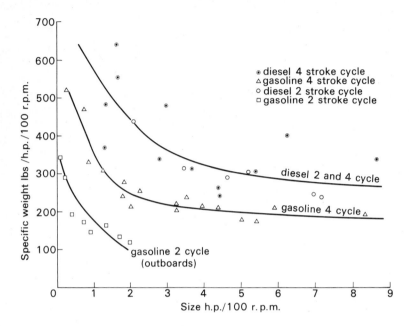

10.2   Specific engine weight as a function of engine size

stroke diesel. The small engines are quite a bit heavier than large engines on the lb per hp per 100 rpm basis. This suggests the magnitude of the weight penalty that a twin engine installation might suffer over a single engine installation.

10.1.3   COST

The cost of various engines can be compared on a common basis. Figure 10.3 shows such a comparison based on listed prices in the United States in about 1970. While these numbers will not be the same at other places and times, the comparative values may remain similar. Figure 10.3 shows that, for the same displacement, the diesel engine costs almost twice as much as the gasoline engine. This large price differential is probably for two reasons:

1. The greater weight of the diesel engine would mean a higher cost even if the price per pound were the same.
2. A higher price per pound is to be expected because of the greater complexity of some of the parts and the smaller scale of production of diesel engines.

The reduction in diesel cost relative to the gasoline engine which has occurred in recent years is probably due to greater production and some continuation along this direction is to be expected.

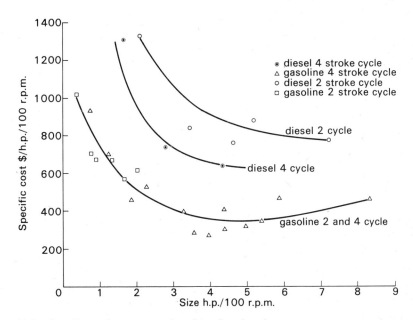

10.3   Specific engine cost as a function of engine size

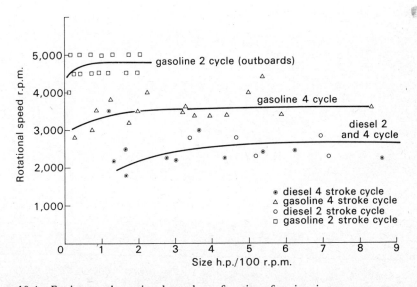

10.4   Engine rated rotational speed as a function of engine size

10.1.4   SPEED

All the comparisons so far have been upon the basis of operating at the same speed. The speed at which the various engines are rated is shown in Figure 10.4. In general the gasoline engine is rated to operate at a greater speed than the diesel engine. Typical speeds are 2500 rpm for the diesel and 4000 rpm for the gasoline engine. If the higher operating speed of the gasoline engine can be used in the installation considered, the weight and the cost advantage of the gasoline engine will be increased in this same ratio. The result of this effect is that the gasoline engine will have about 2·5 times the rated power for the same weight and 3 times as much rated power for the same cost. However, since it is not always desirable or possible to operate the gasoline engine at its full rated speed, this advantage is not always real.

10.1.5   VOLUME

Because of its heavier construction and greater complexity, the diesel engine will usually require a larger space for an installation of the same size and a correspondingly greater space for the same rated power.

10.1.6   FUEL CONSUMPTION

The subject of fuel consumption seems to be one which is often misunderstood. Probably this is because we are used to the high rated power of automobiles and do not realize the small part of this power that is used in most driving. An engine which converted all the useful energy stored in the fuel would require about 0·125 lb fuel per hp hour. Actually, for good reasons, the efficiency of engines is limited to about 20–30% with the result that the specific fuel consumption is increased. Approximate values are:

$$\text{Gasoline engine} \quad 0.5 \text{ to } 0.7 \, \frac{\text{lb fuel}}{\text{hp hour}}$$

$$\text{Diesel engine} \quad 0.35 \text{ to } 0.45 \, \frac{\text{lb fuel}}{\text{hp hour}}$$

Since gasoline weighs about 6 lb/gal and diesel fuel about 7 lb/gal the resulting fuel consumption is

$$\text{Gasoline engine} \quad 8.5 \text{ to } 12 \, \frac{\text{hp hours}}{\text{gal}}$$

$$\text{Diesel engine} \quad 15.5 \text{ to } 20 \, \frac{\text{hp hours}}{\text{gal}}$$

This means that a gasoline engine producing 100 hp will require about 10 gal of fuel per hour and a diesel engine producing 100 hp will require about 6 gal of fuel per hour. These figures are fairly reliable and it may be stated with certainty that an engine burning much less fuel is simply not producing the power.

The part load performance of engines is also important. By 'part load' is meant that part of the total power which the engine is capable of producing at the speed at which it is operating, which is actually produced. The following table gives the per cent of full load fuel consumption which engines require at partial load.

	Full load	$\frac{3}{4}$ load	$\frac{1}{2}$ load	$\frac{1}{4}$ load	0 load
Gasoline	100%	75–90%	60–75%	40–55%	25–40%
Diesel	100%	75–80%	55–65%	35–45%	20–25%

In other words, a 100 hp gasoline engine when operating at full rpm but no load will burn 3 to 4 gallons of fuel per hour and the diesel about $1\frac{1}{2}$ gallons of fuel per hour. It is not economical on fuel to operate a large engine with the throttle nearly closed.

10.1.7   FIRE HAZARD

The hazard of fire is a very important consideration on a boat and the diesel is safer in this respect. The major advantage of the diesel is that it burns a high flash point fuel oil. The flash point of diesel oil is usually greater than 150°F which means that unless the oil is heated to a higher temperature it cannot be ignited by a spark. Gasoline, on the other hand, has a low flash point so that it is always liable to be ignited by a spark. In general, diesel oil will only form ignitable vapours if it is heated by coming in contact with hot parts of the engine.

Another feature of the diesel engine is that the fuel system is totally enclosed and the fuel is not mixed with air except inside the cylinders. This enclosed fuel system reduces the chance of fuel vapours escaping from the engine.

A further advantage of the diesel engine is the absence of a high voltage electrical system. Under the damp conditions that exist on boats, such a system is a continual source of sparks. In fact, no electrical system is required for the operation of a diesel engine itself. It is only needed for auxiliary purposes and starting.

10.1.8   RELIABILITY, CLEANLINESS, AND SMOOTHNESS

The diesel engine is usually considered more reliable than the gasoline engine. More rugged construction plus the independence from the electrical system are probably the main reasons. However, the exhaust of the diesel tends to be somewhat smoky and to have an unpleasant smell. Also, the diesel probably is rougher than the gasoline and gives more vibration. The heavier moving parts and larger forces involved are the principle reasons.

10.1.9   FUEL COSTS

In the past, diesel fuel has generally been cheaper than gasoline. A comparison of the relative price has been complicated, in the United States, by the different tax structure on diesel fuel and gasoline. The price of gasoline sold to marine users includes the motor vehicle tax for which a refund can usually be obtained. Diesel fuel sold to the marine user does not include this tax. Although the price of fuels may rise considerably, it is expected that the price differential will continue to exist.

10.1.10   WEIGHT AND COST COMPARISON

Neither the diesel nor the gasoline engine has a clear advantage in weight or cost. The gasoline engine has the advantage in engine weight and cost, the diesel engine in fuel weight and cost. Using the data on weight and fuel consumption presented, it is possible to determine a typical duration for which both systems give the same total weight of engine and fuel.

	Gasoline	Diesel
Specific weight	200 lb/hp/100 rpm	300 lb/hp/100 rpm
Speed	3500 rpm	2500 rpm
Weight	5·7 lb/hp	12 lb/hp
Specific fuel consumption	0·7 lb/hp hour	0·4 lb/hp hour
Hours of range for equal weight	21 hours	
Total weight of the engine plus fuel for this range	20·4 lb/hp	

A cost comparison is more difficult primarily because of the variations in fuel costs. However, an example based on fuel costs in the United States in about 1970 is instructive.

	Gasoline	Diesel
Specific cost	350$/hp 100 rpm	650$/hp 100 rpm
Cost	10$/hp	26$/hp
Fuel cost	0·30$/gal	0·20$/gal
Specific fuel cost	0·035$/hp hour	0·011$/hp hour
Time for equal costs	667 hours	
Engine plus fuel cost for these hours	33·5$/hp	

This comparison suggests that if an operating range of greater than 21 hours is desired the diesel installation will be lighter and if a total operating life of greater than 667 hours is expected the diesel will be cheaper. The weight comparison is much more reliable than the cost comparison which can change drastically with changes in engine and fuel costs. Weight and cost are also not the only important considerations in selecting a marine engine.

Chapter Eleven
Hull Structural Design

11.1 Materials

Yachts today are made of a variety of materials. Those of interest are wood (natural and plywood), fiberglass, steel, aluminum. In past years wood was the predominent material; steel was used to a limited extent, mostly for larger craft. Since the 1940s aluminum, fiberglass and plywood have become prominent in yacht construction. For the smaller yachts, fiberglass and plywood are both very important. The use of sheet materials, such as plywood, as well as steel and aluminum, have introduced limitations on hull designs to allow the hull to be formed from a few sheets of such materials.

Wood is the traditional material and is still used. It ordinarily comes in rather narrow pieces with very pronounced directional properties. It is fairly light in weight and has reasonable strength for its weight. It may be fastened with either metal fastenings or glue. Glues are not usually considered completely reliable and metal fastenings cause local stress concentrations and loosen with time. Wood absorbs water and swells across the grain when it does so, a feature which has advantages and disadvantages in boat construction. Because of the narrow pieces in which wood is available, a relatively complex structure with many fastenings is necessary. Plywood has been developed to overcome some of the disadvantages of natural wood. It comes in wide sheets and has fairly uniform properties in all directions. However, the result of obtaining good properties in all directions is that it is weaker than natural wood in its preferred direction. Being a sheet material, it can only be applied to hull shapes which curve in one direction and over restricted radii.

Fiberglass is a new material which has excellent properties for use in boat construction. It consists of glass fibers held together by a plastic binder. It is quite strong and reasonably light. A mould must be prepared before a hull can be built so that it lends itself more to production of several hulls of the same design than a single hull. It is reasonably uneffected by water and has a long life, if properly laid up.

Steel has been used for ship construction for many years and has been the standard material for more than the last fifty years. It is very strong but also heavy. It rusts in water and especially in salt water. To prevent rust a protective coating of paint or zinc plating or spray is used. Steel may be fastened with rivets and screws but is more commonly welded. It is a sheet material and can be most easily applied to surfaces designed for sheet materials. However, it is ductile and can be formed to other shapes and because of its easy weldability can be applied in pieces to cover more complex shapes. Aluminum is similar in many ways. It is not as strong but is considerably lighter. It was not until the 1940s that aluminiums that did not corrode badly in salt water were developed. The proper alloys are quite corrosion resistant and do not require paint except for appearance. They are active electrochemically and do require careful insulation from dissimilar metals.

11.1.1 SCALING OF STRUCTURES

A yacht is a structure loaded by its own weight. A simple scaling law can be determined for such structures. For a tension rod, a simple beam, and a column consider the effect as the structure is scaled larger, keeping the ratio of all dimensions the same. Then the stress is proportional to the size ($\sigma \sim 1$) for the first two structures. This statement can be proven for geometrically similar tensile members since the weight is proportional to the a typical dimension 1^3 and the cross-section area is proportional to 1^2.

Therefore

$$\sigma = \frac{W}{A} \sim \frac{1^3}{1^2} = 1 \tag{11.1}$$

For two geometrically similar beams the weight is proportional to 1^3 and the bending moment to 1^4. The section modulus, however, is proportional to 1^3.

Therefore

$$\sigma = \frac{M}{I/y} \sim \frac{1^4}{1^3} = 1 \tag{11.2}$$

For the column the elastic modulus proportional to size, $E \sim 1$, is required if similarity is to be maintained. For a column, the allowable load is given by the relation

$$W \sim \frac{EI}{1^2} \tag{11.3}$$

Since $W \sim 1^3$ and $I \sim 1^4$ then $E \sim W1^2/I \sim 1^5/1^4 = 1$. This simple result indicates that if a boat is scaled up in proportion, then higher stresses will be caused. This scaling accounts for the familiar result that small boats, especially models, are very strong relative to their weight; they can be picked up when poorly supported and even dropped, while large boats are weaker and must be handled more carefully.

11.1.2   COMPARISON OF MATERIALS FOR STRUCTURAL PURPOSES

For structural purposes in a boat, a material must be both strong and stiff. It must resist the local water pressures and the overall loads applied to the hull. From the standpoint of overall loads the hull acts somewhat like a beam producing tension and compression loads so that the strength for a given weight of material is important. In resisting local water pressures the strength of the skin material in bending is important. The stresses in the panels subject to bending decrease rapidly with thickness so that a light material has considerable advantage.

The properties for wood are only in one direction along the grain and therefore should be divided by two if used in such a way that strong properties in two directions are required. When used as plywood the maximum properties are reduced by half. While the comparison suggested in this table is not adequate in all respects, it suggests that aluminum and fiberglass are the strongest for a given weight with the other metals about a factor of two weaker. Wood is very competitive if strength in only one direction is required, but only half as strong if strength in both directions is required. The difficulty in adequately fastening a wood boat makes it difficult to realize this full strength and, being a natural material, it is harder to control reliability.

The following table shows properties of materials of interest to boatbuilding.

Table 11.1   Properties of materials

	w	σ_{max}	E	$\dfrac{\sigma}{w}$	$\dfrac{E}{w}$
	lb/ft^3	lb/in^2	lb/in^2	in	in
Wood					
Spruce	27	3500	$1{\cdot}39(10^6)$	$2{\cdot}24(10^5)$	$8{\cdot}9(10^7)$
Douglas fir	32	3570	$1{\cdot}2(10^6)$	$1{\cdot}925(10^5)$	$7{\cdot}2(10^7)$
Oak	46	8000	$1{\cdot}7(10^6)$	$3{\cdot}00(10^5)$	$6{\cdot}4(10^7)$
Plastic					
Fiberglass	95	$20(10^3)$	$1(10^6)$	$3{\cdot}6(10^5)$	$1{\cdot}8(10^7)$
Metals					
Aluminum	165	$40(10^3)$	$1(10^7)$	$4{\cdot}18(10^5)$	$10{\cdot}5(10^7)$
Steel	485	$60(10^3)$	$3(10^7)$	$2{\cdot}14(10^5)$	$10{\cdot}7(10^7)$
Bronze	530	$60(10^3)$	$1{\cdot}4(10^6)$	$1{\cdot}96(10^5)$	$4{\cdot}55(10^7)$
Monel	552	$80(10^3)$	$2{\cdot}5(10^6)$	$2{\cdot}51(10^5)$	$7{\cdot}83(10^7)$
Lead	710	500		$1{\cdot}23(10^3)$	

A different comparison is required to judge the ability of the material to resist local pressure loading. For a given distance between supports and a given distributed loading, a bending moment will be caused in the material. The stresses caused by this moment are:

$$\sigma = \frac{My}{I} \tag{11.4}$$

and the deflection

$$\delta = \frac{M}{EI} \tag{11.5}$$

where I is the moment of inertia of the section and y is the distance from the neutral axis to the extreme fiber.

For a sheet material:

$$I = \frac{bt^3}{12} \tag{11.6}$$

where b is the width and t the thickness.

If W is the weight per unit length of material

$$I = \frac{W^3}{12b^2w^3} \tag{11.7}$$

and

$$\frac{\sigma}{w^2} = \frac{6Mb}{W^2} \tag{11.8}$$

σ/w^2 is the proper parameter for making a weight comparison of materials subject to bending loads. Similarly

$$\frac{E}{w^3} \sim \frac{b^2}{\delta W^3} \tag{11.9}$$

so E/w^3 is the proper parameter for comparing stiffness. A comparison of the materials considered on this basis is given in Table 11.2.

Table 11.2   Bending criteria for various materials

	$\dfrac{\sigma}{w^2}$ in^4/lb	$\dfrac{E}{w^3}$ in^7/lb^2
Wood		
Spruce	$1{\cdot}435(10^7)$	$3{\cdot}65(10^{11})$
Douglas fir	$1{\cdot}04(10^7)$	$2{\cdot}1(10^{11})$
Oak	$1{\cdot}13(10^7)$	$0{\cdot}906(10^{11})$
Plastic		
Fiberglass	$6{\cdot}55(10^6)$	$5{\cdot}95(10^9)$
Metals		
Aluminum	$4{\cdot}37(10^6)$	$1{\cdot}15(10^{10})$
Steel	$7{\cdot}62(10^5)$	$1{\cdot}35(10^9)$

Wood is definitely superior for supporting the local pressure loads both in strength and deflection because of the greater thickness of the sections which can be used. Fiberglass is fairly good from a strength point of view and poor in deflection, while aluminum is almost as good for strength and better in deflection. Steel is poorest in both these categories. These local loads can be carried by closer spaced frames and other supports so proper design can alleviate these weaknesses in the denser materials.

11.1.3   PLYWOOD

Plywood has become a popular material for boat building. It comes in large sheets that simplify construction and make it easier to provide a waterproof structure.

Plywood has less of the preferred direction features of natural wood and is not as weak as wood in the cross-grain direction. The directional properties of natural wood are overcome in plywood by running the grains of the different plies perpendicular to each other. This system increases the strength in one direction but decreases it in the other direction. Plies with the grain perpendicular to the direction of stress will carry only about $\frac{1}{20}$ the load of plies with the grain parallel to the direction of stress. For direct tension only the plies with parallel grain need be considered, but in some cases of bending, when the *outside* plies have their grain perpendicular to the direction of bending they can contribute a noticable amount.

Table 11.3 lists the properties of common plywood: ‖ plies refers to plies with the grain parallel to that in the surface plies, and ⊥ plies to those with grain perpendicular to the surface plies. The thickness of the plies given is before sanding. The face plies are sanded down so that the total thickness is the value given. The properties of area (A), of inertia (I), and section modulus (S), are given in inch units per foot width of plywood.

Table 11.3　Properties of plywood

Thick-ness in	Plies	Ply thicknesses			‖ plies			⊥ plies		
		faces in	center in	cross-bands in	A in²	I in⁴	S in³	A in²	I in⁴	S in³
$\frac{1}{4}$	3	$\frac{1}{9}$	$\frac{1}{9}$		1·67	0·0143	0·114	1·33	0·0014	0·0247
$\frac{3}{8}$	3	$\frac{1}{8}$	$\frac{3}{16}$		2·25	0·0461	0·246	2·25	0·0066	0·0704
$\frac{1}{2}$	5	$\frac{1}{8}$	$\frac{1}{8}$	$2@\frac{1}{10}$	3·60	0·0926	0·370	2·40	0·0324	0·1995
$\frac{3}{4}$	5	$\frac{1}{8}$	$\frac{3}{16}$	$2@\frac{3}{16}$	4·50	0·251	0·670	4·50	0·171	0·608
1	7	$\frac{1}{8}$	$2@\frac{1}{8}$	$3@\frac{3}{16}$	5·25	0·540	1·000	6·75	0·460	1·131
1		Natural wood			12·0	1·0	2·0	0	0	0

The last line giving properties of 1 in thick natural wood has been included for comparison. The cross-bands are the plies between the center and face plies. The face plies and center plies have the same direction, except in three-ply, and the cross-bands have perpendicular grain.

For three-ply construction it can be seen from the table that the properties are of the ⊥ plies much less than those of the ‖ plies so that there are pronounced directional properties. For 1 inch seven-ply these directional properties are almost overcome, but the properties in either direction are only about half as good as that for natural wood in the preferred direction. For three-ply plywood it is necessary to consider the strength of the plies with grain perpendicular to the stress when bending in ⊥ direction

$$I = I_\perp + \tfrac{1}{20} I_\parallel \qquad (11.10)$$

For $\frac{1}{4}$ in plywood $I = 0·0014 + \frac{1}{20}(0·0143) = 0·0021$. A 50% increase has been obtained from the plies with grain perpendicular to the direction of stress because they are located so much further from the centerline.

11.1.4 FIBERGLASS (GRP)

Fiberglass (GRP) has proven to be an excellent material for small craft construction. It is light and strong and not seriously affected by water. Fiberglass material consists of glass reinforcing fibers bonded together with resin. The glass fibers themselves are very strong, having rupture stress of the order of 250 to 400 thousand lb per sq in. However, laminates contain only about 20% to 60% by weight glass and are considerably weaker than the individual fibers. Fiberglass laminate has a fairly low elastic modulus making it quite flexible, but it is also a brittle material, not ductile like steel.

Glass/fiber filaments are 1 (10^{-3}) to 2 (10^{-4}) in a diameter. A large number of these filaments are combined together into a strand. The filaments are made into roving, mat or cloth. Roving consists of many strands together like an untwisted rope. The roving is then woven together either with most of the strands in one direction (unidirectional) or the roving in both directions. Woven roving is often used in boat construction because it is a fairly cheap form of fiberglass; it gives a thick buildup per ply and has high glass content; and has high directional strength.

Mat consists of chopped strands of fiberglass randomly deposited and held together with binder. It has the following advantages and disadvantages: low cost, being the cheapest form of fiberglass; equal strength in all directions; forms a good water barrier; has a lower glass content than roving or cloth.

Cloth is woven from twisted strands of glass filaments. Its properties are as follows: good surfacing material; consistent and fairly high glass content; poor strength in the diagonal directions; poor interlaminar bond; many layers are required.

The resins used are of two types, polyester and epoxies, with polyester the more common in boat construction. It is cheaper than epoxy but has poorer physical properties.

Polyester resin comes in different types possessing different properties. Rigid polyester resin is the strongest but is less resistant to impact. It has between 0·5 and 3·0% elongation to rupture, and is usually used in small boats with minimum framing. Semi-rigid resin is less brittle than the rigid type. It has 3 to 10% elongation to rupture and is the type usually used in boats longer than 16 ft where stiffeners are used. Flexible resin has greater than 10% elongation to rupture. It is not usually used directly in boat construction but is blended with rigid type to form semi-rigid types.

Epoxy resins have not been used extensively in boat construction, due to higher cost and the tendency of some curing agents to cause skin irritation. They provide greater adhesion and give slightly better physical properties than the polyesters.

Greater strength and stiffness can often be provided by sandwich construction. The sandwich usually consists of layers of high strength material as the outer faces with a lightweight material in between. Fiberglass laminate is used as the facing material. In this way the high-strength fiberglass can be placed further apart and a lighter material used to fill the space in between. Sandwich construction is commonly used for decks and bulkheads where local stiffness is important. The common core materials are wood, foamed plastic, honeycomb and plastic spheres embedded in resin.

Plywood and balsa are the commonly used woods. Plywood is rather heavy for a good core material but contributes considerably to the strength. Balsa is a better material for a lightweight core.

Rigid unicellular plastic foams are often used: pre-foamed polystyrene and cellular cellulose acetate as well as foamed-in-place polyurethane. Polystyrene foam, unless properly coated to prevent contact, will be attacked by some resins. Plastic foam is lightweight, resistant to decay and can be formed in place. Cores of honeycomb aluminum, fiberglass laminate, cotton duck and waterproof paper are available in various sizes and weights. Waterproof paper core sandwich honeycomb is commonly used in boats for interior bulkheads and decks. Gas-filled phenolic spheres embedded in polyester or epoxy resin are used to form a denser foam which can be troweled in place. This material is used where this method of application is advantageous.

The strength of the fiberglass laminate depends upon the nature of the reinforcement. The strength is higher the higher the glass content. Laminates made of mat give non-directional strength properties while woven roving or cloth are directional. Roving can be unidirectional or two-directional while cloth is two-directional; both are weak along the 45° direction.

The specific weight of fiberglass laminate depends upon the glass content and the void fraction. The specific gravity varies between 1·35 and 1·80 depending upon the laminate. The actual specific gravity of the fiberglass reinforcement is 2·55 and of the resin is between 1·18 and 1·24.

Tensile strength varies over the range 5000 to 35 000 psi depending upon the type of reinforcement and the direction of the load. Typical values are given in Table 11.4.

Fiberglass laminate is quite flexible with a low elastic modulus. This property coupled with the high strength makes it very good at absorbing shocks. However, it is a disadvantage when a stiff structure is required. The value of the modulus of elasticity varies for different laminates from 0·7 to 2·5 (10^6) psi.

Fiberglass laminate is not a ductile material. The stress–strain curve shows no yield point characteristic such as steel. Yielding or plastic flow is not observed. Once it has reached its elastic limit it will rupture. It can absorb a fair sized impact elastically but will crack, not dent, if a heavier blow is applied.

Table 11.4   Directional strength properties of different laminates

Laminate	Direction:	0°	45°	90°
2 oz Mat		10 000 psi	10 000 psi	10 000 psi
25–27 oz W.R.		38 000 psi	9 000 psi	37 000 psi
10 oz cloth		24 000 psi	12 000 psi	20 000 psi

11.2   Hull design methods

A boat is a complicated structure and the loads to which it is subject are hard to specify accurately. Boat design methods have been developed based upon extensive experience. Several rules have been developed to specify the size of members and construction techniques. The most prominent ones for wood construction are those by Lloyds, Herreshoff and Nevins. Similar rules have also been developed for steel and fiberglass construction. It is also possible to make direct predictions of the loads and required scantling dimensions by making use of some basic simplifying assumptions. For conventional wooden boats, the use of the established rules is the best approach. These rules will not be reviewed here. In this section, the means of predicting the loads and methods of designing to withstand them will be given.

   Hull design methods must be considered separately for two different classes of materials. The first class is composed of the relatively heavy and strong sheet materials such as steel, aluminum and fiberglass. The second class is lighter and weaker strip material such as wood. Plywood falls in between these two categories. For materials in the first class, local deflections and stresses dominate and if the hull is made adequate to sustain these, it is normally adequate to take the overall loads applied. Materials in the second class are usually used in thick enough sections so that local loads are not dominant but overall strength requirements govern the design.

11.2.1   HULL LOADS

In the first class of materials the scantling and framing dimensions are designed to withstand local pressure loading criterion. For displacement type boats this is given in terms of a static pressure load as follows:

   Displacement motor boat: hydrostatic pressure, 2 ft above main deck for forward two-thirds of hull; 6 in. above main deck for after one-third of hull.
   Sailboat: hydrostatic pressure to the height of the top of the coaming.

   In addition to these hydrostatic pressures, an additional term should be used proportional to the speed of the boat, but it is unimportant at usual displacement yacht speeds. The appropriate relation is:

$$P_v(\text{psi}) = \frac{1 \cdot 8 V^2 (\text{knots})}{1000} \tag{11.11}$$

At various speeds the pressures given by this relation are as follows:

V	P_v
5 knots	0·045 psi
10	0·18
15	0·45
20	0·72

The added pressures, above the hydrostatic loadings, should be applied to the forward two-thirds of the hull.

Stresses on the hull of a planing boat are largely the result of high speed pounding against the water. The unsupported fore part of the hull also imposes major bending loads under conditions of high vertical accelerations.

Probably the best source of knowledge of the loads on high speed planing boats comes from tests carried out by the David Taylor Model Basin on a US Navy torpedo boat, and also by the British on a 68 ft rescue boat. The American tests were run at speeds of up to 35 knots in waves 4 to 6 ft high and a wave length of about 100 ft. The tests were limited to 35 knots because this was considered the highest speed safe for personnel. The boat experienced pressure on the bottom of 36 psi and maximum acceleration at the bow of 11·3 g. These conditions represent extreme military conditions and require extreme hull strength. Lower design requirements can be set for normal civilian craft. Reasonable maximum accelerations are 3·3 g at the bow, 1 g at the center of gravity, and 1·3 g at the stern. These values are about one-third the torpedo boat test values. Suggested design values are 4 g at the bow and 2 g at the center of gravity.

The maximum hull pressure per inch of hull length can be calculated by the relation

$$P_o = \frac{3D}{2L} (1 + a_{cg}) \tag{11.12}$$

where D is the displacement, L is the waterline length and a_{cg} is the acceleration at the center of gravity.

The peak pressure associated with these slamming loads is

$$P_{SM} = \frac{3 \cdot 3 P_o}{G} \tag{11.13}$$

where G is the greatest distance from chine to keel.

The actual design pressures for the boat are obtained by an approximate factor times the maximum slamming pressure plus the hydrostatic pressures.

$$P_d = P_{SM} F_1 + P_{static}$$

where F_1 is shown in Figure 11.1, and P_{static} is the pressure on the surface in question when the boat is at rest. The factor F_1 gives that fraction of P_{SM} to be applied as a function of position along the boat's length.

For framing design, a reduced pressure can be used since the maximum will not occur along the whole frame at the same time. For designing the frames, an extra factor is used:

$$P_d = P_{SM} F_1 F_2 + P_{static} \tag{11.14}$$

F_2 is given in Figure 11.1 for either longitudinal or transverse framing, (F_{2L} and F_{2T}). The abscissa of the F_{2T} curve is based on the per cent of unsupported frame length between keel and chine.

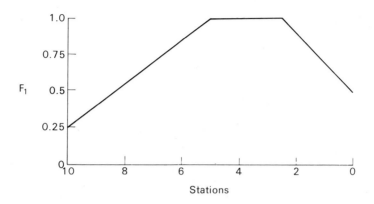

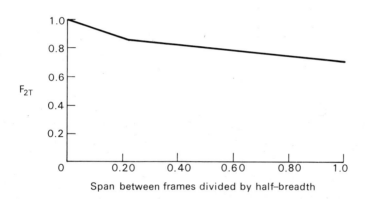

Span between frames divided by half–breadth

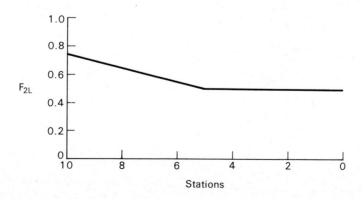

11.1   Structural loading coefficients

An alternate method of obtaining P_{SM} based on the boat's speed is given by the relation

$$P_{SM}(psi) = \frac{2 \cdot 85 V^2 (K) + 1 \cdot 46 V(K) \ L(ft) + 16 \cdot 9 L(ft)}{144} \qquad (11.15)$$

where L is the waterline length. The relation for P_{SM} which gives the lowest value should be used since the operating conditions of the boat will be limited by speed or acceleration conditions. A summary of suggested loading specifications is given in Table 11.5.

Once the design pressures have been established, the scantlings and framing must be designed to withstand this load. The longer the spans of unsupported skin, the thicker the skin must be. Skin thickness can be reduced by an increased number of frames or reinforcements. These frames may be run in either the transverse or longitudinal direction. With materials such as fiberglass, metals or plywood, which have strength in two directions, the type of framing is somewhat arbitrary. With conventional wood construction, the frames are used to tie the planking together and must be run perpendicular to the planking.

11.2.2   HULL PANEL DESIGN

Unsupported sections of scantling are called panels. In general the panels will be supported on all four sides. When the panels are long and narrow, greater than 5 times the width, then simplified formulas which do not consider the support on the ends can be used. Whether the panel is subject to a fixed or a non-fixed edge condition is also important. If the edge of the panel is restrained from rotating, the panel will be stronger and stiffer than if it is allowed to rotate. If two adjacent panels are actually continuous over a stiffener, and subject to similar loadings, then these panels can be considered to have fixed edge conditions. This continuous panel condition is the usual one to which the fixed end condition applies. The following relations should be used for calculating stress and deflection.

All edges supported, not fixed:

$$\sigma = \frac{0 \cdot 75 P_d b^2}{t^2 (1 + 1 \cdot 61 a^3)} \qquad d = \frac{0 \cdot 142 P_d b^4}{E t^3 (1 + 2 \cdot 21 a^3)} \qquad (11.16)$$

All edges supported and fixed:

$$\sigma = \frac{0 \cdot 5 P_d b^2}{t^2 (1 + 0 \cdot 623 a^6)} \qquad d = \frac{0 \cdot 0284 P_d b^4}{E t^3 (1 + 1 \cdot 056 a^5)} \qquad (11.17)$$

Two edges supported, not fixed $(a < 0 \cdot 2)$:

$$\sigma = \frac{0 \cdot 75 P_d b^2}{t^2} \qquad d = \frac{0 \cdot 142 P_d b^4}{E t^3} \qquad (11.18)$$

Table 11.5   Summary of design loads

Boat type	Shell		Framing		Decks		Bulkhead
	bottom	sides	bottom	sides	weather	interior	
High power Planing	Design impact pressure F.S. = 1·5	Same as bottom thickness	Design impact pressure F.S. = 1·5	Water level 6 in. above deck F.S. = 4·0	Water level 2 ft above deck F.S. = 4·0	40 psf F.S. = 4·0	Nominal size or local loads F.S. = 4·0
Cruising Sail	Water level to coaming in heeled condition F.S. = 4·0	Water level to coaming in heeled condition F.S. = 4·0	Same as shell	Same as shell	Water level 2 ft above deck F.S. = 4·0	40 psf F.S. = 4·0	Nominal size or local loads F.S. = 4·0
Cruising Power Displacement Low power	Water level 2 ft above deck fwd 2/3; 6 in. above deck aft $\frac{1}{3}$. F.S. = 4·0	Water level 6 in above deck F.S. = 4·0	Same as shell	Same as shell	Water level 2 ft above deck F.S. = 4·0	40 psf F.S. = 4·0	Nominal size or local loads F.S. = 4·0

Two edges supported and fixed $(a < 0.2)$:

$$\sigma = \frac{0.5P_d b^2}{t^2} \qquad d = \frac{0.0284P_d b^4}{Et^3} \qquad (11.19)$$

where σ is the maximum stress, P_d is the design loading, b is the width, d is the maximum deflection, t is the thickness, E is the elastic modulus, a is the width to length ratio.

Most panels used in boat construction are curved. Sheet material can only be curved in one direction while a moulded material can be curved in two directions which stiffens the panel against bending in the direction perpendicular to the curvature. These curvatures are usually slight and it is general design practice to ignore the effect; nevertheless, there is an increase in strength and panels should be curved when practical.

11.2.3   FRAMING

The framing or stiffeners are designed to support the loads transmitted to them by the panels. They should be designed as non-fixed or fixed end beams depending upon whether they are continuous over the supports. The bending moment is given by:

$$M = \frac{P_d l^2}{12} \text{ fixed ends}$$

$$\qquad (11.20)$$

$$M = \frac{P_d l^2}{4} \text{ non-fixed ends}$$

where l is the length between supports. The required section modulus to support this load can be calculated by the relation

$$S = \frac{M}{\sigma} \quad \text{where } S = \frac{2I}{t} \qquad (11.21)$$

For stiffeners which are rigidly attached to the skin, a certain part of the skin can be considered to act as part of the stiffener. In general this width should be taken as the width of the stiffener at the point it attaches to the skin plus ten skin thicknesses.

11.2.4   BULKHEADS

Modern boat design practice is to combine accommodation and structure. Bulkheads, bunks and other components if designed as an integral part of the structure provide considerable structural strength. A common system of construction is to use bulkheads, with heavy intermediate frames where required, to support longitudinal framing which in turn supports the scantling. Such frames or bulkheads must be designed to withstand the forces imposed by the longitudinal stiffeners. Frames can be designed by the relations previously given and bulkheads must be considered for buckling. In general only bulkheads which are subject to special loads, such as the mast load, need be considered in detail.

11.2.5   DESIGN LIMITS

Most structural parts have both a stress and deflection limit. The factors of safety to be applied to the maximum stress are given in Table 11.5. The deflection limitation generally used is 1 in 200. It is particularly critical for decks where excess deflection will give an unsafe feeling.

11.2.6   STRUCTURAL DESIGN RULES

Structural design rules for boats are available from several sources. Lloyds provides rules for all types of boat construction, wood, metal and fiberglass. There are several other rules for wood boats in addition to Lloyds, such as those of Nevins and Herreshoff. For conventional wood construction, the use of these rules is the best way to proceed. Wood boats must be designed to withstand overall loads; because of the lower density and greater thickness of the wood scantlings, the local pressure loads are more easily withstood by wood and the overall loads provide the more severe restriction. Since these are very difficult to predict, and the overall structure hard to analyse, it is best to rely on general experience as described by these rules.

11.3   Hull designs suitable for sheet materials

The use of sheet materials for scantlings imposes certain restrictions on the shape of the hull. In general, sheet materials can be formed to certain types of surfaces but not to others, as thin sheets are fairly flexible in bending or twisting but cannot easily be stretched or sheared in the plane of the sheet. A surface with compound curvature cannot easily be formed since this involves stretching the material. To understand this effect, consider a sheet of material that is bent into a cylinder. Since a cylinder is made up of parallel straight-line elements there is only curvature in the direction perpendicular to these straight-line elements (Figure 11.2). If we now attempt to take a section of this cylindrical surface and bend it about an axis perpendicular to these straight line elements, the upper elements must stretch and the lower elements compress. The curvature in the initial direction stiffens the sheet so that it cannot easily be bent in another direction. A ductile substance like steel will stretch so that it can be formed into compound surfaces, but this takes a

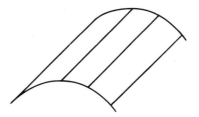

11.2   Surface made up of parallel straight lines, cylindrical

great deal of force and a form over which it can be bent. The whole process can be done with less force if the steel is first heated so that it becomes softer and more plastic. A brittle material like plywood will take very little compound bending before parts of the material will be stretched beyond their limit and crack. Therefore, particularly for plywood, but also for steel and aluminum construction, we should understand how to lay out hull shapes that can be formed without compound bending.

If we restrict our attention to surfaces having straight-line elements, there are three types of surfaces which must be considered (Figures 11.2, 11.3):

1. Surfaces made up of parallel straight-line elements, e.g. cylinders.
2. Surfaces made up of intersecting straight-line elements, e.g. cones.
3. Surfaces made up of skew line elements.

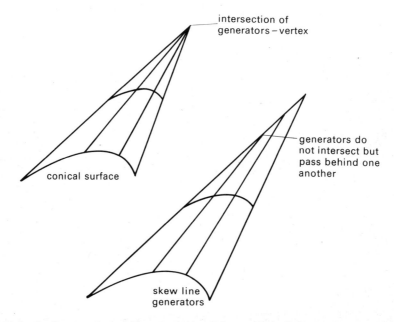

11.3   Surfaces made up of intersecting and skew straight lines

When we speak of cones or cylinders we are not restricting ourselves to the common right circular cylinder or cone but to any surface made up of parallel or intersecting lines. The surfaces can be made up of conical and cylindrical surfaces or be a more general surface using skew generating lines. The first method is more restrictive and increases the work in laying out suitable surfaces.

11.3.1   CYLINDRICAL AND CONICAL PROJECTIONS

First let us consider the more restrictive method and limit our considerations to conical and cylindrical surfaces. Figure 11.4 shows the plan and elevation view of the bottom of a typical small runabout. If we are to require the bottom surface to be a conical or cylindrical surface we are not free to specify the keel and chine in both

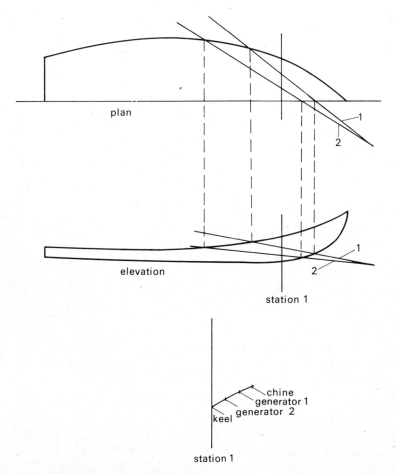

11.4   Conical hull surface development

views. Consider that the plan view of the keel and chine is fixed and also the elevation view of the chine but that the elevation view of the keel is undetermined. Start off by drawing a generator (1) in the plan view and this same generator in the elevation view by projecting into this view the points where it crosses the chine and keel. Another generator (2) may now be drawn in the plan view which either intersects generator (1) at some vertex 0_1 or is parallel to (1); for the case considered, an intersection at 0_1 will be taken. The intersection of generator (2) with the chine and the keel is determined in the plan view. The intersection of the generator (2) with the chine, determined in the plan view, may now be projected onto the elevation view and this intersection determined in this view. Generator (2) may now be drawn in the elevation view since 0_1 and the intersection with the chine are both determined. The intersection of generator (2) with the keel can now be determined from the intersection of this generator with the keel in the plan view, and the projection of this point upon the generator in the elevation view. This construction fixes the point of the keel in the elevation view, which may or may not be at the desired location. If this point on the keel elevation is not satisfactory, then another point for 0_1 may be taken until a satisfactory location for the vertex is found. This process may be continued with other generators in the same way. The vertex chosen may be different for each additional generator or it may remain the same. The vertex for the next generator may be chosen anywhere along the last generator, or it may be parallel to the last generator. The vertex may not be chosen within the area which is to be covered with the sheet material since the curvature at the vertex is infinite. As long as the keel and chine lines are fair then the whole surface should be fair.

The section views can now be developed from the construction already accomplished. The station plane is cut by the series of generators that appear in both the plan and elevation views. The points at which these lines cross the section plane can now be determined by measuring off the vertical and horizontal distances from suitable base lines and plotting in the station plane. In general this line will be curved in the section view since this line intersects the generator lines, and if both are straight the surface is plane.

11.3.2   SKEW LINE ELEMENTS

The skew line development technique is similar to the conical development but less restrictive (Figure 11.5). A generator (1) is drawn as convenient in one view and projected into the other view. Another generator (2) may also be drawn and also projected into the other view. If generators (1) and (2), extended, do not cross in both views at the same point, then they do not actually intersect and they are skew lines. In general this will be true since they have been drawn to pass through the predetermined hull and keel lines in both views. The section views may now be determined by the same process as used in the conical method. Only if the generators have been chosen as perpendicular to the keel so that the sections will also be generators, will the sections be straight lines.

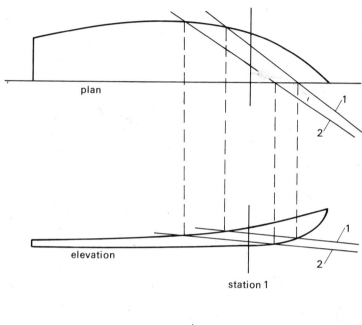

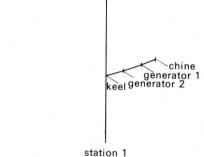

11.5   Hull surface development using skew line generators

Since the skew line construction is easier to accomplish and allows a greater flexibility of design, this is the better method. It can be shown that sets of conical generators can always be found that contain any two skew generators. The method for doing this can be seen in Figure 11.6. If an auxiliary generator is drawn so that it intersects the two skew generators as shown, then the first generator and the auxiliary generator form a conical surface. By shifting the vertex, another conical surface can be found to contain the auxiliary generator and the second skew generator. These two conical surfaces will be tangent to each other along the auxiliary generator. An understanding of the auxiliary generator concept will aid in actually applying a sheet material. The technique to bend the material from one generator to the next is to first bend the material so that it touches the keel end of the generator, and then bend the material to the chine about the auxiliary generators. As long as the lines of the boat are fair, then the sheet material should be fair when it is bent to the lines developed.

For both of these systems of development the curvature to which the material is to be bent must not be too great for the thickness of the material used. The principal curvature can be determined by taking projections of the hull surface perpendicular to the generators. The stress caused by the bending of a thin sheet is

$$\sigma = \frac{Et}{2R} \tag{11.22}$$

where R is the radius of curvature.

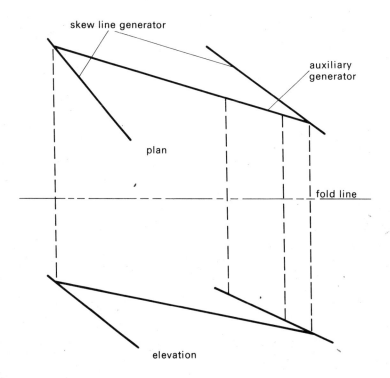

11.6   Development of conical surfaces connecting skew line generators

Chapter Twelve
Sailboat Rigging Design

The mast and rigging of a sailboat form a simpler structural system than the hull. While it is a redundant structure, that is the loads are divided among several supporting members, it is still much simpler than the hull structure. The prediction of the loads on the mast and rigging is quite complicated, but again less so than for the hull. A somewhat more fundamental approach can be made to the design of the rigging, but empirical criteria must still be used in the design process.

12.1 Loads

The loading upon the rigging comes predominantly from the sails. The wind forces upon the sails are transmitted through the sailcloth to the mast and boom, if the sail is directly attached to such members, or via a stay or luff rope to the mast, for sails that are set on stays or flying. Sailcloth and stays cannot sustain bending or compression loads but only tension, while the mast and boom can sustain tension, bending and compression loads. For sails and stays the direction of the loads must be along the direction of the member. Since a stay is a line, this direction is well defined, but it is less so for the sail. Since it is a plane the tension force vector can lie anywhere within this plane. If no loads are applied to the sails and stays, the stays will form straight lines and the sails flat planes between their points of attachment. If a load is applied which does not lie in this line or plane, then the line or plane must deflect into a curve to sustain the load. The wind load is always applied approximately perpendicular to the surface of the sailcloth and the sails apply this load approximately perpendicular to the stays.

The amount of curvature will depend upon the ratio of the tension force to the perpendicular loading force. Consider the simple case of the jib stay shown in Figure 12.1. The division of the load between the stay and the luff rope is not considered here since it depends upon the tension in the halyard and the relative elasticity of the stay and the halyard/luff rope combination: for this discussion

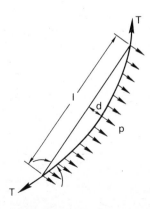

12.1 Deflection of stay under uniform load p

consider the stay to be the combined stay and luff rope. Assume that the sail is applying a uniform load whose total value is p to the stay and which causes a maximum deflection of d from the unloaded condition and an angle δ at the attachment points. The loaded stay will form a parabola in which

$$\frac{d}{l} = \frac{1}{16}\frac{p}{T} \qquad\qquad (12.1)$$

and

$$\delta = \frac{1}{2}\frac{p}{T}$$

Therefore for

d/l	T/p	δ
0·01	6·25	4·6°
0·02	3·12	9·2°
0·04	1·56	18·4°

The relation for the angle is independent of the way in which the load is applied but the maximum deflection is not. For instance, if all the load was applied at the mid-point, then

$$\frac{d}{l} = \frac{1}{4}\frac{p}{T} \qquad\qquad (12.2)$$

giving four times the deflection of the uniform loading condition.

The stress in the sail is more complicated since it consists of tension forces in perpendicular directions lying in the plane of the sail. These forces cannot be predicted simply by knowing the applied loads since the system is redundant and knowledge of the stretch of the cloth and cut of the sails is required to predict the shape and loads on the sail. However, the relation for δ still holds insofar as it predicts the average angle. While prediction of the stress in the sailcloth is not simple, a reasonable approximation is that shown in Figure 12.2. If the sail is loose-footed, the lines of principal stress run from the clew radially to the luff; if it is attached to a boom, then they run parallel to the leech from the boom to the mast. The magnitude of the tension stress is roughly proportional to the length of the principal stress line and inversely to the deflection of the cloth from the straight line. This assumption of sail loading is obviously not complete, in that it ignores the stresses which must exist in the direction perpendicular to the principal stresses described. However, it is both simple and reasonable and allows the wind pressure loads to be transmitted to the mast, boom, stays and sheets in a manner reasonably consistent with the existing restraints. The stress picture for a sail attached to a boom suggests that if cut with the cloths running parallel to the leech, there will be

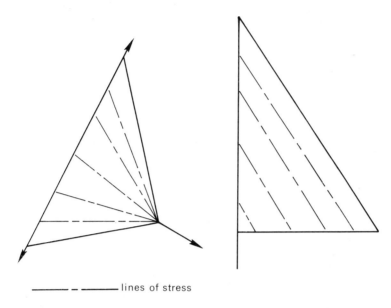

——————— — ———————lines of stress

12.2   Stress pattern in sails

a minimum of stress on the seams. This conclusion is born out by experience, but sailmaking practice indicates that a better shaped sail can be produced by running the cloths perpendicular to the leech, thus putting an increased dependence on the seam stitching. Somewhat similar statements can be made concerning the loose-footed sail resulting in the mitre cut.

Keeping in mind this picture of how the wind loads are supported by the sails and those forces are transmitted to the stays and mast, consider the situation shown in Figure 12.3, showing a sloop sailing closehauled. The closehauled condition is the one which imposes the highest loads on masts and rigging for a given wind strength because the apparent wind is strongest upon this course and because of the need to trim the sails flat. Higher stresses in the sails are required to support the wind pressure loads. The jib is supported by the stem, sheet block attachment, and the masthead (for the masthead rig illustrated). The load on the masthead is in the direction of the jib stay, principally down with a large forward component and a small athwartship component. The heeling of the boat by this athwartship component is one of the principal results observed, but it represents only a minor component of the force applied to the masthead.

The mainsail applies a distributed load along the mast which is conveniently broken into components perpendicular to the mast in the plane of the sail and along the mast. The component along the mast is transmitted to the masthead by the halyard and boltrope while the horizontal component is applied along the mast. The sail applies a force component along the boom and perpendicular to the boom; that along the boom is transmitted to the mast and approximately balances the forces in the direction of the boom applied by the sail along the length of the mast. The sheet, plus the weight of the boom, supplies the downward force and a force towards the centerline of the boat. The sheet would lie in the plane of the sail if the weight of the boom were negligible.

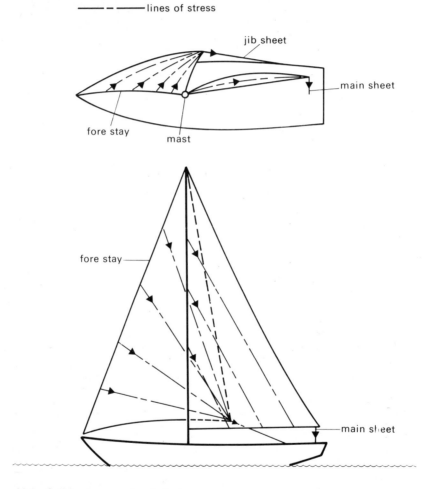

12.3   Sail loads on mast and rigging

Looking at Figure 12.3 again, it is seen that the force from the mainsail on the mast when closehauled is principally towards the stern with a small side component. If there were no jib, the headstay would be essential to resist the downward pull of the mainsheet which is transmitted to the mast by the mainsail. If a jib is present, the jib stay performs this function. If there is no backstay, the fore and aft forces in the jib stay and mainsail must balance if the mast is fairly flexible so that it is free to adjust to this condition. If a backstay is provided, the head of the mast is fairly well located in a fore-and-aft direction, and the load from the jib stay is shared between the mainsail and backstay. In the absence of a backstay, it is obvious that a jib hoisted without the mainsail imposes a rather severe load on the mast. The jib itself imposes a more severe load on the mast than the mainsail because of the multiplying effect of supporting the sail loads on a tight stay and applying these loads directly to the masthead instead of distributing them along the mast.

While the principal loads from the jib stay and mainsail are in the fore-and-aft direction, these loads essentially balance, leaving the athwartship components unbalanced. Shrouds are needed to support these athwartship loads, and because of the narrow base which the beam of the boat provides for them, the loads in the shrouds may be appreciable.

For other points of sailing the loads are reduced relative to the closehauled position. As the sheets are eased and the wind is brought further onto the beam the relative wind decreases and the belly in the sails is increased. The result is that the wind loads decrease and the tension generated in the sailcloth by a given wind also decreases. The load on the mast and stays also decreases. The important change is that as the mainsheet is eased, the backward pull of the mainsail upon the mast decreases. The jib, and especially a spinnaker if used, delivers a strong forward pull on the masthead. Under these conditions, a backstay is necessary and the load on this backstay may be maximized under these conditions.

Since the stays and shrouds are all tension members, they provide a resulting downward pull upon the masthead. The bending loads are minimized by a well designed system of shrouds, but a large mast compression load results.

12.2 Masts

The compression load which the mast is capable of withstanding depends upon its strength as a column. The mode of failure of a long column, such as a mast, is by buckling. The load which can be carried depends upon the stiffness of the section and the end conditions, upon whether the column is fixed and cannot deflect, or the equivalent of a pin end which can deflect.

12.2.1 COLUMN REQUIREMENTS

The maximum column load is given by the formula

$$W = K\left(\frac{\pi}{l}\right)^2 EI \tag{12.3}$$

where K depends upon the end condition and is given in Table 12.1.

Table 12.1   Column formula

End condition	Allowable load
2 pin ends	$W = \left(\dfrac{\pi}{1}\right)^2 EI$
1 pin end 1 fixed end	$W = 2\left(\dfrac{\pi}{1}\right)^2 EI$
2 fixed ends	$W = 4\left(\dfrac{\pi}{1}\right)^2 EI$

The strength of the column can be increased by bracing the mast so that the un-supported sections are shortened, reducing the value of 1 in the buckling load formula.

The shrouds can be used to brace the mast in the athwartship direction and to divide it into short sections. The stays support the mast in the fore-and-aft direction, but it is more difficult to provide support to the mast at points along its length in this direction. With a masthead rig, this becomes even more difficult than with a $\frac{3}{4}$ or $\frac{7}{8}$ rig. Running backstays can be used to support the mast in the aft direction and several forestays can be used forward. The disadvantage of having to trim the running backstays as the ship is brought about and of dividing the foretriangle into separate sections so that a single large jib cannot be conveniently used are features which make it desirable to do away with these intermediate stays where possible. Some fore-and-aft bracing can be obtained by using two shrouds connected to one point on the mast with a maximum fore-and-aft spread between them. While this supplies some bracing it is not as effective as fore-and-aft stays being led to those points. A jumper strut with associated stays can be used effectively with a non-mast-head rig. The result is that the mast itself must generally be stiffer in the fore-and-aft direction than in the athwartship one.

12.2.2   MATERIALS

The mast must be designed as a column to withstand a compression load with minimum weight. Therefore a stiff light material is required. The materials that have been used most for masts are wood (spruce), aluminum, and steel. Maximizing the stiffness means a maximum of EI. Both the weight per unit length and the maximum dimensions are important.

$$EI = \frac{k^2}{r^2} W \frac{r^2 E}{w} = \frac{k^2 W^2}{A} \frac{E}{w^2} \qquad (12.4)$$

where   k = radius of gyration
          r = maximum dimension
          W = weight per unit length
          w = specific weight
          A = cross-sectional area

The first form is appropriate if the maximum dimension r is to be kept the same; k/r will be relatively constant for a hollow section using different materials if r is the same. Actually k/r will decrease somewhat as the specific weight decreases since the additional wall thickness required with light materials will put more material nearer the center. If the maximum dimension is fixed, E/w is a good material criterion with some greater advantage to the heavier material than shown as long as the walls do not become too thin. If a similar geometric shape is to be used, such as a solid cylinder or a hollow cylinder with a constant external to internal radius ratio, then the second form becomes more useful since k^2/A is a constant for geometrically similar shapes. For such conditions E/w^2 is a good material criterion. The appropriate values of those parameters are shown in Table 12.2.

Table 12.2   Stiffness criteria for various materials

Material	Elastic modulus	Specific weight	Criterion of merit	
	E	w	$\dfrac{E}{w}$	$\dfrac{E}{w^2}$
	lb/in^2	lb/in^3		
Spruce	$1{\cdot}4(10^6)$	$0{\cdot}0156$	$8{\cdot}9(10^7)$	$5{\cdot}7(10^9)$
Aluminum	$1{\cdot}0(10^7)$	$0{\cdot}0957$	$10{\cdot}5(10^7)$	$1{\cdot}1(10^9)$
Steel	$2{\cdot}9(10^7)$	$0{\cdot}281$	$10{\cdot}3(10^7)$	$3{\cdot}67(10^8)$
Fiberglass	$1{\cdot}0(10^6)$	$0{\cdot}055$	$1{\cdot}8(10^7)$	$3{\cdot}3(10^8)$

On the basis of constant maximum size, aluminum and steel are about equal. However, for steel, wall thickness often becomes too thin and rust is a severe problem. The proper aluminum alloys do not corrode badly and the walls need not be so thin. Spruce has a reduced index which actually is further penalized by the thicker sections needed which place the material nearer the center. Fiberglass is poor because of its low elastic modulus. On the basis of geometrically similar sections E/w^2 becomes the proper criterion showing that spruce is considerably superior and steel and fiberglass are the poorest. If a solid section is used, wood is the only practical material. It is hard to specify a good wall thickness criterion for a hollow wood section, but a common rule of thumb is that the wall thickness should be 20% of the total dimension in the same direction. For metal, such as aluminum or steel, the structural limit on wall thickness is that caused by local buckling. Until the ratio of radius to wall thickness is greater than 100 (R/t > 100) there seems to be no danger of this mode of failure. A wooden mast could not have equally thin walls because the non-uniform properties of the wood make it impractical in such thin sections.

Other considerations worth mentioning are that aluminum is a more uniform material than wood, which makes its properties more reliable. Manufacturing techniques (extrusion) make it desirable to use an aluminum mast of uniform section all the way to the head, though modifying an extrusion by cutting out a section and welding allows a tapered mast with constant wall thickness. Since the upper part of the mast is usually not as highly stressed as the lower part, the upper part could be thinner resulting in a weight saving in a critical area. Wood lends itself to adjusting the cross-section of the spar as required.

The shape of the section chosen has an effect on the moment of inertia; a thin-walled section is superior to a solid section. The outside shape also has an influence. In order to show this, consider solid symmetrical sections. In the following table three sections have been chosen for comparison.

	A	I
Round	$\dfrac{\pi d^2}{4}$	$\dfrac{\pi d^4}{64} = 0.0796\,A^2$
Square	r^2	$\dfrac{r^4}{12} = 0.0835\,A^2$
Equilateral triangle	$\dfrac{\sqrt{3}}{4}r^2$	$\dfrac{r^4}{32\sqrt{3}} = 0.096\,A^2$

where d is the diameter of the cylinder and r is the length of the side of the cylinder or triangle. For the same cross-sectional area the round section has the smallest moment of inertia and the triangle the most. Other shapes such as T or X sections could give greater moments of inertia but should be more properly compared with the hollow sections since a thin web is involved and the moment of inertia increases as this web is made thinner. For wood sections, the square seems preferable over the round because of its greater strength and ease of fabrication. The triangle, while stronger, is a less convenient shape, but may have advantage in certain applications.

12.3   Masts and rigging design

In usual design practice the loads in the athwartship direction are used to design the mast. This is because these loads can easily be obtained from the heeling stability of the hull. The compressive load in the mast at the step required to heel the boat is given by the relation

$$\text{Mast force} = \frac{RM}{b/2}$$

where RM is the righting moment and b is the distance between port and starboard shrouds. The forces caused by the stays and halyards are added to this value; 30° of heel is taken for the reference condition. The design mast loads are as follows:

Load

Mainmast	$\dfrac{(2\cdot78)RM}{b/2}$
Mizzen mast	
yawl	$\dfrac{(1\cdot05)RM}{b/2}$
ketch	$\dfrac{(1\cdot47)RM}{b/2}$

The moment of inertia of the mast in the transverse and fore-and-aft direction can then be obtained by the relation

$$I = CPl^2(10^{-8}) \tag{12.5}$$

The values of C are given in Table 12.3 using units of lb and inches.

Table 12.3   Values of mast design parameter C

	C (*transverse*)		C (*fore and aft*)		
	Single spreader	*2 or 3 sets of spreaders*	*Masthead rig* *short*	*tall*	*$\frac{7}{8}$ Foretriangle*
Spruce	6·78	8·11	3·9	4·2	3·74
Aluminum	0·94	1·13	0·55	0·58	0·52

These values are for lower sections; increase by 1·50 for upper sections; increase by 1·50 for lower sections if stepped on deck. Increase fore-and-aft value by 10% if single lower shroud.

The loads in stays and shrouds can be expressed relative to the mast load (Table 12.4).

Table 12.4   Shroud loads

Rig	Sets of spreaders	% of mast load		
		lowers	*intermediates*	*uppers*
$\frac{7}{8}$ Foretriangle	1	60		45
	2	45	30	30
Masthead	1	65		45
	2	55	30	30

Recommended factors of safety are, for main shrouds 2·5 to 3; for mizzen shrouds 1·5. Because of the difficulty in predicting stay loads these are usually related to the shroud loads, thus:

Forestay—same as most heavily loaded shroud

$$\text{Backstay—forestay load} \times \frac{\text{Distance from mast to forestay attachment}}{\text{Distance from mast to backstay attachment}}$$

12.3.1   TENSION IN STAYS DEPENDS ON ADJUSTMENT

The tension in the stays depends very much on the way they are set up, and the designer cannot predict the loads without anticipating how the boat will be handled. Equations 12.1 and 12.2 show how the tension forces vary with the sag in the stay and the applied sail loads. Tightening the backstay to prevent all sag in the forestay when going to windward is an impossible goal and can produce very large loads in the stays and mast.

References

1. Sears, R. I., *Wind tunnel Data on the Aerodynamic Control Surfaces of Airplanes.* NACA WR L 663, 1943
2. Ames and Sears, *Determination of Control Surface Characteristics from NACA Plane Flap and Tab Data.* NACA TR 721, 1941
3. Abbot, Ira H.; Von Doenhoff, Albert E., and Stibers Jr, Lewis S., *Summary of Air Foil Data.* NACA ACR No. L5CO5, Mar. 1945
4. Henry, Robert G.; Miller, Richards T., *Sailing Yacht Design—An Appreciation of a Fine Art.* SNAME Nov. 1963, Paper No. 9 also Cornell Maritime Press, 1965
5. Davidson, K. S. M., *The Mechanics of Sailing Ships and Yachts*, Survey of Mechanics, G. I. Taylor 70th Anniversary Vol., Cambridge at the University Press
6. Davidson, K. S. M., *Some Experimental Studies of the Sailing Yacht.* Trans. SNAME Vol. 44, 1936
7. Spens, P. G., De Saix, Pierre; Brown, P. W., *Some Further Experimental Studies of the Sailing Yacht.* SNAME 1968
8. Nigg, D. J., *A Sailing Hydrofoil Development.* Marine Technology Vol. 5, 2 Apr. 1968, pp 150–157
9. Clement, Eugene P.; Blount, Donald L., *Resistance Tests of a Symmetric Series of Planing Hull Forms.* SNAME Vol. 71, 1963, pp 491–579
10. Skene, Norman L., *Elements of Yacht Design.* Dodd, Mead & Co. 1948
11. Lissiman, Peter B. S., Editor, *The Ancient Interface I.* First AIAA Symposium of the Air/Hydronautics of Sailing. Western Periodicals Co. 1969
12. Hammitt, A. G., Editor, *The Ancient Interface II.* Second AIAA Symposium of the Air/Hydronautics of Sailing. Western Periodicals Co. 1970
13. Gentry, A. E., 'The Aerodynamics of Sail Interaction', *The Ancient Interface III.* Third AIAA Symposium of the Air/Hydronautics of Sailing. Western Periodicals Co. 1971
14. Engineers of Gibbs & Cox Inc., *Marine Design Manual for Fiberglass Reinforced Plastics.* McGraw-Hill Book Co. 1960
15. Marchaj, C. A., *Some Physical Aspects of Yacht Instability and Heavy Weather Sailing.* Land's End Yachtman's Equipment Guide, Land's End Publishing Corp. 1970
16. White, F. M., *An Analysis of Flat Plate Drag with Polymer Additives.* Journal of Hydronautics, Vol. 2, 1968, pp 181
17. Sinney, Francis., *Skene's Elements of Yacht Design.* Dodd, Mead & Co. 1962
18. Marchaj, C. A., *Sailing Theory and Practice.* Dodd, Mead & Co. 1964
19. Smith, B., *The 40 Knot Sailboat.* Grosset & Dunlap, Inc.
20. *Practical Methods of Observing and Forecasting Waves by Means of Wave Spectra and Statistics.* US Navy HO 603, Government Printing Office 1955
21. Kowin-Kroukovsky, B. V., *Theory of Seakeeping.* SNAME 1961
22. Lewis, E. V., *High Speed Ships.* International Science and Technology, Apr. 1963
23. C. L. Shuford, *A Theoretical and Experimental Study of Planing Surfaces Including Effects of Cross Section and Plan Form.* NACA Report 1355, 1958
24. *CCA Measurement Rule.* Cruising Club of America, New York

25. Milgram, J. H., *Section Data for Three Highly Cambered Airfoils in Incompressible Flow*. NASA CR 1767
26. Simpson, T. W., *Aluminum Boats*. Kaiser Aluminum & Chemical Sales, Inc.
27. Wallis, R. A., *Axial Flow Fans*. Academic Press, New York, 1961
28. Gerritsma, J. and Beukelman, W., *Analysis of the Resistance Increase in Waves of a Fast Cargo Ship*. International Ship Building Progress, 1972, pp 285–93
29. Gerritsma, J. and Moeyes, G., *The Seakeeping Performance and Steering Properties of Sailing Yachts*. Third Symposium on Developments of Interest to Yacht Architecture, 1973. HISWA, 412 Keizersgracht, Amsterdam, Holland
30. Spens, P. G., Private communication. July 1973
31. Ewing, G., *Slicks, Surface Films and Internal Waves*. Journal of Marine Research Vol. IX No. 3 1950. pp 161–87
32. Sverdrup, H. U. and Munk, W. H., *Wind, Sea and Swell: Theory of Relations for Forecasting*. US Navy Hydrographic Office Publication 601, March 1947
33. Crook, W. M., *More Power to You*. Pamphlet, International Nickel Corp.

Index